Using Randomised Controlled Trials in Education

Paul Connolly, Andy Biggart, Sarah Miller,
Liam O'Hare & Allen Thurston

Los Angeles | London | New Delhi
Singapore | Washington DC | Melbourne

Los Angeles | London | New Delhi
Singapore | Washington DC | Melbourne

SAGE Publications Ltd
1 Oliver's Yard
55 City Road
London EC1Y 1SP

SAGE Publications Inc.
2455 Teller Road
Thousand Oaks, California 91320

SAGE Publications India Pvt Ltd
B 1/I 1 Mohan Cooperative Industrial Area
Mathura Road
New Delhi 110 044

SAGE Publications Asia-Pacific Pte Ltd
3 Church Street
#10-04 Samsung Hub
Singapore 049483

Editor: James Clark
Assistant editor: Robert Patterson
Production editor: Tom Bedford
Copyeditor: Lynda Watson
Indexer: Cathy Heath
Marketing manager: Dilhara Attygalle
Cover design: Sheila Tong
Typeset by: C&M Digitals (P) Ltd, Chennai, India
Printed in the UK

© 2017 Paul Connolly, Andy Biggart, Sarah Miller, Liam O'Hare and Allen Thurston

First published 2017

Apart from any fair dealing for the purposes of research or private study, or criticism or review, as permitted under the Copyright, Designs and Patents Act, 1988, this publication may be reproduced, stored or transmitted in any form, or by any means, only with the prior permission in writing of the publishers, or in the case of reprographic reproduction, in accordance with the terms of licences issued by the Copyright Licensing Agency. Enquiries concerning reproduction outside those terms should be sent to the publishers.

Library of Congress Control Number: 2016961866

British Library Cataloguing in Publication data

A catalogue record for this book is available from the British Library

ISBN 978-1-4739-0282-4
ISBN 978-1-4739-0283-1 (pbk)

At SAGE we take sustainability seriously. Most of our products are printed in the UK using FSC papers and boards. When we print overseas we ensure sustainable papers are used as measured by the PREPS grading system. We undertake an annual audit to monitor our sustainability.

Contents

Series page	viii
About the authors	ix
Acknowledgements	x
Introduction	**1**
Working out what works	2
RCTs: What works and ongoing controversies	4
About this book	6
Prior knowledge and suggested background reading	8
Further reading	9
1. What RCTs Can and Cannot Tell Us	**11**
Pedagogical practice and experimentation in schools	12
Paradigm wars and the critique of RCTs	14
In defence of RCTs	20
RCTs and critical realism	24
Conclusions	26
Further reading	29

2. Logic Models and Outcome Measures — 30

- What is a logic model? — 31
- Components of a logic model — 32
- Programme theory — 33
- Building a programme logic model — 35
- A worked example — 37
- Other functions of logic models — 40
- Defining and selecting outcomes — 43
- Choosing outcome measures — 44
- Conclusions — 48
- Further reading — 48

3. Research Designs for RCTs — 50

- Underpinning principles — 50
- Designs of RCTs — 53
- Ethical considerations — 56
- Sampling and randomisation — 59
- Recruitment and attrition — 66
- Sample size and intended analysis — 69
- Conclusions — 73
- Further reading — 74

4. The Fundamentals of Analysing RCT Data — 75

- Assumptions — 76
- Linear regression — 76
- Linear regression and RCTs — 83
- Analysis of sub-group effects — 91
- Real-life example: analysis of RCT evaluation of 'Doodle Den' — 95
- Conclusions — 105
- Further reading — 106

5. Dealing with the Analysis of More Complex RCT Designs — 107

- Analysing trial data with binary outcomes — 108
- Analysing cluster randomised controlled trials — 121
- Conclusions — 141
- Further reading — 145

6. How to Report RCTs and Synthesise Evidence from Different Trials — 147

Reporting results from RCTs — 147
Synthesising evidence from different trials — 161
Conclusions — 171
Further Reading — 172

References — 173
Index — 182

Series page

Research Methods in Education

Each book in this series maps the territory of a key research approach or topic in order to help readers progress from beginner to advanced researcher.

Each book aims to provide a definitive, market-leading overview and to present a blend of theory and practice with a critical edge. All titles in the series are written for Masters-level students anywhere and are intended to be useful to the many diverse constituencies interested in research on education and related areas.

Titles in the series:

Atkins and Wallace, *Qualitative Research in Education*; Brooks, Te Riele and Maguire, *Ethics and Education Research*; Connolly, Biggart, Miller, O'Hare and Thurston, *Using Randomised Controlled Trials in Education*; Hamilton and Corbett-Whittier, *Using Case Study in Education Research*; McAteer, *Action Research in Education*; Mills and Morton, *Ethnography in Education*.

Los Angeles | London | New Delhi
Singapore | Washington DC | Melbourne

About the authors

Paul Connolly is Director of CESI. He is Professor of Education and Dean of Research for the Faculty of Arts, Humanities and Social Sciences at Queen's University, Belfast. He is also Director of the Campbell Centre for the UK and Ireland.

Andy Biggart is the Lead for the Educational Attainment Research Programme within CESI. He is a Lecturer in Education within the School of Social Sciences, Education and Social Work at Queen's University, Belfast.

Sarah Miller is the Lead for the Health and Wellbeing in Schools Research Programme within CESI. She is a Lecturer in Education within the School of Social Sciences, Education and Social Work at Queen's University, Belfast and is also Deputy Director of the Campbell Centre for the UK and Ireland.

Liam O'Hare is the Programme Manager for Innovation Zones within CESI, with a focus on working with local communities and service providers to develop innovative and effective programmes. He is also a Senior Research Fellow within CESI.

Allen Thurston is Deputy Director of CESI and the Lead of the What Works for Schools Strand. He is Professor of Education within the School of Social Sciences, Education and Social Work at Queen's University, Belfast.

Acknowledgements

SAGE would like to thank the following reviewers for their comments on the proposal of this book:

Tom Clark, University of Sheffield

Alex Sutherland, University of Cambridge

Toby Greany, Institute of Education, University of London

Introduction

Imagine, for a moment, that you are a teacher and you hear about an exciting new approach that has been developed to enhance primary school children's reading skills. The approach has been organised into a clear programme that runs for one school term and includes a range of specific tasks and activities to be undertaken with the children on a whole-class basis. From what you can see, the programme looks convincing and certainly reflects the types of approaches you feel are important and that you wish to develop further with your own children. One of the first questions you will ask as a teacher will be: is this new programme likely to be effective? In particular, and before you risk adopting it with your own class, you will be keen to know if there is any evidence to show that it is likely to work better in terms of improving reading skills than the existing approaches you are using. You will also have in mind the particular characteristics and needs of your children when you are asking this question. You will thus also want to know: what are the chances that this programme would work for your particular class?

This book focuses on the research methods used in education to address precisely these types of questions. Starting with the basics, the book builds up your appreciation and knowledge of the methodological approaches used to test the effectiveness of a wide range of different educational programmes and interventions. It takes you through the process of how to design your study, given the particular type of programme or intervention you wish to evaluate, and then how to undertake that study. All of the key issues involved in the collection and analysis of the data and the writing up of findings are covered in detail. In working through this book you will gain the knowledge and skills required to design and undertake a piece of research that will provide you with strong and robust evidence of whether a particular educational programme or intervention works or not. Even if you do not intend to conduct such research yourself, this book will provide you with invaluable insights into, and an appreciation of, the appropriate methods to use to evaluate the effectiveness of educational programmes and thus the skills you will need to critically assess the strength of the evidence that you will read elsewhere.

Working out what works

Of course, each child is different. What might be effective for one child in your class may not be effective for another. Also, each class and school is different. An approach to reading that may work well, overall, with your children may not work well, or may even have a negative effect, with another class in another school. These questions about what works are therefore, inevitably, questions about general tendencies. It is simply not possible, through research, to predict with certainty that a particular approach to reading will definitely lead to additional gains in reading skills for a specific child or a particular class of children. Rather, all we can do is seek evidence of what is likely to work, for what types of children and in what contexts. Turning back to this exciting new reading programme you have heard about, you may find that there have been several rigorous studies published to date that have all shown, to varying degrees, that this new programme tends to increase children's reading scores by the equivalent of about an additional three months' progress compared to those of children who just carried on as normal. These studies should give you sufficient encouragement and confidence to try the programme out with your own class. However, you will never know whether it will work with your children until you actually try it. Moreover, even if you find it does work, it is unlikely to have the same effect for all of your children. While your class may improve their reading scores by an additional three months' progress compared to what they would have done otherwise, this will only be the average level of improvement. By definition, and being the average, we know that half the children will have made greater gains than this but that the other half will have made lesser gains. Indeed some may have even regressed over this period.

The key point therefore is that research can only ever tell us how particular groups of children are likely to respond, *on average*, to a specific educational programme or intervention. However, the availability of a body of rigorous evidence that can provide teachers with insights of this kind for a wide range of differing educational programmes and interventions is undoubtedly extremely valuable. It is precisely this question of how we can generate robust evidence of whether an educational programme or intervention is effective for a particular group of children that provides the focus for this book. Methodologically, there are a number of clear steps we will need to take if we want to design a research study capable of addressing this particular question in a rigorous and convincing way. As an illustration, let us return to the example of the new reading programme for primary children that has been designed to be delivered on a whole-class basis over one school term. First of all we need to gather some objective data on how much progress the children made with their reading over the duration of the term when they were engaged with the new programme. To do this we could use any one of a number of standardised reading tests at the start of the term and then again at the end to get some measure of how much progress has been made by the children on average. However, we have to take into consideration that they are likely to make some reading progress during this period regardless of the teaching method used, simply due to attending school. As such, if we want to estimate what the *additional* effects are, on average, of introducing this new reading programme, we also need to see how a group of similar children progress over the same period who were not using that approach in class. This is our second step – introducing a comparison, or control group. Ultimately, if the children using the new approach make greater gains in their reading skills compared to those in the comparison group then this would provide us with evidence that the new approach is likely to be more effective, on average, for those particular children. Within this, we can also extend our analysis of the data to compare the progress made by boys and girls separately in each school, and by any other factor that we feel might have an influence on the effectiveness of the programme on average.

The main reason we are able to draw robust conclusions regarding the effectiveness of this reading programme from this type of study design is that we are assuming that the two groups of children are similar. Thus, and to put it simply, if the children in the schools using the new reading scheme are broadly the same as the children in the schools carrying on as normal then the only systematic difference between them is the fact that one group is using the new reading programme while the other is not. If this is the case then any differences in the reading progress made by the two groups of children must be due to the effects of the reading programme, as the two groups are the same in all other respects and are thus subject to the same range of other external social processes and factors within and beyond the school. Of course, this assumption that the two groups are the same is a critical one. It is for this reason that the third step in the research design process is that we need to create two matched groups, and we need to do this through random allocation. More specifically, and in the case of this new reading programme, we could work with maybe 40 or more primary schools and randomly select half of them to run the new programme and the other half to continue as normal. The crucial point to note is that by randomly splitting the schools into two groups we have maximised the likelihood that we have two matched groups. Through the randomisation process, and with a sufficiently large sample, we can be fairly confident in assuming that all of the other myriad of factors that will impact upon children's progress in reading will be evenly balanced across the two groups.

What has been described above is, in essence, a randomised controlled trial or RCT. It is a *trial* of a particular educational programme or intervention to assess whether it is effective; it is a *controlled* trial because it compares the progress made by those children taking the programme or intervention with a comparison or control group of children who do not and who continue as normal; and it is *randomised* because the children have been randomly allocated to the two groups being compared. It is this design that provides the focus for this present book. In the chapters to follow we will look at the broader philosophical and methodological debates regarding the use of RCTs in social and educational research as well as setting out, in some detail, the practical issues involved in choosing the right design for the particular programme or intervention you wish to evaluate. The book also takes you through, step-by-step, how to collect and analyse the data from an RCT and how to report it thoroughly.

RCTs: What works and ongoing controversies

Over the last ten years we, the authors, have collectively run over 30 RCTs in education. To date, these have involved over 800 schools and other educational settings across Northern Ireland, the Republic of Ireland, England and Scotland. Each one has involved working collaboratively and in partnership with a wide range of schools and organisations involved in developing and delivering educational programmes and interventions. Our experience over this time is that the type of approach described above is largely uncontroversial. Put simply, teachers, pupils, parents and other key stakeholders just seem to 'get it'. They understand the need for a control group and, with a little explanation, they soon come to fully appreciate the importance of randomisation. Perhaps most importantly, they are all passionately concerned with the effectiveness of what they do and whether, ultimately, it is having a clear and measurable impact on children's learning and development. This is not to say that the process of undertaking an RCT is easy, or that it is without complications. As will be described throughout this book, running RCTs in education presents many challenges and dilemmas. However, these challenges – of research design, of ethics, of negotiating and maintaining relationships with stakeholders, of analysing, interpreting and presenting findings – are ones faced by all social and educational researchers, regardless of the particular methods they employ. The point about RCTs being uncontroversial is that we have simply not encountered any resistance to the use of trials in education or faced any unique problems with regard to running trials compared to any other type of research.

We make this point about the uncontroversial nature of RCTs *in practice* because they have faced, and continue to face, considerable resistance to their use in education *in theory*, particularly from significant sections of the education research community. Unfortunately, such opposition to RCTs appears to be embedded in the culture of the academic community in education. Take, for example, one of the leading textbooks *Research Methods in Education*, written by Cohen, Manion and Morrison and now in its seventh edition. It is arguably the most popular and widely used methodology textbook in education in the UK. This is how they present RCTs to students:

> This mode of an experiment, premised on notions of randomization, isolation and control of variables in order to establish causality, may be appropriate for a laboratory, though whether, in fact, a social situation either ever *could become* the antiseptic, artificial world of a laboratory or *should become* such a world is both an empirical and a moral question respectively ... Further, the ethical dilemmas of treating humans as manipulable, controllable and inanimate are considerable ... [T]he experimental approach may be fundamentally flawed in assuming that a single cause produces an effect. Further, it may be that the setting effects are acting causally, rather than the intervention itself.
>
> [...]
>
> Schools and classrooms are not the antiseptic, reductionist, analysed-out or analysable-out world of the laboratory ... Generalizability from the laboratory to the classroom is dangerous, yet with field experiments, with their loss of control of variables, generalizability might be equally dangerous ... Randomized controlled trials belong to a discredited view of science as positivism.
>
> (Cohen et al., 2011: 314 and 318, original emphases)

The tone of this criticism is notable, as is the complete mismatch between these trenchant criticisms of RCTs *in theory* and the reality of their use in a wide range of educational settings *in practice*. Indeed, the authors make clear to students reading their textbook – who will become the next generation of education researchers – that 'RCTs are often not possible in education' (Cohen et al., 2011: 66), even though there have been many thousands of RCTs conducted in education successfully to date (Oakley, 2006). Given this mismatch between theory and practice, it is difficult not to agree with Oakley (2006) that much of the critique betrays a fundamental, worrying and widespread ignorance among significant sections of the educational research community of the use of RCTs in reality. It is certainly our experience that the 'constant recycling of stylised objections' to the use of RCTs and the associated failure to recognise or engage with the many detailed discussions that have taken place in the methodological literature regarding these, as Oakley (2006: 69) noted a decade ago, is still commonplace among the educational research community today. Indeed, the polarised nature of the debate over these last ten years, and the relative lack of any real and constructive dialogue between advocates of and objectors to RCTs, would suggest that we have witnessed the resumption of the classic paradigm wars, this time being waged on the site created by the emergence of evidence-based practice (Hammersley, 2008).

About this book

This book will debunk many of the myths and arguments surrounding RCTs as touched upon above. By taking you carefully through the realities of conducting RCTs in practice in education, the book will demonstrate very clearly that the types of criticisms listed above are not just mistaken but are also ill-founded and that they do, unfortunately, betray a fundamental lack of understanding of the use of RCTs in practice. It will be seen, for example, that far from RCTs being done *on* teachers, there are many models of collaborative practice where teachers, pupils and other key stakeholders are centrally involved in the design of trials and in the analysis, interpretation and presentation of findings. Also, the continually recycled concerns about ethics tend to betray a lack of awareness of the many RCTs where no child is denied the programme in question; it is just that there is a delay before the control group are delivered it. In addition, rather than RCTs ignoring contexts and being unable to undertake within-programme analyses, it is quite possible and indeed increasingly commonplace for trials to pay close attention in their design and analysis to the particular contexts within which a programme is delivered, how its delivery varies between contexts, and how – within any one context – the effectiveness of the programme may vary systematically between differing sub-groups of learners. Moreover, many RCTs are multi-method in design and include a parallel qualitative component precisely to help understand the quantitative findings that emerge from the trial, and thus to address directly the questions of *why* a particular programme has (or has not) been effective and/or why its effectiveness has varied between contexts or groups of learners.

Given the widespread misunderstanding of and resistance to RCTs in education, we will therefore begin, in Chapter 1, by looking in more detail at some of the core methodological, philosophical, ethical and political debates touched upon above. The chapter sets out the rationale for RCTs and also the key criticisms levelled at their use in education and social research. These criticisms are each addressed, in turn, with reference to real-life examples of RCTs that we have conducted in practice. Through this, the chapter then sets out a more considered philosophical position for RCTs in education and social research, drawing upon critical realism, that provides a framework for the rest of the book.

Chapters 2 and 3 then move on to look at issues relating to the design of RCTs. Chapter 2 encourages you to take an initial step back from the educational programme or intervention you may be interested in so that you can map out and understand the theory of change that underpins it. The chapter will set out a practical framework for doing this through the use of a technique known as logic modelling. It will be shown how logic modelling is an invaluable tool for helping to think through the theory of change and to identify what the anticipated outcomes are for a particular programme or intervention and precisely how these are expected to be achieved. The chapter then looks, in some detail, at how to choose appropriate measures for the outcomes specified. With the wider theory of change in mind, as set out by the logic model and associated anticipated outcomes, the book then moves on, in Chapter 3, to consider the key issues involved in the design of an RCT. This chapter sets out clearly a range of common designs and which ones are most appropriate to use given the nature of the educational programme or intervention under consideration. Within this, the chapter provides step-by-step advice on how to calculate the size of the sample needed for the RCT, and also how to incorporate a qualitative component to study the process of delivery of the programme or intervention, as well as to help understand the findings that arise from the quantitative trial data.

The next two chapters focus specifically on how to analyse the data gathered from an RCT. While the importance of incorporating a strong qualitative component to the design of an RCT has been stressed, because of the limits of space, these two chapters will focus specifically on the appropriate methods for analysing the quantitative trial data. Chapter 4 begins this by setting out the overall approach to analysing a simple RCT (i.e. when individual children have been randomly allocated to the control and intervention groups). The chapter will take you through the steps involved in determining the overall effects of the programme or intervention concerned and also how to ascertain whether it has been more or less effective for particular sub-groups within the sample. Chapter 5 then extends this general framework by setting out how to undertake these analyses when you have different types of outcome data and also when the data are gathered from a cluster randomised controlled trial (i.e. when the study has involved randomly allocating whole classes or schools to either the control or intervention groups).

The final chapter, Chapter 6, focuses on how to write up and report the findings of randomised trials. Taking the CONSORT statement as the guide, the chapter will set out clearly the information that needs to be reported and in what format. It will also provide you with an appreciation of how the findings of individual RCTs are used in the synthesis of research evidence through the use of systematic reviews and meta-analysis. In all of this, the chapter will stress the need to be tentative in interpreting the findings as well as the claims that are made from these.

Prior knowledge and suggested background reading

This book does not assume any prior knowledge of evaluation methods in general or of RCTs in particular. It has been specifically written for the generalist educational or social researcher who wishes to extend their knowledge and skills to the use of RCTs. In this sense, and as outlined above, the book is designed to take you through each stage of the process of designing, undertaking and writing up an RCT in a clear step-by-step manner. However, it does assume some basic understanding and appreciation of research methods in two respects. Firstly, it is assumed that you already have a good knowledge of qualitative methods and also case study methods. Their importance in the context of an RCT will be stressed in the book and how they can be used will be set out in

Chapter 3. However, and because of the limits of space, the book will not cover the key issues involved in undertaking case studies or in using particular qualitative methods such as semi-structured interviewing, focus group discussions and participant observation. Secondly, it is assumed that you are also familiar with the statistical software package SPSS and that you have some prior knowledge and understanding of basic statistics. In particular, it is assumed that you will be familiar with the key concepts associated with descriptive statistics – namely percentages, means and standard deviations and their graphical display in bar charts and boxplots. It is also assumed that you have some appreciation of inferential statistics and, in particular, of the notion of statistical significance and the associated use of 'p values' and confidence intervals.

If you do not have a sufficient grasp of qualitative methods or basic statistics then you will find it beneficial to consult one or more of the references set out below before reading this book.

Further Reading

Qualitative Methods

Qualitative Research in Education, by Liz Atkins and Susan Wallace (Sage Publications, 2012).
Research Methods for Education, 2nd edn, by Peter Newby (Routledge, 2014).
Introduction to Research Methods in Education, 2nd edn, by Keith Punch and Alis Oancea (Sage Publications, 2015).

Case Studies

Using Case Study in Education Research, by Lorna Hamilton and Connie Corbett-Whittier (Sage Publications, 2013).
The Anatomy of the Case Study, by Gary Thomas and Kevin Myers (Sage Publications, 2015).
Case Study Research: Design and Methods, 5th edn, by Robert Yin (Sage Publications, 2013).

Statistics

Statistics: A Gentle Introduction, 3rd edn, by Frederick Coolidge (Sage Publications, 2013).
Beginning Statistics: An Introduction for Social Scientists, 2nd edn, by Liam Foster, Ian Diamond and Julie Jefferies (Sage Publications, 2014).
Statistics Explained, 3rd edn, by Perry Hinton (Routledge, 2014).

Using SPSS

SPSS Explained, 2nd edn, by Perry Hinton, Isabella McMurray and Charlotte Brownlow (Routledge, 2014).

SPSS Survival Manual, 5th edn, by Julie Pallant (McGraw Hill Education, 2013).

Discovering Statistics Using IBM SPSS Statistics, 4th edn, by Andy Field (Sage Publications, 2013).

1

What RCTs Can and Cannot Tell Us

Introduction

One of the issues which has faced education policy over much of the last century is the pace of change. A range of different educational interventions continues to come and go. Fashions and fads within education are rife and while most may have some common-sense appeal, many have little evidence supporting them as effective pedagogical practices. While most people working in the field of education have good intentions, there remains a lack of robust evidence on the range of different pedagogical practices and whether they are actually effective in improving learning and skills among all or different subsets of learners.

RCTs within education offer the possibility of developing a cumulative body of knowledge and an evidence base around the effectiveness of different practices, programmes and policies. However, and as touched upon in the last chapter, their use remains controversial and they have not been widely accepted among the educational research community. The educational and wider social science research community within the UK has remained largely sceptical of such experimental approaches, which are often defined as part of a positivist paradigm and linked with a neo-liberal audit culture within policy. This, however, has not prevented a number of prominent advocates from arguing for the greater use of trials drawing on the model within medicine and the health sciences (Fitz-Gibbon, 1996;

Hargreaves, 1996; Oakley, 2000, Torgerson and Torgerson, 2001) which has, in turn, stimulated considerable debate surrounding the use of randomised control trials in educational settings over the last decade.

In this chapter we explore some of these debates about the methodological, philosophical, ethical and political issues associated with conducting RCTs in education. We critically reflect on the literature and also draw upon our own experience of conducting trials. We aim to set out an approach to trials informed by a critical realist perspective and one that is post-positivist in outlook. In doing so, we hope to convince some of those sitting on the sidelines of the merits of such an approach to evaluation research, whilst also tempering the calls that have been made by those who would advocate an over-scientific approach.

Pedagogical practice and experimentation in schools

Education as a profession has not had strong links with research. Much of what is taught in classrooms is rooted in tradition, experiential knowledge, expert opinion, or directed through central or local policy perspectives (Hargreaves, 1996). Moreover, teaching practice by its nature is often experimental and the profession often buys into new ideas with vigour. New educational interventions, policies and practices are regularly introduced within schools. In fact, schools continually experiment with different programmes and approaches. However, there is rarely any systematic attempt to evaluate their impact on pupil learning or other outcomes, beyond teacher intuition. Few of these practices, which are often targeted at the most disadvantaged pupils, have been rigorously assessed in a systematic way against the proposed outcomes that they intended to change. As such, educational practice remains vulnerable to fads. Some of the fads which have entered the classroom include left and right brain training and placing a bracelet on the wrist, learning styles, avoiding food additives, whole language approaches, the new maths and open classrooms to name a few (Goldacre, 2013). More worrying still is that, without a robust evidence base, many of the various fashions introduced in schools are ones that had already been abandoned in the past as ineffective novelties, but have now come around again with a new generation of teachers or policymakers (Raffe and Spours, 2007). Whilst innovation is therefore at the heart of the teaching profession, there is a tendency for this to take place in the dark and thus for the constant recycling and reintroduction of fads, with little sense of learning or progression.

In this sense, RCTs have a critical role to play in supporting the natural experimentation and creativity that take place in schools and classrooms all the time. In particular, and as Campbell and Stanley (1963: 2) argued over fifty years ago: '[the experiment] is the only means for settling disputes regarding educational practice, as the only way of verifying educational improvements, and as the only way of establishing a cumulative tradition in which improvements can be introduced without the danger of a faddish discord of old wisdom in favour of inferior novelties'. What RCTs offer, therefore, is not just the opportunity to provide robust evidence relating to whether a particular programme is effective or not, but also – and over time – the creation of a wider evidence base that allows for not only a comparison of the effectiveness of one programme or educational approach against another but also for how well any particular programme works in specific contexts and for differing sub-groups of learners. Moreover, we would suggest that there is also a moral imperative to rigorously test programmes, not just so that we can ensure that we are making the best use of the limited resources that are available but also to make certain that we are neither holding learners back by persisting with an approach that is simply ineffective nor, critically, that we are not actually exposing them to potentially harmful effects.

One classic example of the dangers of fads in education, and the importance of developing a robust evidence base, is the Scared Straight programme designed to 'scare' or deter at-risk or delinquent children and young people from a future life of crime (Petrosino et al., 2013). The programme was introduced by a number of inmates serving life sentences in a New Jersey (USA) prison and involved juveniles visiting the prison and being subject to an aggressive presentation by the inmates on life in prison. A television documentary on the programme was broadcast in 1979 and showed the inmates shocking the juveniles with stories of rape and murder in prison. The documentary also claimed that the programme was successful in the fact that 16 of the 17 delinquents featured in the documentary did not engage in further offending for the next three months – 'a 94% success rate'. Not surprisingly, the programme received considerable media attention and became the latest fad that promised to offer a simple (and cheap) silver bullet in relation to crime prevention. Very quickly, the programme was rolled out in over 30 states across the USA (Petrosino et al., 2013).

However, and by 1982, the first RCT of the New Jersey programme was published reporting that it had found no evidence of an effect on the offending behaviour of participating juveniles in comparison with a control group (Finckenauer, 1982). Indeed, the study reported that those who participated in the programme were actually more likely to be arrested subsequently. Further trials later emerged that also reported similar worrying findings, and in 2003 a research team undertook a full systematic review of the international evidence to date in relation to this programme, conducted through the Campbell Collaboration. This review, updated in 2013, found nine RCTs that had been conducted to date on Scared Straight and similar programmes in eight different US states (Petrosino et al., 2013). The authors of the systematic review were able to combine the data from seven of these in order to conduct what is termed a meta-analysis. In analysing the pooled data, the authors found that, overall, there was clear evidence that participation on the Scared Straight and similar programmes actually increased the odds of juveniles re-offending by between 1.6 and 1.7 to 1. In other words, the odds of juveniles re-offending had increased by between 60 and 70% amongst those who had participated in the programme compared to a control group.

Thus, while having much intuitive appeal, the use of shock tactics in this case was not only found to be ineffective but also the growing body of evidence presented a consistent picture that it actually exacerbated the problem. This is a particularly clear example of the role that RCTs can play in helping us guard against the tendency to be taken in by the latest fads that, on the surface, look as if they should work and that are also often extremely appealing precisely because they present simple and cheap solutions to what are complex underlying problems. In many cases, the findings from RCTs might not be as stark as these found for the Scared Straight programme. For many school-based education programmes it may be that they are just ineffective rather than having a negative effect. However, the implications are no less serious given the direct investment that is required to deliver many programmes, not to mention the often substantial opportunity costs associated with schools and teachers putting their time and efforts into delivering a programme that does not work at the expense of one that does. What we have with RCTs is the promise of not just testing whether a specific programme or intervention works in a particular context, but also the broader goal of building and maintaining a robust evidence base enabling us to understand the relative effectiveness of differing approaches and, within this, which approaches might be most suited for which particular contexts.

Paradigm wars and the critique of RCTs

Randomised trials have a long history in educational research, with Oakley (2000) tracing their use back to the 1920s and noting that the early trials in education predated their use within medicine. While a natural science approach associated with a logical positivist philosophy of science held sway within educational research throughout the 1950s and 1960s, it came under increasing attack from interpretivist and feminist challenges, especially following the publication of Thomas Kuhn's (1962) *The Structure of Scientific Revolutions*. Kuhn's notion of paradigm shifts provided a framework for understanding science not as a linear and objective process characterised by the gradual growth in knowledge, but as a socially constructed process where the dominant paradigm at any one time tends to determine and define what theories, methods and ways of interacting are considered appropriate and often regarded as natural and unproblematic. This, in turn, allowed for existing scientific approaches, most notably the various strands of positivism held together with a belief in an objective and value-free social science, to be effectively challenged.

As a result, interpretivist approaches increasingly came to critique the dominance of positivist research models based on quantification and applying a natural science model to educational and social research from the 1970s (Pring, 2015). Over the years these interpretivist approaches have developed and diversified, and have played a critical role in stressing the importance of qualitative research and the need to appreciate and situate individuals' experiences and perspectives in order to better understand human behaviour and interaction. Whilst initially adopting a realist approach, in recognising the real existence of a social and physical world, many of these perspectives have become more idealist as social constructivist and post-modern perspectives have largely taken hold. Increasingly many of these approaches have questioned the very possibility of knowledge beyond relativistic multiple perspectives. These interpretivist approaches have typically positioned themselves firmly against, and in opposition to, methods rooted in a positivist tradition. Moreover, such debates have resulted not only in the growing dominance of qualitative approaches in educational research, but also an inbuilt scepticism of the value of quantitative methods. It is in this space that the role of experimental methods, and the use of RCTs in particular, has become situated.

Unfortunately, and for many in the educational research community, RCTs would appear to symbolise the old positivist tradition and to represent an existential threat to the large body of work that now exists, located broadly in the interpretivist tradition and later developments in post-modern and post-humanist perspectives. A brief taste of the nature of this opposition to RCTs, and its embeddedness in educational research, was provided in the last chapter through the extracts from one of the dominant methodology textbooks in education (Cohen et al., 2011). However, and

16 Using randomised controlled trials in education

particularly over the last decade, this opposition has increased through the emergence of a strong discourse underpinning this resistance to RCTs. It is a discourse that has tended to create two binary and opposing subject positions: one organised around what has been regarded as the current political hegemony associated with 'what works' and the wider evidence-based practice agenda; and the other representing an alternative political project, based broadly upon critical social research. A clear example of this discourse can be found in the book by Lather (2010), *Engaging Science Policy*, that provides a critique of the move towards a 'what works' agenda in government policy and research funding in a number of countries, including most notably the USA and the UK. The discourse underpinning her book is summarised in Table 1.1.

Table 1.1 The discourse underpinning Lather's (2010) *Engaging Science Policy*

Current political hegemony: 'What works' research	Alternative political project: Critical social research
Right-wing, neo-liberalist, imperialist, masculinist	Left-wing, neo-socialist, democratic, feminist
Positivist	Post-modernist
Quantitative methods (especially randomised controlled trials)	Qualitative methods (an eclectic mix of methods – anything but quantitative)
Objective, de-contextualised, prediction, explanation and verification	Subjective, contextualised, description, interpretation and discovery
Simplistic	Complex
Seeking to establish universal laws of 'what works' through experimentation and replication; based on a view of the social world as simple, unified, fixed and closed	Seeking to show the impossibility of all attempts to represent reality through deconstruction; based on a view of the social world as ambiguous, fragmented, fluid and open

Source: Connolly (2011: 473)

For Lather (2010) this 'what works' agenda has become increasingly apparent in the USA since 2001 and the passing of the No Child Left Behind (NCLB) Act by the new Bush Administration that represented the most wide-ranging reform of the education system in the USA since 1965. One of the key underlying themes of NCLB has been the promotion of a culture of accountability through a focus on setting high standards and measurable goals. Within this, the promotion of 'scientifically based research' has come to be one of the main drivers of this reform, with a clear emphasis on RCTs as providing the mechanism for determining which educational programmes are leading to measurable improvements in outcomes for learners and thus providing the basis for future funding decisions by federal government.

These developments, in turn, have led to a significant increase in funding for RCTs compared to other forms of research and this has been taken forward by the Institute of Education Sciences, formed in 2002 within the US Department of Education, with the mission to 'provide rigorous evidence on which to ground education practice and policy'.

Such developments have been paralleled in the UK with the emphasis placed on evidence-based policy and practice by the incoming New Labour government in 1997. As made clear in the Labour Party Election Manifesto of that year: 'New Labour is a party of ideas and ideals but not of outdated ideology. What counts is what works. The objectives are radical. The means will be modern' (quoted in Oancea and Pring, 2009: 12–13, emphasis added). This emphasis has been taken forward through successive Labour administrations and the following Conservative/Liberal Democrat Coalition Government of 2011–15. The most recent and significant manifestation of this focus has been the establishment of the Education Endowment Foundation (EEF) in England in 2011 by the Sutton Trust, with a founding grant of £125m from the Department for Education. As an independent organisation, the EEF seeks to play a key role in identifying and funding innovative programmes and interventions in education that address the needs of disadvantaged school-aged children in England. It has set itself the goal of securing additional investments to enable it to award as much as £200m in supporting the development, delivery and rigorous evaluation of programmes over its fifteen-year lifespan. In its most recent Annual Report for 2015–16, and within just five years of its formation, the EEF notes that 'more than £75m has so far been invested by the EEF in supporting 127 programmes [in England]. Collectively, these have involved close to one-third of all schools – 75,000 schools and nurseries in England – and reached over 750,000 children and young people' (EEF, 2016: 2).

What these developments have led to, according to Lather (2010), is a new 'what works' political hegemony that is associated with, and serves the needs of, right-wing neo-liberal governments; that privileges quantitative methods and in particular RCTs; and that is overly simplistic and positivist in focus. For Lather, what it rules out are alternative forms of (largely qualitative) research that recognise and help us appreciate the complex and subjective nature of the social world and also recognise the multiple and embedded forms of power and inequalities found within this. This creation of two binary opposite positions – of what works research versus critical social research – is made possible in part by what Oakley (2006) describes as the many 'rhetorical devices' used to encourage rejection of RCTs by the reader. Such devices were clearly evident in the quotations from Cohen et al. (2011) reproduced in the last chapter, which present RCTs as crude, artificial, laboratory-style experiments that are dependent on the ability to control educational settings as natural scientists would control conditions in their laboratories. These rhetorical devices are unfortunately commonplace. Take, as another example, the following description of RCTs:

> Here, all variables are held constant except the one under investigation. Ideally, this one variable is deliberately changed, in two exactly parallel situations as, for example, when a new medical drug is tested against a placebo. If a difference is noted, rigorous tests are conducted to minimize the chances that it is coincidental. Laboratory experiments are repeated, to ensure the results always turn out in the same ways. When involving human populations, inferential statistics are used to determine the probability of a coincidental result. This is the view of research that lies at the heart of the evidence-informed practice movement.
>
> (Hodkinson and Smith, 2004: 151)

This continual construction of RCTs in education, and of the wider evidence-based practice movement, as seeking to ape the methods of medicine and the natural sciences, is also evident in the following quote from Hammersley (2004: 137):

> In this context, we should note that the very phrase 'what works', which the evidence-based practice movement sees as the proper focus for much educational research, implies a view of practice as technical; as open to 'objective' assessment in terms of what is and is not effective, or what is more and what is less effective. I would not want to deny that effectiveness, and even efficiency, are relevant considerations in professional practice. But the information necessary to judge them in the 'objective' way proposed will often not be available – even in principle, not just in terms of the costs involved in gaining it. And any such assessment cannot be separated from value judgements about desirable ends and appropriate means; not without missing a great deal that is important.

Such constructions of RCTs continue to dominate education texts and the thinking of significant sections of the education research community. The ongoing popularity of this view can be understood not just because of the general lack of knowledge or experience of RCTs in practice in education, but also because the key themes associated with this discourse resonate so closely with the strong new managerialist emphasis that is now evident in education with its associated technologies of discipline and performativity (Ball, 1995; Davies, 2003). In the context of increasing government control of the curriculum, of stringent inspection regimes and school league tables, Ball (1995: 265) has previously suggested that there are now attempts 'to monitor, control and instrumentalize all and every facet of educational experience'. This, in turn, has been seen to undermine the professional judgement and craft knowledge of teachers; rendering their role largely to that of technicians where they are required simply to follow the latest diktats set out by government (Hammersley, 2004). In this sense, the portrayal of RCTs as laboratory-style research conducted *on* teachers, rather than *with* them, just adds to this sense of de-professionalisation – especially when RCTs are constructed as artificial experiments that provide simplistic evidence of which programmes work best that teachers are supposed simply to follow, uncritically.

Of course, once this simplistic depiction of RCTs is accepted, once the straw doll has been set up, then it is easy to knock it down. Educational programmes and interventions are more complex in reality, it is claimed. You cannot standardise 'educational treatments' in order to test them as you would do so if you were testing drugs (Hammersley, 2008: 4). The delivery of educational programmes is also never straightforward, as it is claimed RCTs assume – rather they are subject to a myriad of competing interests and negotiations on the ground and in practice (Pawson and Tilley, 1997; Pawson, 2006). The effectiveness of educational programmes therefore needs to be studied in their specific contexts, which RCTs apparently also fail to do (Pring, 2004). In addition, it is argued that there is the need to undertake within-programme analysis that can help us understand the varying effects a programme may have on different sub-groups, something that, again, it is maintained that RCTs are not able to do (Pawson and Tilley, 1997: 43). And all of this is not to mention the ethical problems associated with RCTs that those who oppose education trials often cite, especially the unacceptable practice of denying half the children access to the educational programme or intervention just for the purposes of the research (Cohen et al., 2011).

Ultimately, those opposed to RCTs argue that there is a need to move beyond the very restricted role established for educational research through the promotion of RCTs. As Elliott (2004) suggests for example, in a move that further reproduces this binary divide, there is a need to move away from this narrow focus on 'instrumental effectiveness':

> The primary role of *educational* research, when understood as research directed towards the improvement of *educational* practice, is not to discover contingent connections between a set of classroom activities and pre-standardised learning outputs, but to investigate the conditions for realising a coherent *educational* process in particular practical contexts.

Both the indeterminate nature of educational values and principles, and the context-dependent nature of judgements about which concrete methods and procedures are consistent with them, suggest that *educational* research takes the form of case studies rather than randomised controlled trials. The latter, via a process of statistical aggregation, abstract practices and their outcomes from the contexts in which they are situated. Such case studies entail close collaboration between external researchers and teachers on 'the inside' of an educational practice.

(Elliott, 2004: 175–6, original emphasis)

Moreover, these criticisms from Elliott (2004) are developed further by Whitty (2006) when he contends that there is a need for research that is more broadly based than 'what works' seems to imply: 'Some research, therefore, needs to ask different sorts of questions, including why something works and, equally important, why it works in some contexts and not others' (p. 162).

In defence of RCTs

There are four key elements to the oppositional discourse outlined above that need to be unpicked briefly here. The first point to note relates to the political positioning of RCTs and the criticism that their rise in educational research represents a broader resurgence of a neo-liberal managerial culture of centralised control and audit. This, however, is essentially a political and ideological concern with the way that RCTs are being used rather than a criticism of the methodology itself. Ultimately, an RCT is no more than a research tool for assessing whether a particular programme or intervention is more effective in improving a particular set of outcomes compared to what is normally provided. Of course, the political economy underpinning trials, in terms of who funds them and thus who determines what programmes to evaluate and what outcomes to measure, is an important consideration. If ideologically driven, this can lead to certain educational approaches being legitimised and privileged over others as well as significant gaps in our knowledge in relation to other types of programme and approaches that are overlooked. Moreover, it can lead to the further exclusion of key stakeholders – whether these be teachers, parents or children – as those deemed to be the 'experts' make key decisions regarding what outcomes to focus on and what approaches to improving these are important.

However, this is a fundamental issue for all research, and not just RCTs. All educational and social research is political in the sense that decisions are required in terms of identifying the focus for a study and the key research questions to ask. This, however, does not mean that the research methods used are necessarily political also and thus cannot be used to generate evidence to challenge existing political and ideological orthodoxies. Indeed the effectiveness of using research for such purposes depends on an acceptance that the methods themselves can be neutral so that the findings they produce have the potential to be more broadly recognised and accepted as valid by those who hold differing political perspectives. In this sense, therefore, an alternative view of RCTs is one that promotes their democratic governance and a motivation for their use grounded in broader concerns about social justice. For example, many of the RCTs we have conducted across Ireland, with the support of The Atlantic Philanthropies, have been bottom-up initiatives, whereby baseline surveys of local community needs were conducted and, following extensive consultation, programmes were sourced or designed to meet those needs. RCTs were then conducted to see if they had achieved the intended outcomes, as defined and owned by local stakeholders, with the aim of policy mainstreaming if shown to be effective. Such an approach, that values the generation and use of robust evidence of programme effectiveness, has been critical to promoting and supporting programmes that are effective in reducing inequalities and promoting inclusion. Indeed our challenge to those researchers committed to social justice is how can you justify not including some focus within your work on studying whether existing educational approaches are effective in leading to measurable improvements in the lives of disadvantaged and marginalised groups?

A second key point to note regarding the opposition to RCTs outlined above relates to their intended purpose. We recognise that some advocates of RCTs explicitly adopt and promote a hierarchy of knowledge approach where RCTs are placed towards the top of an evidence pyramid (only surpassed by systematic reviews of RCTs) and are referred to as the 'gold standard' in terms of educational research. This is particularly unhelpful and, unfortunately, only has the effect of furthering the binary divide and type of oppositional thinking outlined earlier. It makes no sense to claim that RCTs are the gold standard unless we are clear what role we are expecting of them. If they are being used to determine the nature and size of the effect of a particular education programme then we can possibly claim that they are the best and most robust method for that particular task. However, they are next to useless as a method for understanding the experiences and perspectives of individuals and the nature of the interactions between them. If this were our focus then the 'gold standard' would be qualitative, ethnographic methods. Moreover, even when it is accepted that RCTs are the most appropriate method for addressing the particular question of how effective a programme or intervention is, the use of the term 'gold standard' limits our ability to recognise that the knowledge they produce, as with all knowledge, is fallible, subject to error and not always conclusive. Questions will always remain regarding, for example, whether the correct outcomes had been identified, did we miss additional programme impacts that went unmeasured, was the trial of sufficient size to draw reliable conclusions and what has been the consequence of some individuals/schools withdrawing from the study.

Moreover, and even if the above points can be addressed, it is also important to acknowledge that an RCT is only designed to answer one specific question regarding whether a programme or intervention has led to measurable change for those who participated in it, *on average*. This is undoubtedly an important question but it is not the only one we are likely to ask. If we find that the programme has been effective, for example, then we will also want to understand why this was the case. Equally, if we find no evidence of it being effective we will also be concerned to understand why. Of course an RCT, which essentially focuses on comparing the average scores of participants before and afterwards with those of a matched control group, is not designed to answer these additional questions. The goals of an RCT are much more modest in telling us whether the programme has led to measurable change rather than why this change has come about. On its own, an RCT is essentially a black box evaluation. This is precisely why multi-method designs, involving strong qualitative research running alongside a quantitative RCT, are so critical to producing a more holistic evaluation. Without detailed qualitative process data it is simply conjecture as to why a programme works or does not work. Fortunately, many RCTs are designed in this way. It is also in this sense that the types of criticism of RCTs offered by Elliott (2004) and Whitty (2006) referred to earlier are not fundamental criticisms of RCTs but of the wider research design, of which an RCT is only a part.

The third point to note, and following on from the last one, is that there is also no necessary reason for RCTs to ignore context and/or to only operate at the most general level of abstraction. With the use of qualitative components running alongside an RCT, it is quite possible to pay close attention to the particular contexts within which a programme is delivered, how its delivery varies between contexts and how, within any one context, the effectiveness of the programme may vary systematically between differing sub-groups of learners. Indeed, and as will be demonstrated in Chapters 3 and 4, even with just quantitative trial data, there are methods for assessing whether a programme has had differential effects for differing sub-groups of learners or for those with particular characteristics. Moreover, with the use of systematic reviews and meta-analysis it is becoming increasingly possible to pool a larger number of trials, which each might have focused on programmes delivered in differing contexts and with some variations in the components they included. In doing this, we are able to then undertake quite sophisticated analyses of the relative significance of differing contexts, processes and programme components for differing groups of participants. Moreover, the most sophisticated research designs should also be capable of staging data collection in such a way as to use the findings from such an analysis to identify case studies for further qualitative exploration, as well as the emerging findings from the qualitative component of the project informing further exploratory statistical analysis of the trial data.

Finally, there are a number of ethical issues raised by opponents of RCTs. The most common criticism is the argument that it is just not morally defensible to deny half of the participants access to an educational programme or intervention simply because of the requirements of an RCT design and the need to produce a control group. In many cases, however, no such ethical dilemma exists as those randomly assigned to the control group are not denied access to a programme, rather their access is simply phased so that they are given access immediately after the trial has finished. In many other cases, however, and especially when piloting a new approach, the resources simply do not exist to deliver it immediately to all eligible learners. Indeed, if this were to be an ethical issue then no teacher would be able to try out anything new or innovative with their class because of the charge that they are denying it to the children in other classes within the school, or other schools in the local area. There is thus always the need to start somewhere in relation to piloting a new intervention or programme. If anything, random allocation is much fairer as the names of all eligible children are effectively placed in the pot and thus they all have an equal chance of participating in the pilot.

Beyond this, the ethical concern regarding the lack of participation in an educational programme or intervention rests on a belief that the programme is actually effective and hence those not able to participate in it are being denied the opportunity to receive a positive boost. However, and in reality, we know that many educational programmes turn out to be ineffective, even those that would appear on the face of it to be clearly likely to be successful. Moreover, and as seen with the example of Scared Straight, there is also the possibility that a programme may have a negative effect. This, in turn, raises what we believe to be the most fundamental ethical issue in relation to RCTs – how can we justify not using RCTs routinely but instead continue to rely upon an education system where experimentation routinely takes place but without any sense of whether the new approaches being introduced are effective or not or whether they might even be causing harm? This ethical issue is even more apparent when we consider programmes that are prioritised and rolled out across an education system, with considerable public investment, but with no evidence of what effects they will have, if any.

RCTs and Critical Realism

Although, as already highlighted, experimental approaches are often dismissed by critics as representing a discredited positivist philosophy of science, one of the key early proponents of experimental approaches in education was Donald T. Campbell who was avowedly anti-positivist in his writing – rejecting the logical positivism of the Vienna circle. Indeed, he can be seen as an early advocate of what has since become termed as a critical realist approach, in that whilst he held onto the belief that there is a social and physical world that exists independent of how individuals perceive it, he also recognised that it was often not possible to accurately capture and measure that reality. Rather, any attempts through social research to understand and reproduce that reality will inevitably be partial and influenced by a range of psychological, social, political, cultural and economic factors. Campbell's approach therefore involved the rejection of the certainty of logical positivists, but equally a rejection of the relativism of some social constructivist and post-modernist perspectives that held there was no reality at all beyond the multiple perspectives of individuals. His was post-positivistic in perspective, rejecting certainty and replacing it with inductive plausibility and statistical probability (Dunn, 1998: 7). Grand claims from an RCT regarding how there is evidence that a particular programme leads to a positive effect for all participants are therefore replaced with more nuanced and tentative claims regarding how the programme is associated with an overall positive effect for a particular group of learners in a specific context, and where, within this, the likelihood of change occurring will vary between participants.

Although, in following Campbell, we consider our approach to RCTs to be informed by a critical realist perspective, many from this tradition are sceptical of the value of RCTs (Pawson and Tilley, 1997; Pawson, 2006). One key criticism levelled at RCTs is that they adopt a simplistic, linear approach to causation that focuses on associations between variables, and thus how change in one variable (brought about by the introduction of a new programme, for example) is directly associated with changes in others (i.e. the outcomes that the programme wishes to improve). In this regard, they see the key purpose of an RCT as being essentially limited and restricted to ensuring that the association between these variables is real rather than a spurious one. This, as highlighted earlier, is achieved by the random allocation of participants to control and intervention conditions so that any difference in outcomes between both groups can be directly assigned to the introduction of the programme. With this done, the focus for an RCT is simply to measure the size and significance of the effect of the programme. In contrast, some of the leading exponents of critical realist approaches to evaluation have stressed the need to adopt what they have called a generative approach to causation. Whilst they believe that there is an external reality that is reflected in measurable regularities and patterns, it is argued that these cannot be captured by a simple set of variables but are generated through complex and inter-connected sets of human activities that are essentially open and located within particular social contexts. They thus contend that our understanding of causality can therefore only be grasped through in-depth qualitative and case study approaches that are able to identify and help explain the mechanisms that generate regularities in behaviour and outcomes.

From such a perspective, an RCT is little more than a black box evaluation and to understand what is really going on, and to learn from this, there is a need to look inside the box to study the actual processes, mechanisms and contexts that give rise to change. Although we would fully concur with this argument, we do not believe that such an approach is incompatible with an RCT. In this respect it is useful to note the distinction made by Shaddish, Cook and Campbell (2002) in their classic text on experimental designs between causal description and causal explanation. As they contend: 'The unique strength of experimentation is describing the consequences attributable to deliberately varying the treatment. We call this causal description. In contrast, experiments do less well in clarifying the mechanism through which and the conditions under which that relationship holds what we call causal explanation' (p. 9). In this respect, and as inferred by Shaddish et al. (2002), a full causal explanation requires a range of methodologies to be employed alongside experimental designs in order not only to provide 'causal description' but also to try and more fully understand the mechanisms at work through 'causal explanation'.

In this respect, there is a sense in which the approach to realist evaluation offered by Pawson and Tilley tends to be limited by allowing itself to remain shaped by the broader binary discourses that we encountered earlier, and as exemplified by Lather (2010), that set what works research in direct opposition to critical social research. Ultimately, quantitative RCT methods that seek to determine effectiveness and in-depth qualitative approaches that seek to uncover generative mechanisms are not incompatible nor mutually exclusive. Indeed it is our contention that both are needed and that, ultimately, they require one another. We have already noted the limited nature of data generated through trials that lack a qualitative component. This type of 'black box evaluation' may provide us with important information on whether a particular programme, operating in a specific context and with a defined group of individuals, is actually effective but it tells us very little about why this might be the case. However, and similarly, even the most sophisticated qualitative accounts of generative mechanisms are of little use without clarity on what they are seeking to explain. As Bonnell et al. (2012) have noted, without an appropriate counterfactual (i.e. a convincing and empirically verified account of what would have happened to the participants had they not participated in the programme or intervention under investigation), any critical realist account, however plausible it may seem, could be entirely wrong. If we take the example of the Scared Straight programme outlined earlier, without the evidence from the RCT, a critical realist account would presumably be left identifying the generative mechanisms that could offer plausible accounts of why it worked whereas, in reality, it was having the opposite effect.

Thus, the current criticism of RCTs from critical realist writers is not a fundamental criticism of RCTs in themselves but, rather, of the limited nature of wider research designs that fail to set an RCT alongside a strong and credible qualitative component. In this sense it is important for us not to be complacent. Although many RCTs now include a qualitative element, these often tend to be limited to studying programme delivery and fidelity rather than engaging with the challenge of developing more in-depth analysis of the generative mechanisms that underpin causal change.

Conclusions

In this chapter we have considered, in some detail, the nature of the opposition to RCTs in education and some of the key criticisms levelled at them. What we have seen is that much of this criticism is based upon a poor understanding of RCTs and a limited awareness of how they have been applied in practice in education. Whilst there are a number of substantive political, ethical and methodological issues that need to be addressed when conducting an RCT, we have argued that none of these is unique to RCTs and that they are all issues that represent significant challenges to educational and social research regardless of the particular methods used.

In attempting to develop a philosophical basis for our work, we have located our approach to the use of RCTs broadly within the critical realist tradition. Ultimately, whilst we hold onto the notion that there is an objective social and physical reality that exists beyond individuals' experiences and perceptions of it, we also recognise the difficulties in seeking to understand and measure it fully. Rather, we seek to promote an approach to RCTs that is tentative in its claims and that avoids simplistic generalisations about causality and replaces these with more nuanced and grounded accounts that acknowledge uncertainty, plausibility and statistical probability. In doing this we recognise that our approach may appear to run counter to that of others who would claim a critical realist approach to evaluation. However, we would suggest that their critique of RCTs tends to reproduce many of the limitations of the broader discourses on RCTs with their construction of binary oppositions. Rather, we would suggest that the use of RCTs and the types of qualitative approaches to developing accounts of generative mechanisms proposed by Pawson and Tilley (1997) are not mutually exclusive but actually require one another (see also Bonnell et al., 2012).

Finally, whilst promoting the use of RCTs in education we also need to be acutely aware of their limitations and the fact that there is not a direct correspondence between how trials are used in medicine and how they can, or should, be conducted in education. Whilst the strength of an RCT rests on strong internal validity, the Achilles heel of the RCT is external validity. In the field of medicine, while external validity of trials is still of relevance, in education and the social sciences it is much more salient. In the medical field it is easier to assume, for example, that the biological action of antiretroviral drugs on HIV is likely to be the same across different individuals and cultural contexts. However, it is still feasible that a particular drug works better on some individuals and not others. In contrast, it would seem naive to assume that a sex education programme found to be effective in schools in Manchester, England, would have the same efficacy among young people in Nairobi, Kenya, without strong consideration of the impact of the different local and cultural conditions. In this respect, within education and the social sciences a range of cultural conditions is likely to influence the external validity of trial results across different contexts. It is precisely for this reason that qualitative components of an evaluation, and particularly the development of plausible accounts of generative mechanisms, are so important.

Also, and in relation to our interpretation and application of the findings from RCTs, we need to be careful not to lose this sense of the importance of context. This was something we witnessed with early attempts to export programmes that had established efficacy from the USA into Ireland. Programme developers were often reluctant to adapt their programme to the different cultural context on the grounds that they were scientifically proven as effective, despite how strange some of the programme components may have been in an Irish educational context. This can lead to a tension between programme fidelity and adaption. That said, a number of programmes have been shown to export well across different national contexts; for example, one of the most evaluated programmes internationally is the Incredible Years Basic Parenting programme that has been shown to be replicable across a range of national contexts including the USA, Wales and Ireland (Webster-Stratton et al., 2008; McGilloway et al., 2009; Jones, 2013). However, the degree to which a programme is transportable in this sense should always remain an empirical question rather than simply being assumed.

Having said this, there is a balance to be struck. Within critical realism there is an emphasis on how the social, and much of the natural, world operate within open systems. They highlight how in open systems, the same causal power can produce different outcomes (Sayer, 2000). However, whilst this underlines the issue of context, time and space, and represents a challenge, we feel it is premature to reject any notion that we can find regularities in the effectiveness of different approaches. Some programmes may produce more enduring impacts than others and be applicable to a wider range of contexts than others. The challenge then is rather than abandoning our search for regularities we need to develop a greater and deeper understanding of them. Ultimately, and within the context of open systems, the search for universal laws may be futile. However, we can still identify a range of regularities (or demi-regularities) that sadly remain all too persistent in relation to the lower levels of educational attainment amongst students from working-class backgrounds, for example, or the enduring inequalities faced by children in care or those from particular minority ethnic groups. And, similarly, there is no reason to believe that we cannot also identify regularities in relation to the effectiveness of particular programmes and interventions on social and educational outcomes for these differing sub-groups within the population. And, ultimately, this should be one of the goals of those committed to promoting social justice in education.

Further Reading

The history of RCTs in education and the social sciences
- *Experiments in Knowing*, by Anne Oakley (Polity Press, 2000).

Paradigm wars and debates concerning RCTs in education
- *Educational Research and Evidence-Based Practice*, edited by Martyn Hammersley (Sage, 2007).
- *Evidence-Based Education Policy: What Evidence? What Basis? Whose Policy?* edited by David Bridges, Paul Smeyers and Richard Smith (Wiley-Blackwell, 2009).

Critical realism and evaluations
- *Realism and Social Science*, by Andrew Sayer (Sage, 2000).
- *Realistic Evaluation*, by Ray Pawson and Nick Tilley (Sage, 1997).
- *Evidence-Based Policy: A Realist Perspective*, by Ray Pawson (Sage, 2006).

2
Logic Models and Outcome Measures

Introduction

This chapter highlights what should be considered during the first stages of designing an RCT. Similar to embarking on any major project, when undertaking an RCT it is a good idea to have a clear plan for the work ahead. The initial plan for an RCT should answer two main questions: 'What is the nature of the programme or intervention we are evaluating?' and 'How are we going to tell if the programme has made any difference to the participants receiving it?' As regards the first question, a logic model can be an invaluable tool in helping us understand the nature of a programme or intervention by specifying its main components and any theory of change that underpins it. In relation to the second question, to assess whether a programme or intervention has been effective we need tools that can measure change in the participant outcomes of interest as reliably and validly as possible. This chapter will help you answer these questions by exploring logic models and outcome measures in more detail.

The chapter begins with a focus on logic models. These are particularly useful for an RCT evaluator because they provide an explicit statement of programme components and programme theory. This provides the opportunity to think critically (and logically) about the programme before conducting an RCT. This chapter focuses on the utility of logic models as an evaluation framework and in particular the parts of a standard logic model that help with programme evaluation, including the identification of anticipated outcomes. Following this, the chapter focuses in on outcomes and how they are measured. Within this, particular emphasis will be placed on the choice of appropriate outcome measures for the purpose of conducting an RCT and also how you can assess the quality of outcome measures.

What is a Logic Model?

A logic model has been defined as a '[g]raphic representation of a programme showing the intended relationships between investments and results' (Taylor Powell and Henert, 2008). In this definition, the term 'investments' refers to the programme we are evaluating. Also, the term 'results' can be used interchangeably with the word 'outcomes'. Therefore, a logic model is a concise visual representation of a programme that explicitly outlines how the programme activities are intended to improve the outcomes of the target group. This explicit description of the relationship between programme actions and outcomes ultimately represents the theory underpinning an educational programme. For some programmes or interventions this may be well developed and explicitly stated whereas for others it remains implicit and may need to be drawn out by the researcher. Ultimately, the programme theory represents the hypotheses that we are testing with an RCT and thus can be used to inform our research questions and research design. This explicit use of theory demonstrates that RCTs are not just about standard, descriptive evaluations but can and should be at the heart of theory testing and generation.

A logic model is very adaptable. It can be used to describe and understand the components and theory behind any programme or organised set of activities that channels resources into producing a defined result, from government food aid programmes in Africa to a phonics programme in a single classroom in England. It can be a very effective tool in facilitating collaboration in the design and evaluation of any programme, particularly because it encourages all stakeholders to form a common language and understanding around the programme they are connected to.

Logic models have been developing over the last forty years both in terms of public awareness and sophistication. They were popularised in the 1990s by large charities and philanthropic organisations such as the W.K. Kellogg Foundation and United Way as a means of identifying programmes to fund and ensuring their resources were being used in an accountable way and that their programmes were delivering on their core organisational outcomes (Kaplan and Garrett, 2005; Kellogg, 2004). The use of logic models has since grown in non-profit organisations with many foundations and government bodies now requiring logic models for grant applications and some even provide logic model building tools for applicants (Child Welfare Information Gateway, 2016). For the purposes of this chapter we will view them through the eyes of an evaluator of an educational programme but they can be a useful framework for any of the stakeholders involved with a programme.

Components of a Logic Model

Logic models can vary in complexity (usually proportional to the complexity of the programme they represent) and include components that relate to a wide range of necessary programme considerations (e.g. collaboration, design and evaluation). However, in its simplest form a logic model has three main components, namely: *outcomes* or the results sought by individuals or groups that have been involved in a programme; *outputs* which are the day-to-day activities, services or products provided by the programme; and *inputs* that represent the resources and investments in terms of the people, time and money required to deliver a programme. These three elements are often presented in boxes in a logic model. Also, these boxes are linked with arrows representing the relationships between programme components. The specific relationships identified between outputs and outcomes represent the core theory of change for the programme, which will be considered in more detail in the next section.

Apart from inputs, outputs, outcomes and programme theory, there are several other terms associated with logic models. Two of the most commonly seen are *external factors* and *assumptions* (Taylor-Powell and Henert, 2008). These two elements are one of the main reasons logic models can grow in complexity. In simple terms, external factors refer to things that may influence the programme but are not under the control of the programme stakeholders. A typical example is a national recession, which results in cuts to government services (such as education programmes) and may result in a programme being scaled down or even discontinued. Assumptions refer to the fact that a logic model is usually an idealised representation of a programme. However, many other potentially controllable factors could be influencing the effects of the programme on outcomes. It could be argued that assumptions are akin to 'implementation factors' (Fixsen et al., 2009). Implementation factors are those that can enable or hinder a programme having its desired effect on outcomes. These are also sometimes referred to as 'mediators'. For example, certain activities may result in a particular outcome, but only if the programme implementation team are well trained, delivering the programme with consistency and fidelity, fully engaged, and working with engaged children and their families. These examples are frequently cited as implementation factors (Gearing et al., 2011).

Programme Theory

Having clarified the components in a logic model there is now a need to think about the relationships between these components, represented by the arrows between boxes in our logic model. We do this by understanding programme theory. There are two main types of programme theory: the *theory of change*, focusing on how programme outcomes influence change in other associated outcomes; and the *theory of intervention*, concerned with understanding how programme outputs or activities impact on programme outcomes.

A single outcome is very often one element in a set of sequential short-, medium- and long-term outcomes. It is at this point that a good theory of change can be useful to help construct and underpin the outcome section of our logic model or, more specifically, the arrows between our outcomes. If we think of an outcome as a single stair in a staircase then progress on the first stair is required before progress can be made on the next and so forth. These stairs represent a 'theory of change'. An example of a theory of change would be in relation to social and emotional development, where Mayer and Salovey (1997) suggest that a child first needs to be able to recognise and label emotions before then being able to recognise emotions in themselves and others. It is suggested that these outcomes, in turn, are required before children can begin to acquire higher level skills such as empathising with others and regulating their own behaviour. Another example is that young children need to develop sufficient print awareness and phonological skills in pre-school before they can develop appropriate reading skills in early primary school (Storch and Whitehurst, 2002).

Alongside our theory of change that sets out the relationships between particular outcomes, we also need to include in our logic model a theory of intervention. A typical child may well progress easily through the stages of cognitive development unaided. However, if a child has a cognitive issue (e.g. dyslexia) then they may require assistance to make progress from one stage to the next. An example theory of intervention would be Vygotsky's 'zone of proximal development' (Chaiklin, 2003) where a child may need scaffolding or support to make it between one or more stages of cognitive development. This type of support is a theory of intervention. Returning to our analogy, a typical child may walk up the staircase without issue, but some children may need a banister (i.e. an intervention or programme) to support them during the climb.

An example of the power of the theory of intervention can be seen in our RCT evaluation of the Mate-Tricks afterschool pro-social behaviour programme (O'Hare et al., 2015). The theory of intervention behind Mate-Tricks was collaborative learning (Dillenbourg, 1999). The programme aimed to use collaborative learning of social skills through the participation of both parents and children in the programme. However, the programme engaged the children but failed to engage the parents despite significant efforts by the programme implementation team, demonstrated through the parents' non-attendance. This led to children learning additional social skills but not the parents. This, in turn, set up a competitive learning situation instead of a collaborative learning one. This competition led to a negative effect on parenting outcomes, which then resulted in a negative effect on child behaviour outcomes (incidentally, demonstrating a theory of change between parenting outcomes and anti-social behaviour outcomes). Unfortunately, there was no explicit logic model at the beginning of this programme's implementation, which would have highlighted the importance of collaborative learning as the programme's theory of intervention and thus informed programme design elements to ensure parental engagement. Therefore, this is a cautionary tale about the importance of careful consideration of the programme theory from the beginning in the design and evaluation of an educational programme.

Theories of change and theories of intervention can be drawn from a wide range of sources. In addition to the examples of popular theories outlined above, there are many others you can draw on, for example: the theory of planned behaviour (Ajzen, 2011) for behaviour change; the social ecological model (Bronfenbrenner, 2009) for social interaction; and SAFE practices (Durlak et al., 2011) for social and emotional learning. However, practice wisdom and the evidence base (e.g. from systematic reviews) are also useful sources to decide on the change and intervention theories underpinning the programme.

The utility of specific theories may alter depending on the stage of the programme and also to whom the programme is being delivered. For example, a literacy programme may be most appropriately underpinned by developmental theories for young learners but older learners may respond better to a programme based on theories of motivation or different mixes of the two depending on the age group. Furthermore, it is not always about change – rather it can be concerned with maintaining the status quo. For example, older adults may require a programme to maintain cognitive capacity (e.g. memory) rather than improving it. In this sense, simply resisting decline in relation to cognitive capacity would be a good outcome.

These issues and other related issues related to theory are discussed at length in Funnell and Rodgers (2011) who also offer a word of caution: even though an outcome chain appears in a logic model and may even seem eminently plausible, it is not necessarily the case that they do follow in a chain. As Funnel and Rogers suggest (2011) there may well be alternative theories or competing theories that describe the chain more appropriately. Luckily though, RCTs are an excellent tool for exploring outcome chains and their causal nature.

Building a Programme Logic Model

Now that we have discussed logic model components and programme theory we will consider the practical aspects in building a logic model. The most important aspect of developing a logic model is collaboration as there are usually many people involved in delivering and receiving a programme. As such, and to ensure the successful representation of a programme, it is important that they are able to feed their knowledge and experience into the logic model. A combination of practice knowledge most typically from teachers, user experience in the form of feedback from pupils, robust evidence of what works elsewhere (e.g. Higgins et al., 2014), evaluation know how and existing theory is a powerful mix for constructing a programme logic model, but rarely does one person have all these insights. Therefore, collaboration using the logic model framework offers the best chance for designing an effective educational programme. Different stakeholders may well have different views on what are the target outcomes of a particular programme. For example, some may wish to see change in social, emotional or behavioural outcomes. Others may be more inclined towards improving academic attainment. Discussion of the logic model upfront can draw out these differing orientations and provide the basis for reaching agreement and shared understanding.

There may also be differing views on the theories of change and intervention, but if these are agreed while developing the logic model then it is most likely that everybody will work in an engaged, informed and synchronous way behind these theories. Finally, the importance of collaboration increases as the programme elements stretch across knowledge areas such as health, social care and education. Different disciplines and areas of work may have differing terminology even for the same outcomes and theory. Thus, from the starting point, discussion stimulated by collaborating on the development of a logic model can provide a common understanding of concepts as well as agreement on the core elements and theory behind any intended programme.

When embarking on building a logic model, it is helpful to see logic models as a statement of programme components and theory (both the theory of intervention and theory of change) in a series of causal statements about a programme and, as a result, they can be summarised into six sequenced questions:

1. What measurable things are you intending to change (outcomes)?
2. What is the pattern of change between these outcomes (theory of change)?
3. What are you intending to do (outputs) to make these outcomes change (theory of intervention)?
4. What do you have at your disposal to do these things (inputs)?
5. What is the context or situation surrounding the programme (external factors)?
6. What needs to be in place for the programme to be implemented properly (assumptions)?

Considering the first four questions above, they have intentionally been set in this sequence because it is best practice to start with a focus on outcomes as it sets them as the central point of the logic model and the emerging programme. The main reasons for this are that the whole programme is designed around an outcome that the programme team actually want to change. Secondly, it leaves no room for activities that do not contribute to change in the chosen outcomes and as a result limits the unnecessary use of resources. This is an important point given the general pressure on educational budgets and need for cost-effectiveness. The final two questions refer to external factors and assumptions. These are acting on all parts of the logic model. They also act on the logic model even after it has been constructed as the external situation and assumptions may change. These two factors can change for a number of reasons, which we will look at later in the chapter.

Figure 2.1 shows a visual representation of the core elements of a logic model and how they interact with each other. The key point in this diagram is that the direction of thinking about a logic model is opposite to the direction of programme implementation over time. This technique of thinking backwards, from outcomes to the outputs required to change them and finally to the inputs that resource them, is an important one. This may seem counter intuitive as the thinking is in the opposite direction to the typical direction of programme implementation where, normally, programmes start with a finite set of resources that then generate activities which then seek to achieve a set of outputs that, hopefully, will achieve change in outcomes.

However, and in reality, outputs and inputs are often a limiting factor. There is only so much money, time and expertise available. Therefore, it is more likely to be an iterative process where adjustments have to be made throughout the development of the logic model based on practical considerations. Ultimately though, it is still critical to get into the mindset of continually thinking backwards from outcomes when constructing a logic model and developing the associated programme.

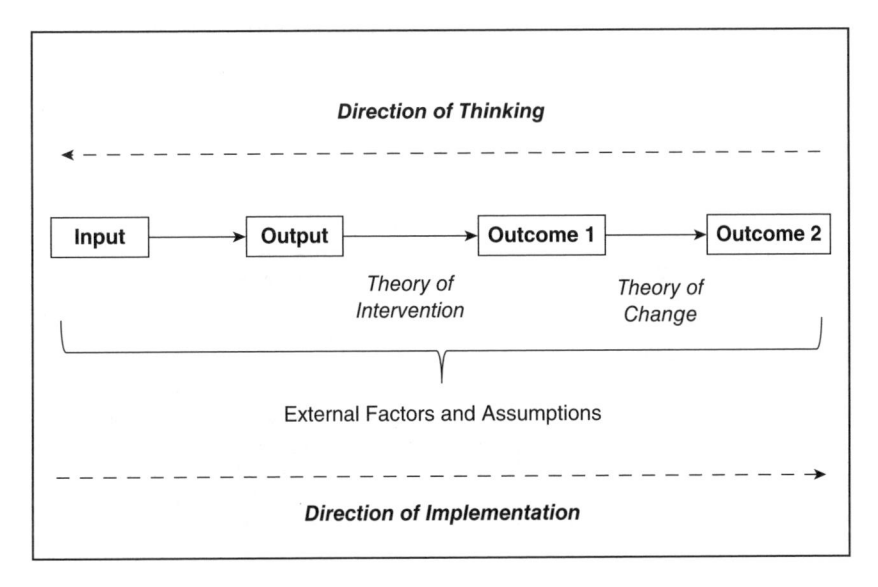

Figure 2.1 Key elements of a logic model and how they interact

A Worked Example

You are most likely to start thinking about a logic model as set out in a series of boxes and arrows. One useful approach is to produce a large printout of a blank logic model where stakeholders can collaboratively add sticky notes regarding their views on inputs, outputs, outcomes, external factors, assumptions and programme theories. These can easily be moved around until an agreed model is produced which then can be laid out more concretely in a further blank template.

Building a logic model is best demonstrated through a worked example. The following example of a logic model (presented in Figure 2.2) uses a book-gifting programme for two-year-old children called Bookstart+, which was provided by the UK national reading charity Booktrust (see O'Hare and Connolly, 2014). In essence, Bookstart+ is a pack of reading resources delivered to parents/carers by health visitors during their statutory visit to a two-year-old child. The pack contains baby books and guidance materials intended to promote early reading habits between parents and their young children. In this example the health visitors also receive training on how to gift the Bookstart+ packs and how to conduct a short demonstration aimed at priming or encouraging parents to read to their child. The training comprises a Booktrust coordinator attending health visitor training meetings and providing a 30-minute presentation on priming families to read together. This includes telling parents that children need stories as an essential part of their development and should be part of their daily routine from as early as possible. This is followed by a question and answer session with the Booktrust coordinator. The health visitors were also provided with an administration pack describing how to gift the packs, and further background on the programme.

Inputs	Outputs	Outcomes		
		Short	Medium	Long
Staff and Participant Time; Money; Infrastructure; Networks	Health Visitor Training by Booktrust; Parent Gifted Bookstart Packs; Parent Primed by Health Visitors	Improved Parent Reading Attitudes and Skills; Increased Library Attendance	Increased Shared Reading Behaviours; Improved Literacy Environment	Improved Child Reading Ability

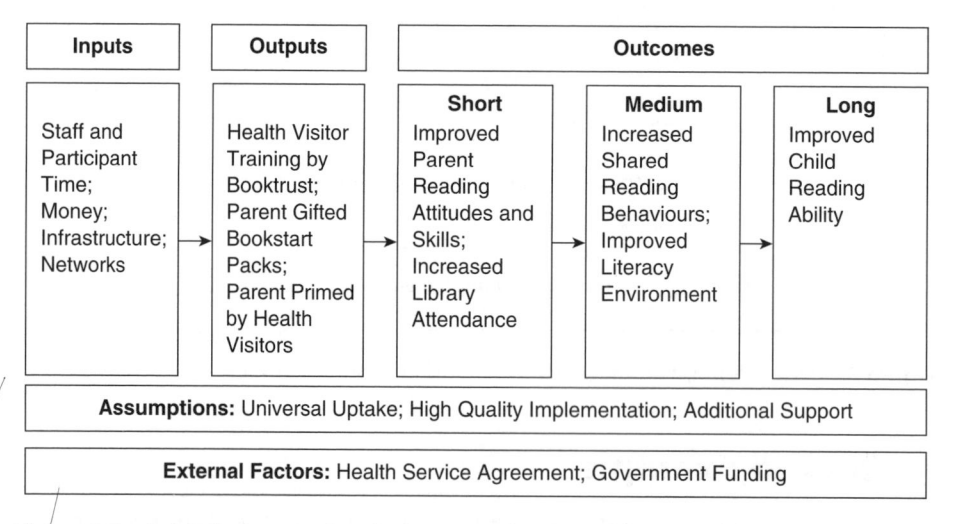

Assumptions: Universal Uptake; High Quality Implementation; Additional Support

External Factors: Health Service Agreement; Government Funding

Figure 2.2 A worked example of a logic model

The *inputs* for this programme outlined in Figure 2.2 are staff time, money, infrastructure, and networks. Basically, time from Booktrust staff and health visitors combined with money from their public and charity funders which allows for preparation and implementation of outputs. The core *outputs* of this programme are the Bookstart+ packs, the health visitor training and health visitor demonstrations to parents. The outputs section, as in this case, also usually highlights the main implementation team (e.g. health visitors and Booktrust staff) and programme participants (e.g. parents).

The *outcomes* in this logic model are broken down into short-, medium- and long- term outcomes. It is expected that the outputs will have short-term effects on parental attitudes to sharing books and reading with their two-year-olds (this is the programme theory of intervention). It is also intended that the programme will have a beneficial effect on increasing library membership, which is another aspect of the theory of intervention. The accompanying theory of change specifies how these initial short-term outcomes are expected to lead to improvements in medium- and long-term outcomes. In this case, medium-term outcomes that are expected to flow from change in these short-term outcomes is a resultant impact upon the reading behaviours of the family, including increased shared reading practices between parent and child and a better literacy environment with increased numbers of books in the home. Ultimately, it is intended that these short- and medium-term changes will have beneficial results longer term in the child's reading ability.

There are also several *external factors* at play in this model. Two clear factors are that Booktrust (as a charity) must maintain a working relationship with a statutory service, in this case health visiting teams, and that the programme is partially funded by government, requiring this investment to maintain the programme. Finally, the main *assumptions* underlying this programme are that the programme is a universal service, such that it is engaged with by families of all two-year-old children in a given area regardless of their demographic characteristics (e.g. child gender and family socio-economic status), and that the pack is gifted as intended, which means that a health visitor gifts the pack and follows the instructions and guidance they received during their training. A final assumption here is that the programme requires additional support for families to capitalise on these initial activities to see the benefits in the longer-term outcomes and ultimately child literacy improvement.

As it happens, we subjected this particular programme to an actual RCT evaluation of its effects on intended short-term outcomes (O'Hare and Connolly, 2014). The study found that there were some significant short-term improvements in parents' attitudes to reading and books. However, the study also found a short-term decrease in library attendance. The first result supported the theory of intervention of the programme on parent outcomes, but also rejected the second theory of intervention on increasing library attendance. Incidentally, and in attempting to make sense of these findings, it was hypothesised that parents receiving the books felt less of a need to go to the library in the short term as they had just received a pack of new books. It is worth noting that this study was conducted in a relatively short period (three months). As such, although the parents may have showed improved attitudes towards reading, this may take longer to be reflected in the medium-term outcomes of shared reading behaviours.

Furthermore, longer-term improvement in child reading outcomes may also only begin to improve over an extended period of time of their parent reading to them.

It should be said that this theory of change between these three reading-related outcomes is offered as a sequence of change. This is sometimes referred to as an *outcome chain* and is a common feature in logic models. As indicated, very often you can see programme logic model outcomes split into short-, medium- and long-term outcomes as demonstrated in this example. One general caveat here is it may be misleading to think of this as a real chain as very often there are iterative, cyclical and concurrent relationships between the outcomes in the chain. Again, the underpinning theories of change and intervention can be helpful for explaining these iterations and cycles. A real-world example of concurrent outcome change was the RCT evaluation of the Doodle Den after-school literacy programme that we undertook (see Biggart et al., 2013) where the programme simultaneously improved literacy ability and pupil concentration in class. It would be hard to argue in this case that one was changed first and then led to a longer-term change in the other. What is more likely is that the programme was simultaneously supporting the development of these two outcomes.

Finally, it is worth noting that logic modelling can be considered to be a developing field. In fact, the first publication that mentioned them was by Joseph S. Wholey in 1979. Since then there have been many conceptual and practical innovations with logic models and it is likely there will be many more in the coming years. Therefore, if there is a need to go 'off script' please do so, as these creative tangents may form future best practice in the further methodological development of logic modelling. Thus, a logic model should be used as a framework and not a definitive map. This allows some flexibility in the process and can help you avoid 'design paralysis' when trying to fit things in linear boxes and arrows that do not suit a particular programme.

Other Functions of Logic Models

The last few sections have shown us how to build logic models and their utility for designing a programme or intervention. It is now useful for us to consider other functions that a logic model can be used for. Additional related functions include using logic models for collaboration, dissemination, and most pertinently for the purposes of this present book, evaluation.

Firstly, and in relation to collaboration, logic models are particularly useful in collaborative contexts for forging a 'common language' around a particular programme. This is an important consideration in the development of educational programmes as there are often many different stakeholders invested in their success and these stakeholders may have different terminology even for basic components such as inputs, outputs and outcomes. Stakeholders can include teachers, pupils, parents, school leadership, voluntary organisations, statutory bodies and policymakers. Therefore, dialogue between these partners is important to understand different perspectives and terminology. A salient point here is that the underlying assumptions and external factors are often influenced by these stakeholders. As such, effective and meaningful collaboration is important for stabilising these two factors to allow the smooth running of a programme. For example, if a programme is to be funded by a government department for education it makes sense to include them in the development of the logic model so that it aligns with government policy initiatives and objectives.

Secondly, related to collaboration is dissemination. Although there may be a wide range of stakeholders involved in developing the logic model you will not be able to include input from all of those who will ultimately deliver and use the programme. This is where a logic model can be useful. It can be used to communicate the aims and objectives to a wider audience. This is beneficial for the effectiveness of the programme because everybody is then clear about, and working towards, the explicit outcomes of the programme. Also, it can help individuals locate themselves in what can often be a quite complex system and it can show them how their contribution is making a difference to improving outcomes for participants. However, because different stakeholders have differing capacities and interests in a programme, many different versions of the same logic model may be required. As programme complexity increases so often does the logic model and as a result the capacity required to understand the logic model. Therefore, capacity building in a workforce around logic models, understanding outcomes and programme theory are useful considerations when working with logic models.

There are some interesting innovations in the burgeoning world of logic models that try to facilitate stakeholder communication. These innovations attempt to let people know where they fit into the programme and generally increase understanding of that programme. Strategies include providing interactive maps, the inclusion of hyper-links to raw data and evaluation reports. For example, the Oregon Paint Stewardship Pilot Programme (Paint Stewardship Program, 2016) uses advanced graphic design interfaces to show stakeholders their role in the logic model of a programme designed to improve the disposal of waste paint.

The third and final function of a logic model to be considered here is the most important one in the context of this book, in relation to how logic models act as an evaluation framework. In this sense, a completed logic model provides an important reference point for designing an evaluation. On the one hand, the logic model sets out a set of core outcomes that should provide the basis for the *impact evaluation* and thus the quantitative data to be collected through the trial itself. We will look in more detail at outcomes and measures shortly. On the other hand, the logic model provides an important starting point and framework for designing the *process evaluation*. The process evaluation will include various components and is likely to draw upon quantitative and qualitative data. The overall aim of the process evaluation is to 'get inside the black box' to help inform our understanding of the effects (or lack of effects) of the programme. In this sense, the process evaluation will include a focus on three key aspects: how the programme was delivered; how it was experienced; and how it has worked (or not worked).

In relation to how the programme was delivered, the process evaluation needs to capture and record what was actually done, when and to whom. There is often some type of manual or guide setting out exactly what the programme involves and this should be the reference point for determining what information needs to be collected. The information from this element of the process evaluation is typically used to develop some type of 'fidelity measure' or score to indicate how well the programme was delivered by each school, class and/or to each child. This, in turn, is then taken into account as part of the quantitative analyses (see Chapter 4). Other information will be used to identify where there has been most variation in the delivery of the programme and this, in turn, can be used to inform the focus on semi-structured interviews with participants and key informants to help understand why there has been such variation.

With regard to how the programme has been experienced, this can involve the use of broader questionnaires to capture overall levels of satisfaction with the programme as well as more in-depth semi-structured interviews and focus groups to explore experiences and perspectives in more detail and possibly to investigate particular issues emerging from the wider satisfaction survey(s). Finally, and in relation to how the programme has worked (or the reasons why it did not work), this is where a range of typically qualitative data is drawn together, often in the form of case studies, to seek to identify the particular sets of processes and interactions (or 'generative mechanisms' as we referred to them in the previous chapter from a critical realist perspective) that are the most plausible explanations for the change (or lack of change) in outcomes. These, in turn, will be determined by the broader contexts represented by the assumptions and external factors that have been identified.

In all three regards, the logic model is a critical component in identifying what the core activities and outputs are, who the key participants and stakeholders are, what the core assumptions and external factors are that are required to be in place, and what the theories of intervention and change are that link these together. These, in turn, provide practical reference points for mapping out who needs to be interviewed, what needs to be observed, and what processes need to be identified and studied.

Defining and selecting outcomes

There are many interpretations of what an outcome is and they can also vary in the terms used to describe them (e.g. result, indicator, construct and measure). However, and in the context of RCTs, it is probably most appropriate to think of outcomes as measureable characteristics of human development that can change over time. At this point it is worth returning to what an outcome is not. In education, and more generally in children's services, outcomes are often confused with outputs. As we have seen in relation to logic models, an output is the activity, programme or service available and who participates in them. For example, a school may provide 20 places on an additional maths class (an output) and 15 children will take up those places (another output), but these outputs are only the processes used to change what we consider to be the outcome, which in this case would be an increase in maths ability in pupils.

Conceptions of outcomes vary greatly across academic disciplines. Well-recognised outcomes in medicine include survival rates, mortality rates and obesity levels. Sociology and social policy (where the term indicator is more frequently used than outcome) often considers employment and socio-economic outcomes. In psychology, outcomes are often referred to as constructs, that is, characteristics that are relatively stable and frequent in human populations (Cronbach and Meehl, 1955) such as intelligence, personality and attitudes. The interdisciplinary field of education necessarily draws upon all these concepts. Public health outcomes are now a substantial research agenda in schools, such as child obesity (Gortmaker et al., 1999). Psychological constructs are also key considerations for schools, not least cognitive ability (Rutter and Maughan, 2002) and emotional health and wellbeing (Connolly et al., 2011).

The use of logic modelling in identifying the core anticipated outcomes for a particular programme or intervention has been discussed above. Where a programme does not have a logic model then it is recommended that the research team should attempt to develop such a model in order to provide the framework for their process evaluation and also the identification of outcomes. Having identified what these core outcomes should be, the next step is to operationalise these outcomes or, in other words, to identify how they can actually be measured. A useful mnemonic to bear in mind when considering the operationalisation of outcomes is *SMART* which stands for outcomes that are specific, measureable, achievable, realistic and time-bound (Rubin, 2002). Being *specific* emphasises that the closer your chosen outcome is to what you want to change the better. For example, if you want to implement a comprehension programme then instead of just having reading ability as the outcome it is better to have reading comprehension skills for 8–10 year old children, which is much more specific. Being *measurable* highlights the importance of identifying outcomes that can be realistically and practically measured and this, in turn, raises a number of specific issues in relation to the reliability and validity of outcome measures that will be mentioned briefly at the end of this chapter.

Achievable relates to the likelihood that a given programme is going to change the chosen outcome. In relation to our previous discussion of Bookstart+ it has been suggested that it is unlikely that a short, one-off book-gifting programme such as this one is going to have a far-reaching impact on reading ability amongst children. Rather, it is more likely to act as a catalyst for changing reading attitudes and paired-reading habits between parents and their children. These are likely to be the achievable outcomes, whereas the programme would require significant additional levels of literacy support for children and parents in order to change the children's reading ability.

Linked to outcomes being achievable is the need for them also to be *realistic*. This relates to choosing outcomes that are in the domain of any given programme. For example, you would not realistically expect Bookstart+ to have any effect on a child's physical health outcomes. Lastly, *time-bound* refers to the notion that a programme sets the timeframe for making a change on a particular outcome. This is particularly useful for an RCT because it can help researchers arrange for post-test measures to be timed so that it can pick up expected change in the chosen programme outcomes at the appropriate time.

Choosing outcome measures

As we have seen there is a wide range of outcomes of relevance to education. There is also a wide and intimidating number of accompanying measures for these outcomes, growing by the day. As such, and in order to simplify the process, it is useful to categorise the quantitative measures we tend to use in RCTs into four different types under a single framework called the 'ABCD model' representing attitudinal, behavioural, cognitive, and demographic elements. The first three represent the three core types of outcome measures whereas the fourth represents broader data that are sometimes needed for the purposes of the analysis of trial data. Before proceeding to a description of these it should be stated that you may not be interested in measuring all of these elements in a single RCT but it is useful to have an overview of the potential outcome measures to improve instrument choice.

Attitudinal measures reflect internally held beliefs, perceptions, opinions or thoughts. They can be on a range of issues, for example: pupil attitudes towards school subject areas (e.g. motivation to read); children's views on their participation in decision making (O'Hare, et al., 2016); and school leaders' attitudes towards improving pupil health and wellbeing (Connolly et al., 2011: 38). Attitudinal measures usually collect categorical data typified by Likert scale measures. Likert scales are a series of repeated options (usually between three and six options) for a list of statements. The participants then choose one of the several Likert options and repeat this for a series of statements using the same options. We tend to use a series of statements and not single statements because we are looking for underlying trends through composite scores to ensure measurement reliability. An example scale is provided in Figure 2.3 representing the 'Pupils Motivated

---

Do you read for any of the following reasons?

Show how much you agree with each of these statements.

Tick one box for each row.

	Agree a lot	Agree a little	Disagree a little	Disagree a lot
a) I like to read things that make me think	[ ]	[ ]	[ ]	[ ]
b) It is important to be a good reader	[ ]	[ ]	[ ]	[ ]
c) My family like it when I read	[ ]	[ ]	[ ]	[ ]
d) I learn a lot from reading	[ ]	[ ]	[ ]	[ ]
e) I need to read well for my future	[ ]	[ ]	[ ]	[ ]

Figure 2.3 Pupils motivated to read scale

Source: Twist et al. (2012)

to Read Scale' from the Progress in International Reading Literacy Study (Twist et al., 2012). You can see that it has five questions around similar issues that combine to give an overall score for a pupil's motivation to read.

Behavioural measures explore a participant's actions. Again, they can look at a range of issues, for example anti-social behaviour (Achenbach et al., 2008) and children's eating behaviour (Wardle, et al., 2001). As a result, behavioural items often have responses like 'never true for me', 'very often true', 'always true', or are even defined by time, such as 'once a week', 'once a month', etc. As behaviour can be an observed action it does not have to be self-reported. Teachers or parents can provide information on child behaviour based on their observations (e.g., Stone et al., 2015). Furthermore, some behaviours will be simple but they may have very powerful longer-term consequences on outcomes, e.g. the decision to go into higher education (Oreopoulos and Petronijevic, 2013) or engagement in extracurricular science and maths activity (Gottfried and Williams, 2013).

One last type of measure similar to behavioural measurement worth mentioning is physiological response measures. These measures assess unconscious physical responses to various types of stimulus or activity. Physiological measures although not often associated with education are becoming increasingly used in educational contexts. There is a growing usage of physiological indicators such as: salivary cortisol, which is a measure of stress (e.g. Schonert-Reichl et al., 2015); galvanic skin response, an indicator of stimulation/arousal (e.g. Vallabhajosula et al., 2016); and electroencephalogram (EEG), which looks at brain activity through sensors placed on the scalp (e.g. Gruzelier et al., 2014).

Cognitive measures are generally associated with performance. Often called ability tests, they usually assess skills or knowledge on a specific subject. Examples of cognitive measures include school exams (e.g. UK GCSE grades), standardised achievement tests (e.g. New Group Reading Test – GL Assessment, 2016) and thinking skills tests (e.g. California Critical Thinking Skills Test – Insight Assessment, 2016). These tests can have a range of items from multiple-choice questions through to short answer and essay questions. In an RCT of an education programme it is always good to include a cognitive measure if possible, because these are often the outcomes of most interest to potential programme funders like governments. Furthermore, cognitive measures often have the most secure operational definition (as discussed before) and as a result are more predictive of future outcome change than their attitudinal counterparts (e.g. O'Hare and McGuinness, 2015), thus providing greater evidential support for a longer-term theory of change.

Demographic measures typically gather information on personal and social attributes of the individual. They can include characteristics such as poverty, gender, religion, educational level and employment. These items are usually in a multiple-choice format providing several suggested response categories. In an RCT evaluation, these measures are typically used in exploratory analysis where we consider whether, for example, a programme or intervention has been differentially effective for different sub-groups of participants.

In relation to sourcing specific measures, articles and reports publishing the findings of related trials are usually an excellent resource because studies often publish the measures they have used either in the methods, results or in the appendices. There is also the ETS test link (ETS, 2016), which is a database with over 25,000 measures that is searchable by outcome. In addition, there are also a number of commercial organisations that produce standardised measures specifically for educational assessment, for example, GL Assessment (2016) and Hodder Education (2016). However, such tests provided by commercial organisations will tend to incur a cost that is usually charged per test ordered.

More complex measures will come with a set of instructions for administration and these are often found with a test manual. It can include a whole range of administration requirements including details on time limits and equipment required (e.g. pens, calculators). There are occasionally verbatim instructions that need to be read out to participants. Also, some measures need to be administered on an individual basis rather than on a group basis. For example, younger children in the early years often need one-to-one administration whereas older children with good literacy skills can often have measures administered on a whole-class basis. Occasionally, you will require a particular qualification to administer a test. This is because some tests require professional experience to work with vulnerable participants (e.g. pupils with autism) and specialist skills to interpret or analyse the data collected. These requirements are usually found when ordering a test from the test publisher. If this is the case, and you do not have the qualification to administer the test, you may need to ask a suitably qualified person to become part of the research team to order and administer the measures for the project.

Finally, despite the wide range of standardised measures and tools for assessing educational outcomes, there are many more educational outcomes of interest that have no widely accepted or widely utilised measure. As discussed before it is important to focus on the outcome of interest rather than what has an available standardised measure. Therefore, this is where measure development becomes relevant. There is not space in this chapter to provide a full treatment of test development but there are a number of guides that specifically focus on test development provided in the Further Reading section at the end of this chapter.

Conclusions

This chapter has focused on the first stage in undertaking an RCT. Developing a logic model may seem like an unnecessary distraction, especially if timescales are tight and there is a need to begin recruiting schools and collecting baseline (pre-test) data. However, and from our considerable experience in running trials, we have found the use of logic modelling to be critical to the effective and successful design of a trial. As we have seen in this chapter, logic models provide the basis for setting out clearly and explicitly the nature of the programme or intervention under investigation, its key components, its underpinning theories of change and, crucially, the main outcomes that it seeks to address. Having clarity at this stage is essential in order to map out the design of the process evaluation and also to identify and agree the outcomes that will form the basis for the trial. This latter element is extremely important, as is the need to do this collaboratively. Programme providers and funders need to be actively involved in identifying and agreeing outcomes from the outset, otherwise there will be a significant risk that these will be challenged at the end of the trial should it not provide evidence of positive effects. In such circumstances it is not uncommon for key stakeholders to claim that the trial was not properly designed and, usually, that the wrong outcomes were selected.

We have also seen in this chapter the importance of selecting outcome measures carefully so that they are specific, measurable, achievable, realistic and time-bound. Equally importantly, they should as far as possible be measures that have been used before and for which there are good data demonstrating their reliability and validity. The use of existing measures not only gives more confidence in your trial but also allows for a more direct comparison with other trials that use the same measures.

Further Reading

Logic models
- *The Logic Model Guidebook: Better Strategies for Great Results*, by Lisa Wyatt Knowlton and Cynthia Phillips (Sage, 2012).
- *Logic Model Development Guide: Logic Models to Bring Together Planning, Evaluation & Action* (Kellogg Foundation, 2001).

- *Program Development and Evaluation: Logic Models* (University of Wisconsin-Extension), retrieved from http://fyi.uwex.edu/programdevelopment/logic-models/

Programme Theory and Evaluation
- *Purposeful Program Theory: Effective Use of Theories of Change and Logic Models*, by Sue C. Funnell and Patricia J. Rogers (John Wiley & Sons, 2011).
- *New Directions for Evaluation*, by P. Rogers, T. Hacsi, A. Petrosino and T. Huebner (eds) (Jossey-Bass, 2000).
- *Handbook of Practical Program Evaluation*, 4th edn, by Kathryn E. Newcomer, Harry P. Hatry and Joseph S. Wholey (Jossey-Bass, 2015).

Outcome Measurement
- *Measuring Program Outcomes: A Practical Approach*, by Harry Hatry, Therese van Houten, Margaret Plantz and Martha Taylor (United Way of America, 1996).
- *Reliability and Validity Assessment*, by Edward Carmines and Richard Zeller (Sage, 1979).
- *An Introduction to Psychological Assessment and Psychometrics*, by Keith Coaley (Sage, 2014).
- *Personality, Individual Differences and Intelligence*, by John Maltby, Liz Day and Ann Macaskill (Pearson, 2013).

3
Research Designs for RCTs

Introduction

This chapter focuses on the key steps involved in designing an RCT. It sets out a range of key designs used in education that involve either the random allocation of individuals (simple RCTs) or the random allocation of classes or schools (cluster RCTs) to intervention groups or control (often 'treatment as usual') groups. The principles of different methods of randomisation are discussed and how these are done using SPSS is illustrated. The chapter concludes by explaining how to calculate the sample size required for a particular research design and provides step-by-step guidance on how to do this using the freely available software package *Optimal Design*. The need to link this to proposed analysis is also discussed. Throughout the chapter case studies are used to present practical examples from real-life RCTs to contextualise the challenges and opportunities that planning RCTs in educational settings can offer.

Underpinning Principles

As described in the Introduction, RCTs are fundamentally based upon the principle that if you have two broadly equal groups and one gets an intervention while the other does not, then differences between the groups are likely to be due to the intervention. As we will see in the next chapter, with RCTs we often separate out the variations that exist among participants in a trial between that due to the signal (i.e. the intervention or programme) and that due to background noise (i.e. natural variation between individuals). The essential logic that underpins our approach to RCTs is that if the two groups are the same at the beginning, and then one receives an intervention but the other does not, then any difference at the end is due to the intervention because this is the only systematic difference between the two groups.

As we saw in Chapter 1, education RCTs are often criticised by detractors as being based in a positivist framework. It is often argued that whilst it is relatively easy to distinguish cause and effect when studying how chemicals interact in a laboratory, the social worlds of classrooms, lecture halls, schools, colleges and universities are too diverse in their geographic, social and academic variables for cause and effect to be determined in any direct and measurable way. As outlined in Chapter 1, it is argued that such contexts are essentially open systems and that the myriad of different factors and processes that operate and articulate between one another, not just within but between these contexts, means that we can never control for all of the possible intervening variables that might exist and thus pinpoint the effects of a programme or intervention on particular educational outcomes. Yet, teachers and lecturers continually strive to make improvements for their learners, and students do learn new things in these settings. Therefore, if change can happen, then it must be possible to improve practice, no matter how complex this process may be.

The key purpose underpinning the design of RCTs is to explore the potential effects of a programme or intervention on outcomes amongst learners and to try to rule out other alternative causes. In considering causality, there is an important distinction to be made between events that are established as *cause and effect* – i.e. where one event causes an effect – and a situation where there is just a *correlation* between two events – i.e. two events happen at the same time, but one does not cause the other. A good example of this is that ice-cream sales are correlated to higher homicide figures in New York City, USA (Rumsey, 2016). This could indicate that your next ice-cream cone could be bad for your life expectancy. However, it is more likely that hotter weather not only increases the likelihood of people buying ice-cream but it also increases the likelihood of violent crimes occurring. For example, consumption of alcohol, increased house break-ins due to windows being left open or some other factors are actually more likely to have caused the rise in the homicide rate. It just so happens that these behaviours increase at the same time as more ice-cream is consumed. Therefore they are correlated, but neither causes the other.

The key aim of an RCT when studying the differences between two groups is therefore to rule out all other potential causes of such differences so that we are left with the programme or intervention being the only plausible explanation for these differences above and beyond the natural variation that exists (i.e. the background noise). This is where having a reference or comparison group is essential as it helps us to rule out anything external to the programme or intervention that would have impacted on the participants and improved their outcomes anyway. The key idea here is that anything external will have impacted upon both groups of participants, if they are similar, and thus will have led to improvements in both groups. As such, our main focus is not on the raw and absolute change that has occurred amongst those getting the intervention from pre-test to post-test, but the additional change that has occurred *above and beyond* what would have happened anyway (as represented by the change in the comparison group).

However, and as we noted previously, this logic depends upon the fact that we are comparing two essentially similar groups at pre-test. This is where the randomised aspect of RCTs is so critical. The key point here is that we do not need to be able to identify and control for all of the possible alternative causes of differences between our intervention and comparison group. So long as we have a sufficiently large sample and we randomly allocate participants to both groups, then the random allocation process will ensure that such potential causes are evenly distributed across both groups and thus can be ruled out as possible explanations for any differences we ultimately find between the two groups. Thus with sufficiently sized groups and the use of random allocation, the only systematic differences between the two groups at post-test is that one has received the intervention or programme whilst the other has not and therefore we can be confident that any differences between the two groups in relation to outcomes must be due to the intervention (Torgeson and Torgeson, 2001). As such, the underpinning philosophy is that appropriately designed *randomised* and *controlled* trials take into account hidden and/or unknown factors and variables that, if not controlled for, could increase the *effect sizes* of a particular intervention (Campbell and Stanley, 1963; Holland, 1986; Tymms et al., 2008). In addition some of the other threats presented by single case studies or quasi-experiments such as history threats, maturation threats, testing threats, instrumentation threats, mortality and regression threats are effectively dealt with by RCTs spreading the distribution of these potential confounding variables evenly between control and intervention groups (Trochim, 2012). RCTs, provided that the sample size is large enough, with their random distribution of these background threats/factors, should ensure 'that the only difference between the two groups was the intervention' (Torgeson and Torgeson, 2001: 319).

Designs of RCTs

RCTs come in a number of forms in education. The basic premise is that some form of intervention is used as opposed to 'treatment as usual'. In this basic respect the educational RCT can differ from medicalised models of RCTs. Students who do not receive an intervention are invariably involved in some form of educational alternative. This may be because they are of statutory school age, or because the intervention takes place in a college/university. The alternative is often referred to as 'treatment as usual' as compared to a 'control' sample. This phrase probably better reflects the diversity in provision that those not receiving an intervention experience. Placebo designs, where students receive an 'alternative intervention' that may give the sample the perception that they were involved in the trial intervention, but in reality has negligible effect, are very rare in educational RCTs. The reason for this is fairly obvious. Those at the statutory schooling level must receive that schooling. Those at college/university level are often paying significant fees to receive an intervention.

The two main underpinning designs for an RCT involve either simple or cluster randomisation. In the simple RCT design, students will be assigned to condition of intervention or control at the individual level. An example of this was our evaluation of the after-school literacy programme, Doodle Den, that provides one of the examples we will use in the following chapter when covering how we analyse data generated from an RCT. Doodle Den was targeted at struggling beginning readers aged five to six in an area of significant socio-economic disadvantage and involved the children attending three after-school sessions per week that each lasted one-and-a-half hours. The programme ran for 36 weeks and was delivered by two staff – a qualified teacher and a qualified youth worker or childcare professional. Doodle Den is a very structured programme, with each session beginning with a snack and sign-in routine and then followed by a variety of literacy educational activities before concluding with a 'fun' element based on a literacy theme. The children were referred by their teachers from eight different schools. The total number of children referred (n = 621) were then randomly allocated, on an individual basis, to the intervention (n = 311) or control (n = 310) groups.

The alternative to the simple RCT is the cluster RCT. A cluster RCT looks at the class (or indeed the school) as the unit under study. These tend to be the most common type of trial in education as most programmes or interventions tend to be delivered on a whole-class or even whole-school basis. As such, it is often practically not possible to separate students individually for the purposes of a trial. Rather, a number of classes or schools are recruited and then they are randomly assigned to either deliver the programme or intervention or act as the control group. An example of this, which will also form one of the examples we will use in Chapter 5 to illustrate how to analyse a cluster RCT, is our evaluation of the Media Initiative for Children: Respecting Difference Programme. This is a preschool programme aimed at three-to-four-year-old children that runs for one year and is delivered on a whole-class basis using a range of activities and resources and supported by training of the teachers and workshops with parents. Our trial involved the recruitment of 74 preschools in Northern Ireland and the border counties of the Republic of Ireland. The preschools were then randomly allocated to either a control group or intervention group and the latter delivered the Media Initiative programme for one school year.

Finally some forms of RCTs, whether single or clustered, can also incorporate 'factor designs'. In this design randomisation is used to assign to condition to explore the effect of a number of variables, and explore how the variables may interact with each other to influence outcomes. Such designs are particularly useful when we are not just dealing with a single, unified intervention but where the intervention has two or more components. A factor design would thus be used to attempt to measure the effects of each of these components singularly and then when combined. An example of a factor design is the Fife Peer Learning Project, which studied the effects of three interacting variables. This project used peer tutoring in schools to try and enhance reading and mathematics attainment in primary schools. There was debate over what intensity of peer tutoring was best (30 minutes or 90 minutes per week), whether peer tutoring worked best with students the same age (either same age tutors from Year 4 or same age tutors from Year 6) or those who were separated by two school years (Year 6 and Year 4), and whether peer tutoring just in reading, just in mathematics or in both would be most effective over a two-year period. So for this randomised trial we used a factor design that looked at the interaction in outcomes between each of these variables. The eventual sample looked as indicated in Figure 3.1.

Eventually a total of 120 schools were evenly randomised to condition, resulting in 10 schools being studied in each cell. This was undertaken as follows (Tymms et al., 2011). At the time of the allocation of interventions, 120 schools had volunteered to participate in the study and this number fortuitously meant that the initial assignments could be carried out so that equal numbers of schools fell into each category. In order to

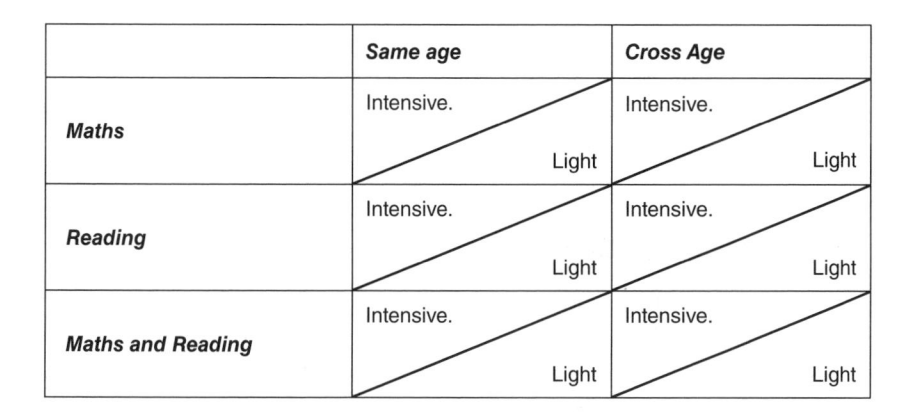

	Same age	Cross Age
Maths	Intensive. / Light	Intensive. / Light
Reading	Intensive. / Light	Intensive. / Light
Maths and Reading	Intensive. / Light	Intensive. / Light

Figure 3.1 Composition of factor design in Fife Peer Learning Project with 10 schools in each cell*

*Each cell defined by whether: the subject focus (maths, reading or both); the age (same age peer-tutoring or cross-age); and intensity (delivered in a light format for 30 minutes per week or more intensively for 90 minutes).

allocate the 120 schools Minitab was used to create a column of 40 'ones', followed by 40 'twos', followed by 40 'threes'. These represented reading, mathematics, or reading and mathematics respectively. In the second column representing same-age or cross-age there were 20 'ones', followed by 20 'twos', followed by 20 'ones', followed by 20 'twos' and so on. Then in the next column representing 'light' or 'intensive' there were 10 ones, followed by 10 twos, followed by 10 ones, followed by 10 twos and so on.

The columns were combined by adding 100 times the first column, 10 times the second column, and 1 times the third column, and then the columns were added up so that the sum of the columns started off 111 for 10 schools, and then 112 for 10 schools, 113 for 10 schools, and so on. In another column a random number was placed in each column between 1 and 120. This number was used to randomly order the columns of the random assignment to the schools. This was undertaken by alphabetically listing schools that had agreed to be randomised and assigning the schools a number between 1 and 120. The number assigned to the alphabetical list of schools was matched to the randomly allocated number for each column to give school assignment to each condition.

Some of the larger primary schools had more than one class per year-group. These schools were asked to select one class to participate on the basis of the class teacher's last name. The teacher with the first letter of their last name being closest to the start of the alphabet was to take part in the project. Next, the schools were asked to work with Primary 4 or Primary 6 if they were doing same-age tutoring. Cross-age tutors were always in Primary 6. They were allocated by inserting alternating '4' and '6' down the column on the spreadsheet corresponding to Primary 4 and Primary 6.

Ethical considerations

We have already addressed a number of key ethical issues that have tended to be raised regarding the use of RCTs in education in the Introduction chapter. These include the ethics of having a control group and the perception of 'denying' some participants access to a particular programme or intervention simply for the purposes of the trial. As we made clear, the actual practice in relation to RCTs is often more complex than this and, in many cases, the use of a wait-list control group means that all participants eventually receive the programme or intervention. Alongside the various counter-arguments made about the ethics of schools pushing ahead with implementing programmes when they have no evidence of whether they work or not (or whether they may actually have negative effects), the bottom line in relation to trials is that no participants should be denied a programme or intervention they would have otherwise received simply because of their involvement in a trial. Beyond these debates, there are three additional points worth briefly outlining here in relation to ethical considerations.

Consent and permission and professional standards

Greater use of cluster-randomised trials has presented ethical dilemmas that need addressing. If assignment to condition occurs at the school or classroom level then what chance do the individual pupils have to truly give informed consent to take part in the research? The requirements in the ethical guidelines of both the American Educational Research Association and the British Educational Research Association, are exactly the same and state that research subjects should give 'informed consent before participating in the research' (American Educational Research Association, 2000: 4; British Educational Research Association, 2000: 1). This would assume that in cluster randomised trials consent should be obtained before randomisation is undertaken. In practice, most ethics committees understand that if the trial is taking place in an educational setting, delivered by teachers during their normal timetable course, and is composed of non-invasive pedagogical development then opt-out consent would be appropriate. In this instance a pupil would be assumed to participate in the trial unless a parent actively decides to withdraw their child from the study. Beyond this, even if a parent is happy for their child to participate in the study, it would be normal practice to also provide the pupil themselves with the opportunity to opt out of the study. In such circumstances, if a programme is being delivered to the whole class as part of the normal school day, the pupil may still be required to participate in the programme but would have the opportunity to opt out from the evaluation of the programme and thus from completing any tests, surveys or interviews.

Equipoise

One important aspect of ethical RCTs is that of equipoise. This is the fact that when trialling a new development there should be genuine and true uncertainty over whether the technique will be effective at the scale and in the context being investigated. The ethical issue here is essentially avoiding the unnecessary application of research, and the burdens this places on participants, in situations where the main findings are already clear and known.

Research participants as partners

This third issue develops further our concern with the development of collaborative approaches to RCTs discussed in the previous chapter. RCTs in schools often adopt a pragmatic design, recommended for educational experimentation. As the trial setting is a real-world environment it strengthens confidence in the ecological validity of the findings, and produces the most useful information for practitioners to judge whether or not an intervention should be introduced in schools (Torgerson and Torgerson, 2008). However, working in authentic contexts can bring issues of transference and implementation integrity. One way to address these issues is for researchers to develop partnerships with school samples prior to conducting a full trial. Refining an intervention using a development study prior to an RCT is recognised as a vital component of a study in health, education, and the social sciences (Torgerson and Torgerson, 2008). Before running a full-scale randomised trial it can often be beneficial to run a development study, treated as a 'run-in' phase of the definitive study to fully develop the intervention for the identified cohort, in readiness for a full trial (Lancaster et al., 2004). There is of course inevitable sacrifice of some standardisation for realism, expected to result in natural variability in delivery (Gorard, 2013). To enhance fidelity to treatment during the full trial when the intervention is tested at scale in schools, the 'run-in' study designed can be particularly important.

58 Using randomised controlled trials in education

Three key considerations gave rise to the delivery of a run-in study that engages teachers as part of school teams, in the design process of an intervention (Cockerill and Thurston, 2015). The first of these is ensuring contextualisation prior to the intervention; the second is providing structures to facilitate whole-school engagement with the intervention; and the third is promoting teacher buy-in through credible resources including authentic professional voices. When integrated into the work plan of a trial, a run-in study can enhance fidelity to treatment during a pragmatic RCT.

When considering the challenges posed in school reform, research indicates that overcoming these requires systematic subscription to the proposed change (Ravitz, 2010) together with collective moral purpose and a shared theory of action (Gifford, 2010). These factors echo Social Interdependence Theory (Johnson et al., 2010; Johnson and Johnson, 2012), as school reform requires three elements: *goal structure* (teachers work with senior management and the researchers with the goal of school improvement); *positive interdependence* (for the new pedagogy to work teachers have set resources and pedagogies to implement in their classroom); and *individual accountability* (all working on the initiative need to buy into the process and deliver/engage with professional development).

Furthermore, factors such as improvement culture and improvement processes can influence reform outcomes positively (Reezigt and Creemers, 2005). Assuring credibility when implementing a new intervention entails both involvement from the leadership and buy-in from teaching professionals within the school, accessing appropriate training (Muijs and Harris, 2006). This includes hearing authentic voices of what is important from other teaching professionals and bringing people together to share ideas and experiences (Magolda and Ebben, 2007). With this in mind, Ravitz (2010) argued in favour of 'a systematic model that provides guidance and ensures adequate focus on and capacity for instructional reform' (p. 309) including a 'top-level vision for instructional changes' (p. 310).

To enhance fidelity to treatment for a subsequent 128-class RCT of peer tutoring in secondary schools, we developed a model that included teacher engagement in the intervention design process, using a development study phase in the identified geographic area where the pragmatic RCT followed as an integral part of their study (Cockerill and Thurston, 2015). The development study was undertaken to take into account contextual factors (Cartwright and Hardie, 2012). The intervention focused on cross-age peer tutoring, for which there was strong evidence of a positive impact in previous research (Cohen et al., 1982; Higgins et al., 2014). However, only one large-scale trial in the UK had been completed, and this had focused on the Primary stage and was conducted in Scotland (Tymms et al., 2011). The study focused on the Secondary stage thus requiring adaptation of previous materials in existence from the Primary stage. In addition, the present study is situated in northeast England, a distinctly different geographic area from that of Scotland, requiring the adaptation of materials for context appropriateness. Due to these contextual factors it was deemed necessary to run a development phase prior to the pragmatic trial.

The development study involved 295, 11–13 year old students, taught by 12 teachers across three secondary schools in northeast England. Using this model the potential of teacher involvement in research design to promote more effective interventions was explored. This development study aimed to build capacity for improved practice in the school setting, in a sustainable way that enabled reform. During the development study phase of the project, Cockerill and Thurston instigated such an approach. They did this by creating structures within schools that included a senior leader who oversaw the new intervention, an operational lead who worked to promote a common approach working with intervention teachers and a network mechanism whereby teachers met regularly and discussed implementation issues and supported one another. The groups within each school received adequate training, including support and feedback to build capacity in school for the planned intervention. Importantly, during the development study phase of the project, the model provided crucial opportunities through professional development sessions for groups across schools so ideas were shared and teachers were provided with feedback and were able to be fully engaged in the necessary adaptation and refinement of materials for ongoing delivery. Such developmental work proved essential in developing pedagogic content knowledge of the interventions as well as providing a support infrastructure to facilitate the subsequent scaled RCTs.

Sampling and randomisation

There are a number of issues to do with sampling that can pose a threat to validity. One of the basic issues is sample size. If the sample is too small there may be a sample effect, unique to that context or group of individuals. The sample has to be large enough to be representative. In addition it needs to be the right size such that we can be sufficiently confident that other effects have not caused significant differences between intervention and control groups. We can illustrate this with a simple experiment. If we took two sets of coins of different denominations and tossed them each 20 times, recording which side landed face-up on each denomination, it is unlikely one would get 10 heads/10 tails for each denomination. Most observers would agree that the differences are caused by chance, rather than some other cause such as physical force dictating the pattern of fall for each denomination of coin.

As with any research there are pitfalls and dangers associated with undertaking either simple or cluster RCTs. These dangers centre around the fact the scientific process that surrounds undertaking an RCT can lull researchers into having an inflated sense of security regarding data validity. RCTs can still be susceptible to sample selection bias. It is still possible to select a skewed sample even when participants are randomised to condition. In fact it is suggested that randomisation should take place independently from the core research team to minimise the risks of this and other sampling effects such as issues surrounding differential uptake and attrition rates in different groups (Puffer et al., 2003). Systematic reviews are starting to show that inherent design characteristics appear to cause variability in effects even when similar, or indeed the same, programme is being investigated (Zeneli et al., 2016). This aspect is discussed in more detail in Chapter 6.

In addition, there is still a need to collect data to establish the causal validity of changes measured during any RCT. It is not enough to assume causal validity and subsequent generalisability just because an RCT is used as the design for a piece of research (Briggs, 2008). In addition it needs to be remembered that if cluster RCTs are used, in order to provide the statistical power necessary to analyse outcomes from the research then sample sizes will have to be larger than if randomisation occurred at the individual student level. By necessity this will make cluster RCTs more expensive to fund (Slavin, 2008a).

There are a number of key approaches to randomisation. These could be referred to as true/simple randomisation, block randomisation of the whole sample or block randomisation of sections of a sample to ensure that covariates that are likely to influence outcomes are evenly distributed between intervention and 'treatment as usual' groups. The latter form of randomisation is often termed 'adaptive randomisation', of which the most commonly used in educational RCTs is 'minimisation'. Minimisation is so-called as the technique tries to avoid intervention and comparison groups being differentially affected by covariate imbalance. In the simplest form this may be by current test performance at the start of an intervention being the largest predictor of post-intervention test performance. If there were an imbalance in test performance between intervention and 'treatment as usual' groups at the start, this may account for some of the differences between the samples at the end (often termed a Type 1 error).

True/simple randomisation and block randomisation

In this form of randomisation, each school/class/participant would be randomised to condition by generation of a random number. Low-tech examples would be use of a coin (heads or tails) or a die (even numbers/odd numbers). However, random number generator software is available for most smartphones and computers. One of the potential issues of this method is that one can end up with samples of uneven size and even uneven composition, leading to increased risk of a Type 1 error (where pre-test differences are the cause of any post-test differences observed). This can be illustrated by our next example involving a pilot study of implementing 'Maths Peer Tutoring' in Irish Medium Schools. In pilot work to extend the use of Maths Peer Tutoring materials developed during the Fife Peer Learning Project (see p. 54), a small number of schools volunteered to be part of a small trial. The aim of the trial was to use a small sample of schools to pilot translated materials. Table 3.1 shows some of the average pre-test scores (marked out of 50) obtained from the schools. As can be seen, given we only had a small sample of schools, if they were randomly assigned to either intervention or control, there would be a possibility that the four highest schools could all have been assigned to the same condition. This could have skewed the result as there was obviously something already happening in relation to those schools that was leading to better mathematics attainment.

Instead of a true randomisation, they were randomised on a pairwise basis to condition. In order to do this they were rank ordered by mean

Table 3.1 Pre-test differences and possible Type 1 error

School	Mean pre-test mathematics score
A	39.74
B	29.62
C	40.09
D	26.10
E	23.83
F	39.16
G	23.42
H	32.95
I	33.12
J	24.96
K	23.83
L	35.29

62 Using randomised controlled trials in education

class pre-test mathematics score from top attainment to lowest attainment. Schools were then organised into pairs, each matched to its closest pair, and each pair was randomly assigned one to intervention and one to control. This method of randomisation gave the best method of ensuring parity between the two 'conditions' of the research.

Another common issue with simple randomisation is that it can result in uneven numbers of individuals or classes being assigned to intervention and 'treatment as usual' conditions. This can be avoided by specifying how many of the sample need to be in intervention and 'treatment as usual' groups. Then when randomisation takes place it can be ensured that samples have the required number in each condition. This is the simplest form of block randomisation and can easily be achieved using SPSS. From the main menu in SPSS choose **Data → Select Cases …** This opens up the dialogue box shown in Figure 3.2. In the box select the option 'Random

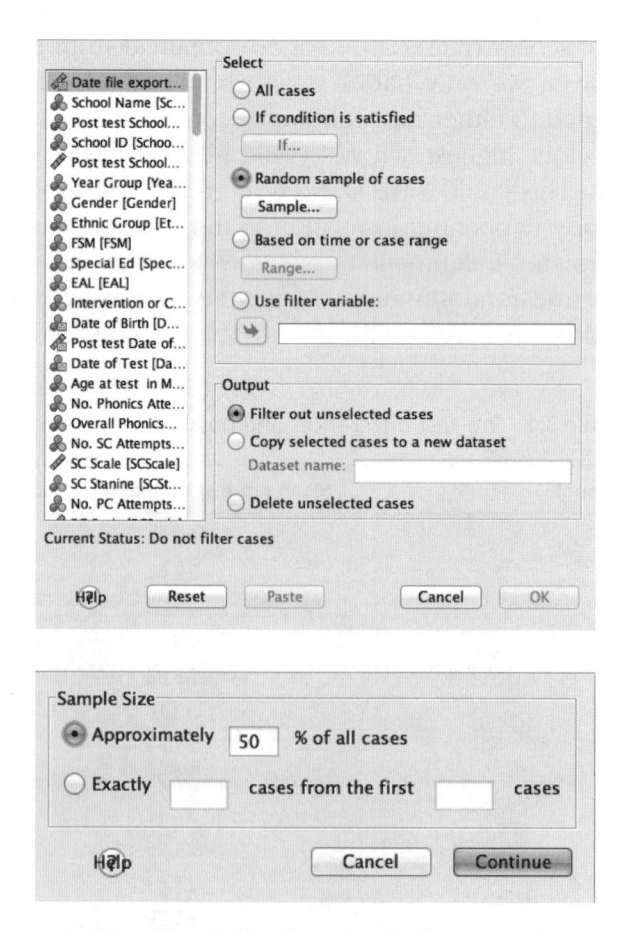

Figure 3.2 How to achieve simple block randomisation in SPSS

Reprint courtesy of International Business Machines, © International Business Machines Corporation

Research Designs for RCTs 63

sample of cases' and then click on the 'Sample' button. In the additional dialogue box that opens (see also Figure 3.2), select the number of cases that you want. You can either select an approximate percentage (obviously some samples may not be able to generate exactly 50% random sampling) or an exact number of cases. Do this and then click 'Continue' and then 'OK' in the main dialogue box. SPSS will then randomly select the number of cases/percentage of cases that you require. Cases will appear as struck through or left in the sample (see Figure 3.3). All that remains is to identify the selected cases with a code in a new variable.

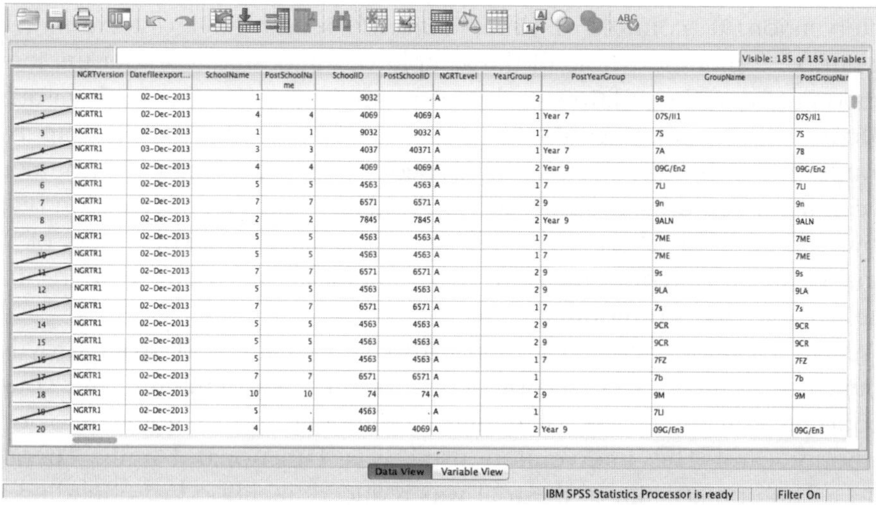

Figure 3.3 SPSS screenshot of randomly omitted cases appearing as struck through

Reprint courtesy of International Business Machines, © International Business Machines Corporation

Adaptive randomisation

True/simple block randomisation may not be enough to guarantee that control and intervention samples have an equal distribution of variables that may influence outcomes even if they have equal numbers of the sample in each condition (Lachin et al., 1988: Slavin, 2008b). There is still a risk that randomisation will create two unequal samples by chance. One way to counteract these risks is to use adaptive randomisation (Lachin et al., 1988). Adaptive randomisation is the process of assigning to condition from a list that is rank ordered on a pre-test variable that may be a predictor of outcomes. It has the advantage over true/simple randomisation in that it helps to generate intervention and control groups that are broadly equal at the start of an experiment. This could be undertaken in a number of ways. The basis of the technique is to decide what variables, available to the research designers at pre-test, are most likely to influence the post-test result. It stands to reason that those most like the post-test measure that will be the primary outcome would be most likely to predict this, e.g. if the main outcomes measure is reading attainment, then using current performance in reading would be the most logical way to ensure the intervention and control samples are evenly distributed to avoid Type 1 error. As in any simple randomisation one would rank order the sample from lowest score to highest score and, after generating a random number for the first of the sample, sequentially rank order the sample to condition; e.g. in a simple randomised sample RCT if 1 represented intervention and 0 control, and a random number of 1 was generated then the sample would be labelled 1 (intervention)/0 (control)/ 1 (intervention)/0 (control)/ 1 (intervention)/0 (control) … until the whole of the sample was allocated to either the intervention or control condition. To be even more secure in the randomisation process then numbers could be generated to split the sample into two groups, and only after this has happened then the designation of numeral to condition could be determined (to avoid any criticism of selection bias). However, in cases where a pre-test variable is likely to explain less of the variance in an outcome measure then minimisation based on more than one variable may be required.

As an example, we worked in partnership with staff from Croydon Council to evaluate a new approach to dealing with children and young people in families at risk of criminal offending and/or going into local authority care. The intervention used was Functional Family Therapy (FFT). The primary aim of the trial was reduced likelihood of offending by young people, but secondary outcomes included school attainment and school attendance. FFT had a history of systematic research that dated back many years (Alexander and Parsons, 1973), resulting in 13 published clinical trials, which suggest that FFT was effective in reducing recidivism between 26% and 73% with offending, moderate, and seriously delinquent youth as compared to both no intervention and juvenile court probation services (Alexander et al., 2000). In one research review it was reported that the use of FFT reduced the likelihood of offending by 27% (Sexton and Alexander, 2002). A design experiment involving 54 'juvenile delinquents' (original term) from rural, lower socio-economic backgrounds in Ohio, USA, reported reduced offending due to FFT. In the study the offending rate for a sample of 27 'treated' individuals was 9% as compared to a rate of 41% amongst a sample of 27 who received 'treatment as usual' (probation) (Gordon et al., 1995). A meta-analysis of the effectiveness of family-based crime prevention programmes reviewed 40 programmes of family therapy and concluded that reduced offending rates were observed in studies with a mean effect size = +0.321. Effect sizes were generally greater for those programmes that focused on behaviour change and were situated outside of the school setting (Farrington and Welsh, 2003).

An initial literature review indicated that gender, prior offending behaviours and ethnicity were likely to be associated with the outcomes of FFT. Literature supported a hypothesis that these factors were likely to explain substantive amounts of variance in the sample. It was reported that in a UK sample of 22,205 youth offenders aged 10–17 that 67% of youth offenders were male (of these 64% were recorded as white and 14% were recorded as black) and of the 33% female youth offenders 72% were white and 13% black (Youth Justice Board for England and Wales, 2010: 50). In a study of FFT involving 917 families in 14 counties in the USA, gender (being male) and prior offending behaviours were reported to be the most significant predictors of post-FFT offending (Sexton and Turner, 2010). In the UK there are reports that in some areas, particularly those with higher than national average black and minority ethnic youths, ethnicity can predict appearance in the youth custody system (Youth Justice Board for England and Wales, 2010: 18 and 40). Therefore, there was a risk that if gender, ethnicity and prior offending behaviours were not evenly balanced across intervention and a 'treatment as usual' group then there was a risk of Type 1 error. To counteract this risk a block randomisation approach was undertaken. In this study a flow diagram was developed. This split the referred families on the basis of the gender of the at-risk young person into male and female. Each gender group was further split into two sub-groups on the basis of having prior offender behaviours or not having prior offending behavior, creating four sub-groups. Each of these four sub-groups were further subdivided into ethnic groups of white or black/ethnic minority, giving eight sub-groups as listed below:

1. Male, prior offender, white
2. Male, prior offender, black/ethnic minority
3. Female, prior offender, white
4. Female, prior offender, black/ethnic minority
5. Male, not a prior offender, white
6. Male, not a prior offender, black/ethnic minority
7. Female, not a prior offender, white
8. Female, not a prior offender, black/ethnic minority

For each sub-group a random number was generated to start the randomisation and families were sequentially allocated to condition as they were referred within these blocks. This ensured that even numbers of the

66   Using randomised controlled trials in education

sub-groups were allocated to intervention and 'treatment as usual' groups, minimising Type 1 error and also allowing the sample size to be modelled for multivariate regression analysis on the basis that variance would not be predicted most strongly by sample composition (Thurston et al., 2015).

Cluster RCTs are widely reported to be effective for measuring the effectiveness of interventions (Eldridge et al., 2008), reducing within-sample contamination (Campbell, 2004), and are particularly effective as they provide an appropriate methodology to detect changes at the organisational level (Campbell and Grimshaw, 1998), thus allowing a greater ability to generalise research findings to other contexts and settings of a similar nature. Of course, good practice in implementing cluster-randomised trials is essential in designing cluster trials. It is important to ensure the following:

- An appropriate sample size is identified for the trial, e.g. there are well-established guidelines in medical trials (Torgerson and Torgerson, 2008).
- Clear design and implementation are used, e.g. the Consolidated Standards of Reporting Trials (CONSORT) agreement is the standard for undertaking cluster RCTs (Campbell et al., 2004).
- Clear reporting procedures are followed, e.g. CONSORT has a 22-item checklist that should be followed when reporting findings (Campbell, 2004), and the What Works Clearing House (Institute of Education Services, 2006) has study design specifications for RCTs.
- Analysis is undertaken at the level of the cluster (Campbell and Grimshaw, 1998).

Recruitment and Attrition

Recruitment to large-scale randomised trials can be problematic. Email requests and mailshots may provide low yield or return of schools that may participate. Typically recruitment through these means can end up being between 10% (Thurston et al., 2008) and 20% (Dunne et al., 2016). Recruitment events can be more fruitful. During the Fife Peer Learning a recruitment event for head teachers (Tymms et al., 2011) and similar recruitment events during the 'Talk of the Town' (Thurston et al., 2015) yielded recruitment in excess of 90% in each local authority approached. However, recruitment to the RCT is only halfway to obtaining the sample for a trial. The trial must keep the sample after assignment to condition. Although equipoise should exist in the design of a trial, most volunteer schools/head teachers/teachers/students have probably volunteered in the first place because they have an interest in the work. This is not always the case. Often a head teacher can decide that the school is going to take part. After that the teachers can find themselves co-opted into a trial that might not have been their preferred choice. This can present a number of problems with recruitment and/or fidelity. One approach to counteract this and improve adherence to fidelity is taken by Success for All (SFA). Teachers in schools undertaking trials using SFA must vote to participate. A majority of teachers (80%) must vote in favour of moving forwards with SFA (Slavin and Madden, 2008: 47). This approach has the potential to improve the fidelity of the intervention.

Sometimes the characteristic of a sample of schools indicates that there would be great potential for skewness in the sample if simple randomisation were used. An example of this is our evaluation of the Cancer Focus NI smoking prevention programme Dead Cool under a grant from the Public Health Agency in Northern Ireland. The developers of the programme were not involved in school recruitment, or any other aspect of the evaluation. We recruited post-primary (Secondary, Grammar, Integrated, Independent, Single-sex and Coeducational) schools to the sample. Northern Ireland has a complex post-primary school composition. This includes Grammar and Secondary sectors which are split between those associated with Catholic and Protestant churches. In addition there are Integrated schools with a presence from both Catholic and Protestant churches and Independent schools. Obviously, this disparate mix of school types would need to be balanced to ensure parity between intervention and control schools on the basis of prior attainment, gender, ethnic background and socio-economic status. During recruitment to this sample the evaluation team paired schools of a similar nature together. So two girls-only, Catholic Maintained, Grammar schools were paired, two co-educational, Protestant Controlled Secondary schools were paired, and so on. Then randomisation took place at the pair level to ensure that there was balance in the type of school in the intervention and control samples (Dunne et al., 2016).

To randomise using block randomisation a more complex procedure may be required than for true/simple randomisation. To undertake this when the dataset is constructed in SPSS it is important that groups of similar schools should be listed together. This is relatively easy to do by selecting **Transform → Rank Cases ...** from the main menu in SPSS. Of course the way in which cases are ranked can depend upon which variables are important to balance in the sample.

In the following example from Northern Ireland, schools of a different type (Grammar and Secondary sectors split between those associated with Catholic and Protestant churches, Integrated schools with presence from both Catholic and Protestant churches and Independent schools) were grouped together and then rank ordered by free school meal percentage (see Figure 3.4). In this study it was important to ensure not only representation from different sectors, but also balance in free school meal percentage between control and intervention groups. Once the sub-groups were created, a random number generator was used to randomly select the first school of each type to intervention (1) or control (0). Schools of the same type were then sequentially allocated to intervention (1) or control (0) to ensure balance in the sample.

Secondary	1.00	1.00	RC Maintained	Urban	Male	764.0	310 (40.6%)	40.6	1.00
Secondary	2.00	1.00	RC Maintained	Urban	Female	1516.0	563(37.1%)	37.1	1.00
Secondary	3.00	1.00	Integrated	Urban	Co-Ed	710.0	293(41.3%)	41.3	.00
Secondary	4.00	1.00	Integrated	Urban	Co-Ed	864.0	338 (39.1%)	39.1	1.00
Secondary	5.00	1.00	Integrated	Rural	Co-Ed	1260.0	204(16.2%)	16.2	1.00
Secondary	5.00	2.00	Integrated	Rural	Co-Ed	1260.0	204(16.2%)	16.2	.00
Secondary	6.00	1.00	controlled	Urban	Co-Ed	463.0	154(33.3%)	33.3	1.00
Secondary	7.00	1.00	controlled	Urban	Co-Ed	650.0	191(29.4%	29.4	.00

Figure 3.4 SPSS screenshot of schools of different type grouped together and then rank ordered by free school meal percentage

Reprint courtesy of International Business Machines, © International Business Machines Corporation

Schools that have volunteered for trials may become disheartened if they end up being assigned to a control condition. One way to try and counteract attrition is to have a 'wait-intervention' control. That is a control group that will receive the intervention after the RCT is completed. Another way is to undertake contracting with schools prior to assignment. This can be that schools gain a very full understanding of the wait-intervention control option or that they agree to underwrite the costs associated with pre-testing undertaken prior to assignment to condition (this can amount to a considerable cost if commercially available tests have been used). Once the RCT is underway then a wait-intervention group gets closer each day to a point where they will receive the intervention. One of the other advantages to them is that they often get an enhanced version where issues have been addressed and the intervention may have been fine-tuned on the basis of experience.

Another issue with attrition can be that schools assigned to an intervention group find that the time commitment expected is problematic for them. Again this issue can be overcome by setting clear expectations and having clear information sheets/recruitment events prior to schools signing up. As noted above, the 'Success for All' organisation takes this one step further whereby a certain percentage of teachers must sign up to undertake the intervention before they will work with a school.

Sample Size and Intended Analysis

The issues of sample size and intended analysis are inextricably linked. Generally speaking, the larger the anticipated effect of an intervention, the smaller the sample size that will be required to detect that effect. Conversely, the smaller the effect then the larger the sample size that will be required to detect that effect. The exact sample size required will also be dependent upon the proposed method of analysis. This means that both sample size and proposed analysis need to be determined before an experiment is undertaken. Normally in RCTs, either an intention to treat or a treated analysis is undertaken. The former would deal with all schools/units selected to intervention/'treatment as usual', even those who drop out of the trial, and the latter would deal only with those who received the full 'intervention'. Sample sizes are normally calculated using software. A good piece of software for this process that is freely available is Optimal Design, created for the Windows platform. Further information and a free manual on how to use the software are available from https://sites.google.com/site/optimaldesignsoftware/home

To undertake a calculation to determine the correct sample size there are a number of things that need to be decided in the design of the RCT. The first of these is whether the trial will be randomised at the individual or 'clustered' level. For instance if you have a new reading intervention, will individuals within classes be randomised to condition or will whole classes be randomised to condition (a cluster RCT)? The power that will be used and the probability levels also need to be determined. By convention, and in the case of Optimal Design, the default settings for these are 80% power and to detect effects with a probability of $p < 0.05$. There are two more parameters that need to be known. The first of these is the anticipated effect size. Put simply, this is the fraction of a standard deviation difference between the intervention and control groups that is expected at post-test that could be attributable to the intervention (assuming that the intervention and control groups were equal at the start of the experiment). The final factor that needs to be estimated is the proportion of the variance in the outcome variable that could be explained by known factors (called the R^2 in statistical notation). This value is included in the sample size calculation as a covariate. These values generally have to be estimated from previous studies and existing literature. The following study illustrates how estimates of these factors were tied to pre-existing literature and used with Optimal Design to calculate sample sizes for the research protocol.

There are a couple of other decisions that need to be made regarding the research design. The first of these is whether the design will result in individuals with individual outcomes, or clusters of individuals with group outcomes who will be assigned to condition. These parameters must be stipulated in the Optimal Design menu entitled **DESIGN**. Clicking on the design tab brings four options:

- Person randomized trial
- Cluster randomized trial with person-level outcomes
- Cluster randomized trial with cluster-level outcomes
- Meta-analysis (we will not deal with this option in this chapter)

Each of these menus has sub-menus associated with it, which must be selected dependent upon your experimental design:

Person Randomized Trial

- Single level trial
- Multi-site (or blocked) trials
- Repeated measures

Cluster Randomized Trials with person-level outcomes

- Cluster randomized trials
- Multi-site (or blocked) cluster randomized trials

Custer Randomized Trials with group-level outcomes

- Cluster randomized trials
- Multi-site (or blocked) cluster randomized trials.

To determine sample size select **Person randomized trials → Single level trials** then choose 'MDES' on the y-axis and 'number of people (*N*)' on the x-axis. Next the Power should be set (at 80%) by clicking on the **P** button and the estimate of R^2 also needs to be set by clicking on the **R²** button (this will depend on how much variance could be predicted by covariates). This will produce a graph with a curve showing *effect size* (on the *y* axis) plotted against sample size on the *x* axis. By clicking along the trajectory then the number of subjects required for a study of various *effect sizes* is revealed. For a detailed explanation of using Optimal Design for different experimental designs consult the Optimal Design manual which is available for free download at http://hlmsoft.net/od/od-manual-20111016-v300.pdf.

As an example, we will return to our trial of Functional Family Therapy in Croydon. Here we will look at the influence that the estimated effect size and predicted variance of known factors had on calculations for the sample size in this RCT. The core characteristics (gender, education level, age, deprivation) of the intervention and 'treatment as usual' groups will be described and compared at baseline. At the end of the RCT the effects of the intervention will be estimated using a series of multivariate regression models for each outcome measure. For each model the post-test score will form the dependent variable and a number of independent variables will be added, including a dummy variable representing group allocation (where 1 = intervention group and 0 = 'treatment as usual' group) and other covariates representing core characteristics and pre-test scores on relevant outcome measures. The main outcome analysis will use logistic regression to estimate the relative risk of reoffending and entering care for young people due to family breakdown for those in the intervention and 'treatment as usual' groups. Linear regression will be used to determine the impact of the intervention on continuous outcomes. The estimated coefficient associated with the dummy variable that represents 'group allocation' (once other covariates have been controlled for) will be the focus of the analysis in terms of its value in the model as a significant predictor of the outcome.

Calculations to determine sample size were undertaken using Optimal Design version 3.01 software (Raudenbush et al., 2011). The regression has been modelled with: Alpha = 0.05; Power = 80%; Proportion of explained variation by level 1 covariates (R^2) = 0.7. The estimate of *effect size (ES)* for this RCT was based on aggregated studies during initial literature search. It was noted that targeted interventions tended to yield larger *ES*. The Croydon intervention was targeted and therefore the 'historical' *ES* reported in previous literature for FFT interventions of this nature was used. This turned out to be +0.32. For a minimum detectable *ES* of +0.32 Optimal Design calculated that the design required a total sample size of $N = 95$. This gave 48 in FFT and 48 in 'treatment as usual'. Optimal Design also modelled for a minimum detectable lower *ES* of +0.25 and indicated that we would need a total sample size of $N = 154$ i.e. 77 in FFT and 77 in 'treatment as usual'. Further modelling indicated that if $R^2 = 0.5$ on level 1 covariates, then the design could detect an *ES* of 0.32 with a sample of 154. The finite sample from which to draw families into the trial was nearly 250 families per year who will be referred to the team at the EIF Centre in Croydon. Given the extent of the infrastructure at Croydon the team will be able to offer FFT. For this design the decision was taken that if initial data collected during the run-in phase of the RCT indicated that the reported *ES* would not be realised, or assumptions of the strength of level 1 covariates of R^2 proved to be overestimated, then the protocol indicated that there was an option

72 Using randomised controlled trials in education

to recruit up to 154 families into the study to cater for the possibility that a smaller *ES* of +0.25, or indeed a level 1 covariate $R^2 = 0.5$, to enable analysis to retain the correct power in subsequent analysis. We are aware that different software would calculate the sample size slightly differently.

The graph of sample size plotted with *ES* for the model produced by Optimal Design is illustrated in Figure 3.5 for $R^2 = 0.7$ and the way in which sample size prediction is affected by a lower R^2 value ($R^2 = 0.5$) is illustrated in this figure. As can be seen, a lower level 1 covariate R^2 value would require a larger sample size to maintain adequate power in post-project statistical analyses.

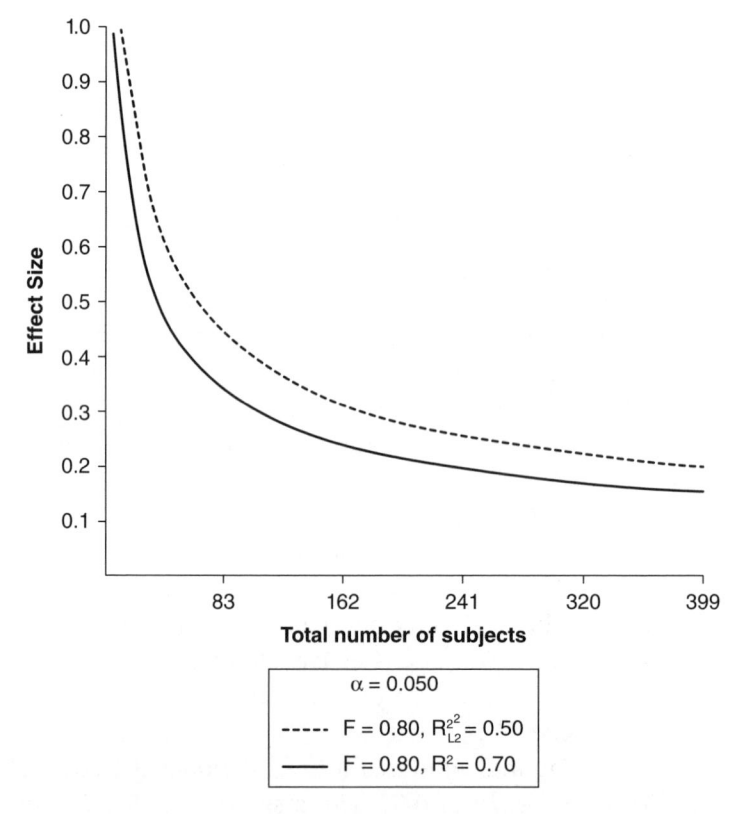

Figure 3.5 Optimal design sample size plotted with *Effect Size* for our model for $R^2 = 0.5$ & $R^2 = 0.7$

Initial thinking is that the level 1 covariates used in the model are likely to be gender and prior offending behaviours (with a possibility of ethnicity also being included). Literature supported a hypothesis that these factors are likely to explain substantive amounts of variance in the sample. It was reported that in a UK sample of 22,205 youth offenders aged 10–17, 67% of youth offenders were male (of these 64% were recorded as white and 14% were recorded as black) and of the 33% female youth offenders 72% were white and 13% black (Youth Justice Board for England and Wales, 2010: 50). In a study of FFT involving 917 families in 14 counties in the USA, gender (being male) and prior offending behaviours were reported to be the most significant predictors of post-FFT offending (Sexton and Turner, 2010). In the UK there are reports that in some areas, particularly those with higher than national average black and minority ethnic youths, ethnicity can predict appearance in the youth custody system (Youth Justice Board for England and Wales, 2010: 18 and 40). Therefore, there could be confidence that if gender, ethnicity and prior offending behaviours were selected as covariates then the variation in the model explained by these could be reasonably estimated at 0.7. However, the study has a run-in phase, and although the model would be finalised before the start of the RCT, there would be a chance to consider the covariates used in the model to ensure the correct covariates are chosen to obtain maximal efficiency in the model. In respect of this, analysis will also examine the likely contribution of diagnosis of conduct disorders and the pre-test SDQ measure as detailed in the full proposal to see if they would be better covariates (Thurston et al., 2015). Therefore, the estimate of R^2 was not considered to be overly optimistic, but there was a contingency in the study protocol to select different level 1 covariates if the run-in phase of the study revealed that outcomes would be better explained by using a different set of covariates.

Conclusions

This chapter has worked through the process of how to design and conduct an RCT. It is assumed that the type of preparatory work outlined in the previous chapter with regard to logic modelling has been undertaken and that we therefore have a clear outline of the programme, its intended theories of intervention and change and the hypothesised outcomes that it is expected to impact upon. With these in mind, we have covered the key issues that then need to be considered in relation to the actual design of the trial. These involve the type of randomisation that is most appropriate (simple, clustered and/or involving a factor design), the calculation of the sample size required and then some of the key ethical considerations involved as well as issues associated with recruitment and dealing with attrition.

Given the limited space available, we have focused specifically on the setting up and operation of the trial element of the study. As covered in the previous two chapters, it is also highly desirable to run strong qualitative components alongside the trial so that we avoid limiting ourselves to simple 'black box evaluations'. Some of the key issues involved in designing these qualitative components have been covered in the previous chapter, particularly as they relate to using the logic model to inform the types of data to be collected and the individuals and groups to interview and activities to observe.

Further Reading

Design of RCTs

- *Field Experiments: Design, Analysis and Interpretation*, by A.S. Gerber and D.P. Green (WW Norton and Company, 2012).
- *Designing Randomised Trials in Health Education and the Social Sciences*, by D.J. Torgerson and C.J. Torgerson (Palgrave McMillan, 2008).

Websites

- All Psych Online: The virtual psychology classroom http://allpsych.com/researchmethods/quasiexperimentaldesign.html
- Optimal Design Manual http://hlmsoft.net/od/od-manual-20111016-v300.pdf
- Web Centre for Social Research Methods www.socialresearchmethods.net/kb/index.php

4

The Fundamentals of Analysing RCT Data

Introduction

The following two chapters will focus on how to analyse RCT data; this chapter will begin by setting out clearly and comprehensively the overall approach to analysing RCT data whereas Chapter 5 considers important extensions to this main approach for dealing with different types of data. At the heart of the analysis of data from RCTs is a technique known as linear regression. How we analyse RCT data and interpret and report the findings from such an analysis requires a solid understanding of this technique. This chapter will therefore provide an overview of the technique in general before then looking at how it is used, more specifically, in the analysis of RCT data. We will therefore begin with a fairly detailed discussion of linear regression. Although the relevance of this to RCTs may not be immediately clear, we would ask you to bear with us as you will soon come to see how it is then applied to the analysis of trial data. Moreover, you will also come to appreciate how this basic understanding is essential for you to be able to understand how it can be applied to address the specific research questions you will have for your own trial. After providing an overview of linear regression and how it can be applied to the analysis of trials, the chapter will then take you through a real-world example using actual data from an RCT and will also take you through all of the steps involved in the process of analysing the data and drawing out and interpreting the key findings. As we will see in the following chapter, the approach

76 Using randomised controlled trials in education

to be covered here provides the essential foundations that can then be built upon when analysing more complex designs, including RCTs that have binary outcomes and also cluster randomised controlled trials.

Assumptions

This chapter and the next assume that you already have a good understanding of the basics of statistical analysis, which you should have covered in any undergraduate research methods module. This will include:

- familiarity with the statistical software package SPSS and an understanding of how to create and save a dataset, how to manage and manipulate variables and how to conduct simple analyses of the data using SPSS;
- a good understanding of key concepts in *descriptive statistics* such as *means*, *standard deviations* and *standardised scores (or z scores)* and how to read and interpret graphical displays of quantitative data using techniques such as *scatterplots* and *clustered bar charts*;
- a sound appreciation of key underpinning concepts in inferential statistics and, in particular, the notion of *statistical significance* and associated concepts such as *standard errors* and *95% confidence intervals*; and
- knowledge of some of the key tests for statistical significance – including *chi-square tests*, *t-tests* and *Pearson's correlation* – and how to interpret the findings from these, most notably the *p values* that they generate.

If any of the terms highlighted above are unfamiliar to you and/or your knowledge of them is now a little 'rusty' then we would suggest you spend some time reading up on these first and before continuing on with this and the next chapter.

Linear Regression

At the heart of linear regression is a dependent variable that provides the focus for our analysis and then one or more independent variables that we believe may influence or explain variations in our dependent variable. In this sense, the dependent variable is assumed to be *dependent upon* one or more independent variables. The dependent variable is also sometimes referred to as either the 'outcome variable' or 'response variable' and

* Dependent variable → outcome variable
* Independent variable → predictor

Fundamentals of analysing RCT data

independent variables as 'predictor variables'. To give some practical sense of what this might look like in practice, let us assume that 40 children have been tested on their reading comprehension at two time points: initially at the start of the school year, at what we can call 'pre-test', and then again at the end of that school year, at what we will call 'post-test'. Figure 4.1 shows a scatterplot illustrating the relationship between these two variables. The 40 children are depicted by the 40 dots in the scatterplot and their pre-test and post-test scores can be read off from the respective axes. For example, it can be seen that Child A achieved a pre-test score of 35 and a post-test score of 42. Similarly, Child B achieved a pre-test score of 45 and 57 at post-test whereas Child C gained 66 at pre-test and a score of 80 at post-test.

In this instance, the post-test score is the dependent variable and the pre-test score is the independent variable. It is this way around as we can assume that at least some of the variation in the children's post-test scores may be influenced by (or be dependent upon) how they have scored previously, as measured by their pre-test scores. Thus, it would be reasonable to assume that a child who achieved a high score at the beginning of the school year, at pre-test, will be more likely to achieve a higher score at the end of the year, at post-test. Similarly, we can assume that a child who was struggling with reading and achieved a low

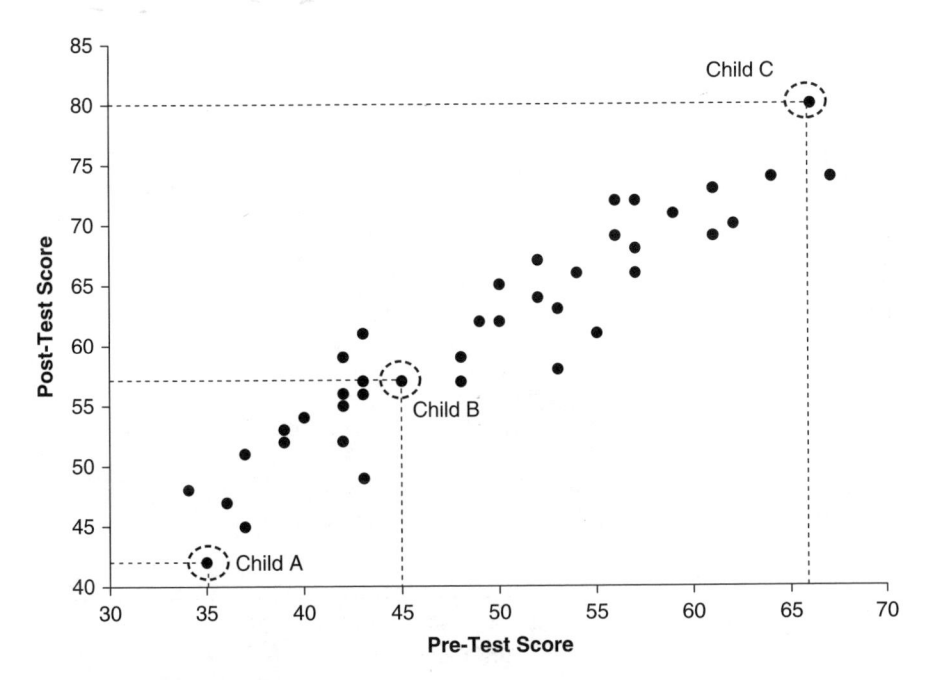

Figure 4.1 Reading comprehension scores at pre-test and post-test for 8–9 year old children (n = 40)

score at pre-test will be more likely, on average, to do the same at post-test. It should also be clear why the two variables cannot be labelled the other way around. In particular, it makes no sense to think about a child's pre-test score being potentially influenced by what they are to achieve one year later and as measured by their post-test score. As a general rule, and as shown in Figure 4.1, the dependent variable usually goes on the 'y axis' (the vertical axis) and the independent variable on the 'x axis' (horizontal axis).

When looking at the data in this way it can be seen that there appears to be a relationship between the pre-test and post-test scores such that the higher the child's pre-test score, the higher their post-test score on average. Moreover, this relationship – or correlation as we refer to it – also appears from the scatterplot to be linear. With this in mind we could depict this linear relationship by getting a ruler and drawing a straight line through the dots, with the position of the line being chosen so that it runs through the middle of the dots and is thus as close to the dots as possible. This has been done with the current data in Figure 4.2. This line, known as the *line of best fit*, is drawn so that the vertical distance between each dot and the line is as small as possible and thus that the line captures the nature of the general relationship between the pre-test and post-test scores as well as possible.

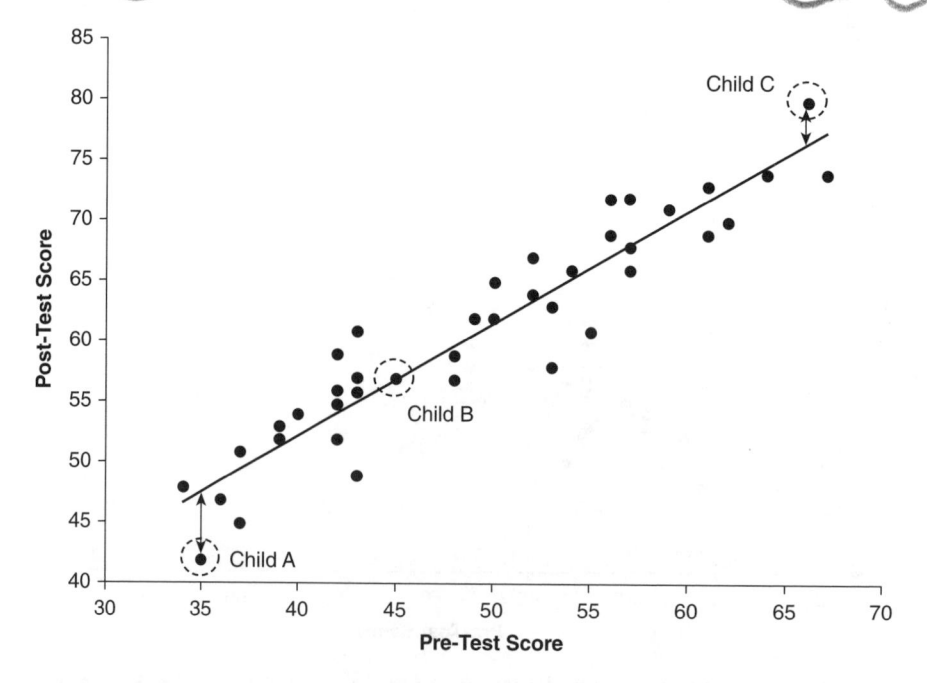

Figure 4.2 Reading comprehension scores at pre-test and post-test for 8–9 year old children (n = 40) with line of best fit

Fundamentals of analysing RCT data 79

Whilst it can be seen that the line of best fit does appear to align well with the dots representing the 40 children, it is not perfect. Only a handful of children actually fall on or very near the line (including Child B). For others, they are either below the line (as with Child A) or above the line (Child C). If the line was perfect in its representation of the relationship between the two variables then all the dots would fall neatly on the line itself. However, and in reality, there is always some degree of discrepancy between the actual position of our subjects (in this case the children) and our line of best fit. These discrepancies, in turn, tell us something about how well the line is as a representation of the relationship between the two variables.

In terms of linear regression, this line of best fit can also be regarded as our best statistical model to represent the relationship between pre-test and post-test scores. Moreover, we can depict this model as a simple equation in the following format:

$$\text{post-test score} = a + b*(\text{pre-test score}) + e$$

Error – distance between dots and line of best fit.

In this equation, 'a' is a constant value and represents the point where the line of best fit cuts across the y-axis when the pre-test score is zero, 'b' represents the gradient of the line and 'e' is the vertical distance between the line and the actual position of each child, sometimes referred to as representing the error in the model. These are illustrated in Figure 4.3, which also shows how we can derive very approximate estimates of 'a' and 'b' (or what we often refer to as the *parameters* of the model) from the scatterplot by visual inspection.

As can be seen, the scatterplot has simply been adjusted so that both axes now start at zero. The line of best fit has been extended and it can be seen that it roughly crosses the y-axis at about 15 (i.e. when the pre-test score is '0' the post-test score is '15'). This, then, is the estimated value for 'a' in the model. As for the gradient, this represents how much the post-test score increases for every one unit increase in the pre-test score. To calculate the gradient we can draw the vertical (dashed) lines shown in Figure 4.3 from the pre-test score values of 50 and 60 on the x-axis up to the line of best fit and then continue them horizontally across to the y-axis. We can do this with any two values but in this case we have chosen pre-test scores of 50 and 60 just for convenience.

In this case we can use the dashed lines to read off from the axes that a 10 point increase in the pre-test score (from 50 to 60) roughly corresponds to a 9 point increase in the post-test score (from about 61 to 70). The gradient is then calculated as the difference in post-test scores divided

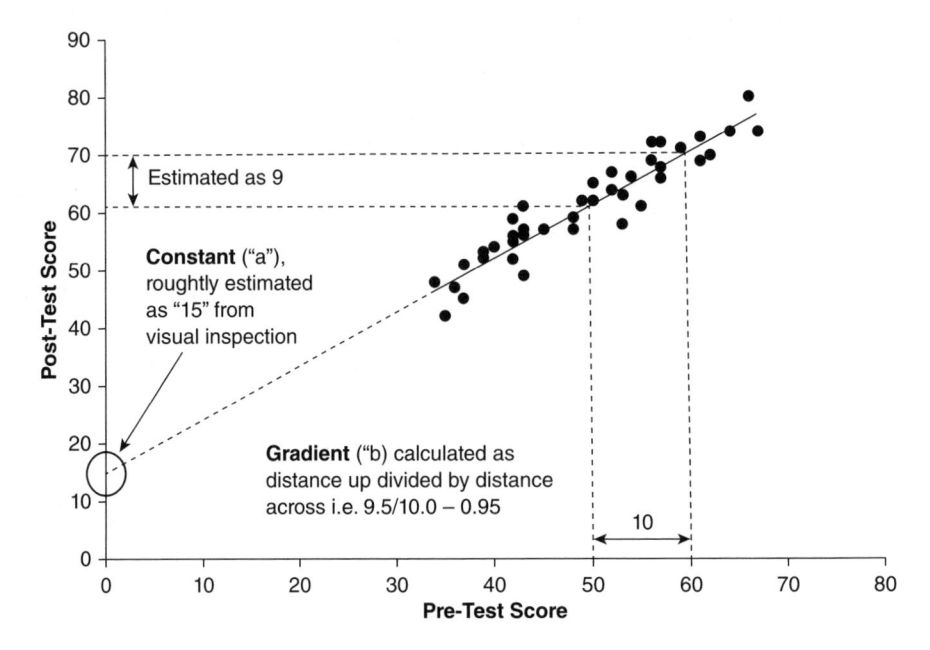

80 Using randomised controlled trials in education

Figure 4.3 Reading comprehension scores at pre-test and post-test for 8–9 year old children (n = 40) with line of best fit and how to calculate its constant and gradient

by the difference in pre-test scores i.e. (70 − 61)/(60 − 50) = 9/10 = 0.9. What this shows us, therefore, is that for every one unit increase in the pre-test score, the line of best fit is telling us that there will be a corresponding increase of about 0.9 in the post-test score on average.

From this, we can conclude that the line of best fit can roughly be depicted by the following formula:

$$\text{post-test score} = 15 + 0.9*(\text{pre-test score}) + e$$

As can be seen, the model is essentially seeking to predict what the value for the dependent (or outcome) variable would be for any given value of the independent (or predictor) variable. To understand how this works in practice, let's take Child A whose pre-test score, we will recall from Figure 4.1, was 35. If we put this into the model we get:

$$\text{post-test score} = 15 + 0.9*(35) + e$$
$$= 15 + 31.5 + e$$
$$= 46.5 + e$$

Fundamentals of analysing RCT data 81

As can be seen, if we use the model (i.e. just going by the line of best fit) then we would estimate that a child with a pre-test score of 35 would, on average, attain a score of 46.5 at post-test. Of course, and for Child A, we can recall from Figure 4.1 that s/he actually achieved a post-test score of 42. This difference between their actual score (42) and their predicted score (46.5) is the discrepancy of about '-4.5' that was illustrated in Figure 4.2. It is also the value for 'e' for Child A that we would need to put into the above model to correct for the inaccuracies in the model represented by the line of best fit.

There is obviously going to be a separate value for 'e' for each individual child. It is included in the model just to ensure that the model is described fully and accurately. In reality, however, we tend to drop 'e' from the model and replace 'post-test score' with '*predicted* post-test score' so that we would have:

predicted post-test score = 15 + 0.9*(pre-test score)

This is our statistical model – our best estimate of the relationship between pre-test and post-test scores based upon the actual data from the 40 children that we have. Of course, and as seen, it is not a perfect depiction of the actual data but is, rather, our best reflection of what this relationship is likely to be on average.

It is worth just taking a moment to look at the above model and to compare it with Figure 4.3. Think about what happens when you put in different values for the pre-test score. If we start with a pre-test score of '0' then 0.9*0 = 0 and thus we are left with a predicted post-test score of '15'. As we have seen, this defines the starting point of the line as it touches the y-axis. Then, for each one point increase in the pre-test score from there we see the predicted post-test score increasing by a value of 0.9. Hence, if the pre-test score is '1' then the predicted post-test score is 15 + 0.9*(1) = 15.9. If the pre-test score is '2' then the predicted post-test score is now 15 + 0.9*(2) = 16.8 and so on. As you can see, this model describes the line of best fit perfectly.

Of course, because we have dropped the error term, this model is no longer completely accurate. Although it represents the line of best fit accurately, as we noted earlier, it does not accurately represent all of the data. For linear regression therefore, alongside calculating the constant and gradient to help us build the model, we can also calculate a figure that gives us a measure of how accurate the model is. This figure is labelled r^2 (or *r-squared*) and you may remember this from the previous chapter and the discussions regarding sample-size calculations. It represents the proportion of variation that all of the independent variables in the model share with the dependent variable. It runs from 0 (meaning there is no relationship at all, and would be shown by all of the dots in the scatterplot being completely randomly placed) to 1 (indicating that there is a perfect relationship, which would be shown by all the dots falling directly on the straight line). In our present case, where there is just one independent variable, then r^2 is calculated simply as the square of the correlation coefficient between the two variables.

So far we have created this model depicting the line of best fit by hand. In reality we would want to do this properly, and accurately, and this is done through the technique referred to as linear regression. The actual mathematics behind linear regression are quite complex but, in essence, the technique seeks to calculate the exact line of best fit where the vertical distances between each point and the line are at an absolute minimum and it estimates, precisely, the value for the constant ('a') and gradient ('b') for the line. The data for this present example can be found in the dataset on the companion website called **regression.sav**. To undertake a linear regression with these data in SPSS, from the top drop-down select **Analyze → Regression → Linear ...** and then select and place the variable *posttest* into the 'Dependent:' window and the variable *pretest* into the 'Independent(s):' window. Click 'OK' and you will obtain the output shown in Output 4.1.

There are three points to note from the SPSS output. First, we can use the estimated coefficients to build our actual model as follows, which shows how our own rough estimates were not too far off the actual values calculated through linear regression:

predicted post-test score = 15.287 + 0.927*(pre-test score)

Second, from the fourth column headed 'Sig', we can see that both of these terms are statistically significant. This means that they can both be considered to be adding something notable to the model. If either of these were not statistically significant (i.e. their values were above 0.05) then we would conclude that we have no evidence to suggest that they are associated with the dependent variable and thus we could remove them from the model. This is an important point when considering how we interpret linear regression models for trial data as we will see shortly. Third, the adjusted R-squared for the model is reported as 0.883, suggesting that the model is a fairly good fit to the actual data given that it can account for 88.3% of the variation in the dependent variable.

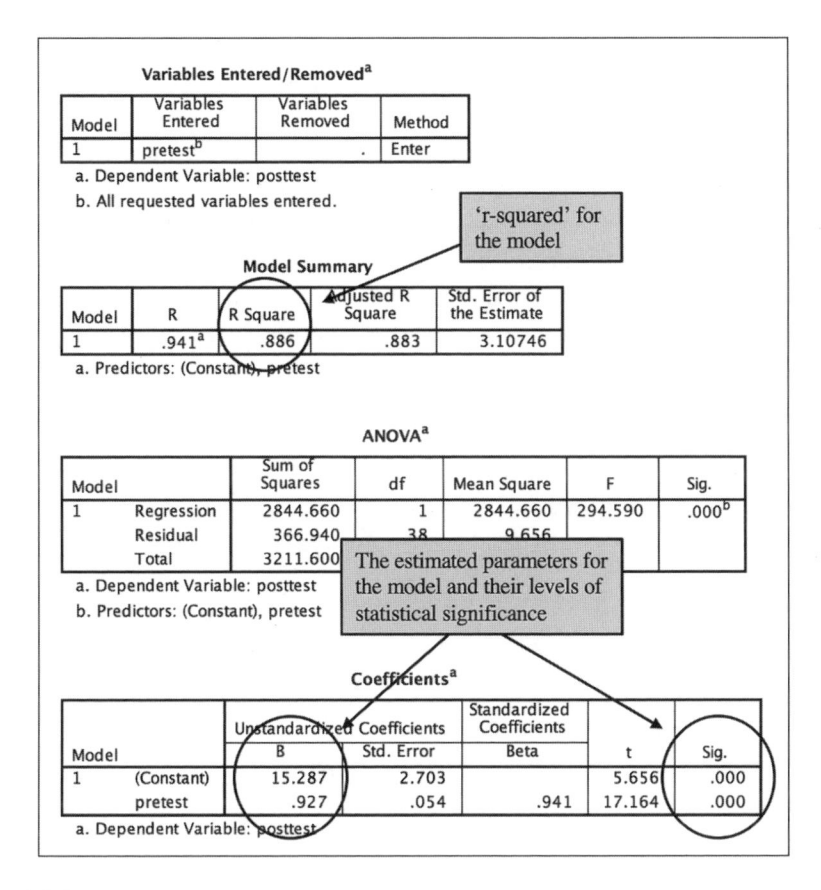

Output 4.1

Variables Entered/Removed[a]

Model	Variables Entered	Variables Removed	Method
1	pretest[b]	.	Enter

a. Dependent Variable: posttest
b. All requested variables entered.

Model Summary — 'r-squared' for the model

Model	R	R Square	Adjusted R Square	Std. Error of the Estimate
1	.941[a]	.886	.883	3.10746

a. Predictors: (Constant), pretest

ANOVA[a]

Model		Sum of Squares	df	Mean Square	F	Sig.
1	Regression	2844.660	1	2844.660	294.590	.000[b]
	Residual	366.940	38	9.656		
	Total	3211.600				

a. Dependent Variable: posttest
b. Predictors: (Constant), pretest

The estimated parameters for the model and their levels of statistical significance

Coefficients[a]

Model		Unstandardized Coefficients B	Std. Error	Standardized Coefficients Beta	t	Sig.
1	(Constant)	15.287	2.703		5.656	.000
	pretest	.927	.054	.941	17.164	.000

a. Dependent Variable: posttest

Linear Regression and RCTs

In relation to the analysis of RCT data, you will recall from the previous chapter that we will typically have data in this format, namely a pre-test score for each individual and also a post-test score. The type of linear regression model described so far is therefore not far off what we need for the analysis of trial data. Our main focus when analysing RCT data is the post-test score, and so this is correctly designated as the dependent (or outcome) variable. We also want to include in our analysis a baseline measure of where each individual started from before the intervention or programme began, and so this is where we would include the pre-test score. Indeed, the only essential piece of information missing from the above model is a variable that tells us whether each individual is a member of the intervention group or the control group. With this in mind, let us

84 Using randomised controlled trials in education

continue with the dataset we have been analysing so far and we will now assume that the data have been collected from a trial of a reading programme involving the 40 children from the same school. Moreover, let us assume that the 40 children were randomly split into two groups, with half of them (n = 20) attending an additional after-school reading programme for the whole of the school year and the other half (n = 20) just continuing as normal and thus not attending the after-school programme. With this in mind, let's return to the original scatterplot and indicate for each child, as we have done in Figure 4.4, whether they were a member of the intervention group or the control group.

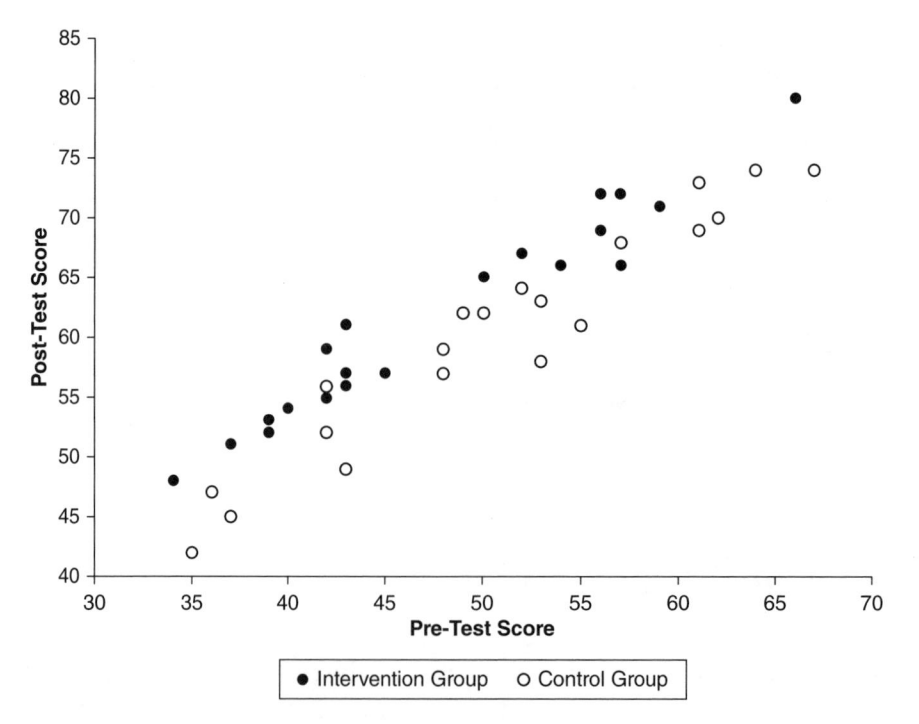

Figure 4.4 Reading comprehension scores at pre-test and post-test for 8–9 year old children (n = 40) by intervention and control group

From an initial visual inspection of the data, it would appear that the two groups of children are not just randomly mixed up. More specifically, if we take any pre-test score and work upwards in a vertical line it does appear that there is a tendency for those in the intervention group to be higher than those in the control group. In other words, it does seem to be the case that children with similar pre-test scores tend to have higher post-test scores if they are in the intervention group compared to the

Fundamentals of analysing RCT data 85

control group. If this pattern does turn out to be the case then what we are looking at here is the effect of the reading programme that appears to be giving a boost in reading scores at post-test for those involved in the programme compared to those that were not.

One way to help with our visualisation of this potential effect is to draw two lines of best fit – one for the control group and one for the intervention group. We would do this just as we did earlier but, this time, drawing our line of best fit for the intervention group by only focusing on the 20 intervention children and, similarly, drawing our other line of best fit for the control group focusing just on our 20 control children. This has been done and is illustrated in Figure 4.5. What we can see here is that the two lines of best fit do appear to be different. In particular, they both appear to be broadly parallel and with the line of best fit for the intervention group being higher than the control group. On visual inspection, the vertical distance between both lines seems to be about five points in relation to the children's post-test score. This is illustrated in Figure 4.5 by taking the case where a child's pre-test score is '51'. As can be seen, if we then follow the scatterplot up vertically then the two lines of best fit suggest that her/his predicted post-test score if they were in the control group would be approximately '60' whereas if they were in the intervention group it would be '65' on average.

This gap of '5' between the two lines of best fit therefore represents the difference in post-test mean scores between the intervention and control groups when we are comparing like-with-like (i.e. when we are comparing children with the same initial pre-test scores). Looking at it another way, it also represents the average estimated effect of the reading programme such that we can conclude that a child who participates in the programme is likely to experience a boost of five points, on average, in their reading scores at the end of the programme.

Now, and in terms of linear regression, we could calculate all of this by splitting our sample into two (one with just the control group children and the other with just the intervention group children) and doing a simple linear regression for this in order to calculate the values (or parameters) for our two lines of best fit. However, there is a neater way to do this by just extending the existing statistical model we have been dealing with and including a second independent variable representing which group a child belongs to. This second variable is what we often refer to as a 'dummy variable' and is always coded '0' or '1'. In our case, and for the purposes of analysing trial data, it makes most sense to code it such that '0' = control group and '1' = intervention group, and to name the variable after the category that is coded '1' (i.e. in this case we have

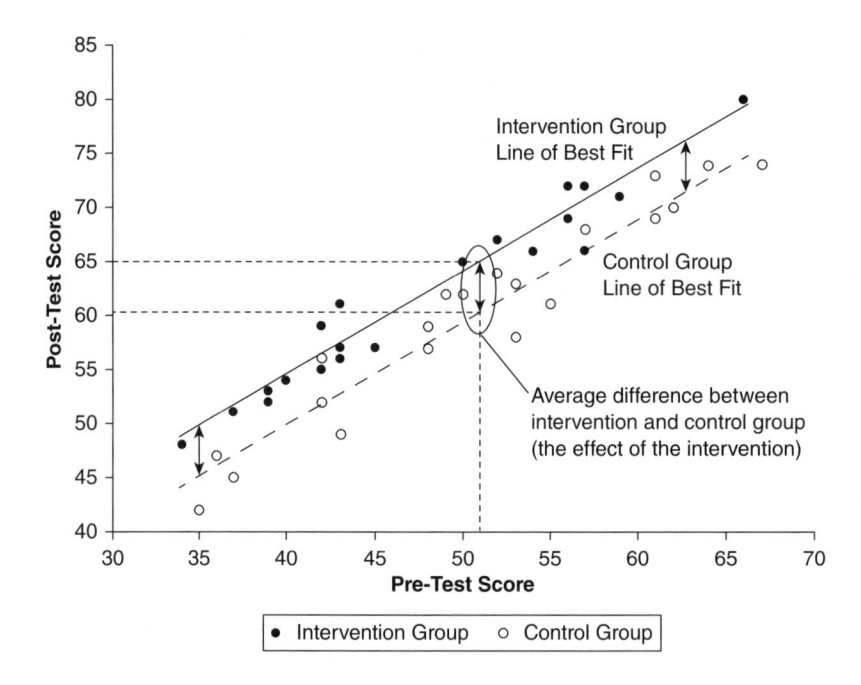

Figure 4.5 Reading comprehension scores at pre-test and post-test for 8–9 year old children (n = 40) by intervention and control group and with lines of best fit added

called the variable 'intervention'). Alongside adding in this second independent variable, the other thing we tend to do is convert all of our other independent variables into standardised scores so that they have a mean of zero and a standard deviation of one. Whilst this does not impact upon the main results of the linear regression model, it does make its interpretation much simpler as we will see shortly. To create a new variable representing the standardised score for pre-test in SPSS, from the top menu select: **Analyze → Descriptive Statistics → Descriptives …** and put the variable *pretest* into the 'Variable(s):' window and also select the option of 'Save standardized values as variables'. Click the 'OK' button and you will see that SPSS has created a new variable labelled *Zpretest* that represents the standardised scores (or z scores) for the variable *pretest* for each child.

To run the linear regression, follow the same procedure as last time in choosing **Analyze → Regression → Linear …** from the top menu and then selecting the variable *posttest* as the dependent variable and the variables *Zpretest* and *intervention* as the two independent variables. Click 'OK' and you will obtain the relevant output. We have only included the final table this time in Output 4.2.

Fundamentals of analysing RCT data 87

Coefficients[a]

Model		Unstandardized Coefficients B	Std. Error	Standardized Coefficients Beta	t	Sig.
1	(Constant)	58.777	.513		114.637	.000
	Zscore(pretest)	8.901	.370	.981	24.071	.000
	intervention	4.245	.730	.237	5.814	.000

a. Dependent Variable: posttest

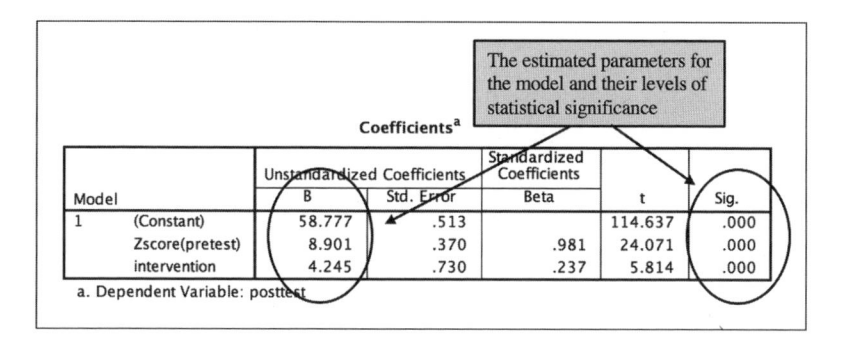

The estimated parameters for the model and their levels of statistical significance

Output 4.2

This output represents the core analysis from a simple RCT. To understand what it is telling us, it is helpful to take the coefficients and write out the model as a formula as we have done previously. To keep things simple, we have rounded the coefficients to one decimal place. Have a look at the resulting model below and compare with the output in Output 4.2 to ensure you can see where the figures have been taken from:

$$\text{predicted post-test score} = 58.8 + 8.9*(\text{pre-test score}) + 4.2*(\text{intervention})$$

As we did previously, it often helps us understand what the above model is telling us by putting in some values. Let us start with the variable *intervention* and see what happens when we put in the values of '0' (representing children in the control group) and '1' (representing those in the intervention group):

Control Group:

$$\text{predicted post-test score} = 58.8 + 8.9*(\text{pre-test score}) + 4.2*(0)$$
$$= \mathbf{58.8 + 8.9*(\text{pre-test score})}$$

Intervention Group:

$$\text{predicted post-test score} = 58.8 + 8.9*(\text{pre-test score}) + 4.2*(1)$$
$$= 58.8 + 8.9*(\text{pre-test score}) + 4.2$$
$$= \mathbf{63.0 + 8.9*(\text{pre-test score})}$$

In essence, and rather neatly, what we can see from this is that the dummy variable for *intervention* has the effect of creating two lines of best fit (highlighted above in bold). Both lines have the same gradient

('8.9') but those in the control have a constant of '58.8' whereas those in the intervention group have a constant of '63.0'. In other words, and if we were to draw these two lines then they would be parallel (as they both have the same gradient) but the intervention group line would sit higher than the control group line by 63.0 − 58.8 = 4.2 points. This is, indeed, what we found with the lines drawn in Figure 4.5 (although we can see that the size of the gap, when calculated accurately, is 4.2 points rather than our visual rough estimate of 5 points).

Another way to interpret the original model is that the coefficient (or estimated parameter) for the variable *intervention* tells us what the average difference is in the post-test scores of those in the intervention group compared to those in the control group. In other words, and looking at the formula, it is telling us that if the child is a member of the intervention group then, on average, their predicted post-test score is boosted by 4.2 points. This is one of the reasons why it was useful to call the variable 'intervention' as it helps us interpret the model in this way. The other key point we can draw out from the findings set out in Output 4.2 is that this coefficient is statistically significant (see the value for it in the fourth column headed 'Sig'). This is a critical finding as it tells us that this average difference in post-test scores between the control and intervention groups is statistically significant, and thus unlikely to have occurred by chance. This, in turn, is the key piece of evidence that the reading programme has had a measurable (and statistically significant) effect.

Beyond this, we should also remember that we are now using the standardised scores for the pre-test variable (*Zpretest*). As such, the variable now has a mean score of '0' and a standard deviation of '1'. Thus, if we are wishing to input values for the pre-test score into our two models then the obvious one to put in would be '0' as this now represents the average child. If we do this for both models then we get the following:

Control Group:

$$\text{predicted post-test score} = 63.0 + 8.9*(0) = \mathbf{63.0}$$

Intervention Group:

$$\text{predicted post-test score} = 58.8 + 8.9*(0) = \mathbf{58.8}$$

What we have here are the estimated mean post-test scores for the control and intervention group children for the average child at pre-test. To put it another way, these are the estimated post-test scores for both

Fundamentals of analysing RCT data 89

groups once we have controlled for any differences between the two groups at pre-test. We therefore refer to these as the 'adjusted mean post-test scores' and, when we are reporting them, we make a note somewhere that they have been adjusted by controlling for differences between the groups at pre-test.

So far, then, we have used our linear regression model to estimate the adjusted mean post-test scores for the intervention and control groups and to determine whether the difference in the two scores is statistically significant. The only other bits of information that we need to derive to report these findings are: the corresponding standard deviations for the intervention and control groups; the sample sizes for both groups; the estimated effect size for the difference in adjusted mean scores at post-test; and a 95% confidence interval for this effect size. We will look at how we derive each of these pieces of information in turn.

First, and in relation to standard deviations and sample sizes, we simply calculate these from the raw data for the post-test scores for each group in turn. To do this in SPSS we first need to use the **Data → Split File ...** command. In the resultant window, select the option 'Organise output by groups', place the variable intervention in the window 'Groups Based on:' and then click 'OK'. Having done this, we just need to select: **Analyze → Descriptive Statistics → Descriptives ...** and place the variable *posttest*

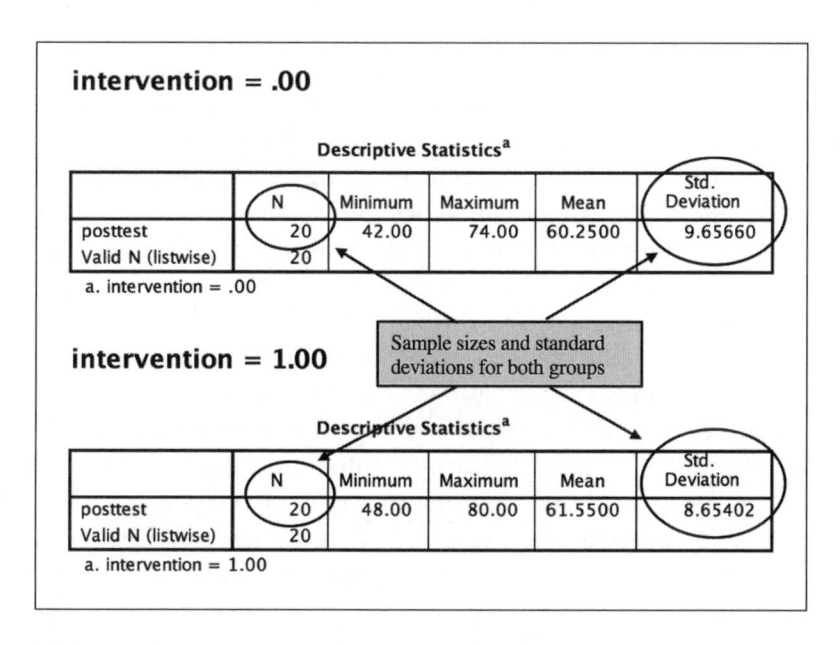

intervention = .00

Descriptive Statistics[a]

	N	Minimum	Maximum	Mean	Std. Deviation
posttest	20	42.00	74.00	60.2500	9.65660
Valid N (listwise)	20				

a. intervention = .00

intervention = 1.00

Sample sizes and standard deviations for both groups

Descriptive Statistics[a]

	N	Minimum	Maximum	Mean	Std. Deviation
posttest	20	48.00	80.00	61.5500	8.65402
Valid N (listwise)	20				

a. intervention = 1.00

Output 4.3

in the 'Variable(s):' window and then click 'OK'. The resultant output is shown in Output 4.3. We can see from the output that for the control group the standard deviation is 9.66 and the sample size is 20, and for the intervention group the figures are 8.65 and 20 respectively.

There are two points to note from this. The first is that this technique works well when we do not have any missing data. In the real-life example to be reported later in this chapter we will run through a slight workaround method for calculating standard deviations and sample sizes when we have some missing data. Secondly, notice how the mean post-test scores for the control and intervention groups are 60.3 and 61.6 respectively; much closer than those we calculated using our linear regression model. The reason for this is that, although we randomly split the sample of 40 children into two groups, this did not result in completely balanced groups at pre-test. Indeed if you were to use the technique above to calculate the mean scores for the pre-test variable for both groups you would find that the mean pre-test score for the intervention group was actually lower (mean = 47.7, sd = 8.9) compared to the control group (mean = 50.8, sd = 9.5). If we just used the raw mean scores at post-test of 60.3 (control group) and 61.6 (intervention group) respectively then this would give a notably under-estimated sense of the amount of progress those in the intervention group made compared to those in the control group. In particular, and just going by the raw scores, those in the control group achieved an average improvement of 9.5 (from 50.8 at pre-test to 60.3 at post-test) whereas those in the intervention group achieved an average improvement of 13.9 (from 47.7 at pre-test to 61.6 at post-test). This is precisely why we prefer to report adjusted rather than raw post-test mean scores.

Finally, we need to derive the effect size for this difference and its 95% confidence interval. In this case, as we are dealing with a scale variable, we would typically report the standardised mean difference as the effect size and this is calculated by dividing the difference in the two mean scores by the pooled standard deviation for the sample as a whole. As such, the resultant value tells us what the difference is between the two mean scores in standard deviations, so that an effect size of '0.5' for example indicates a difference between the two mean scores of half a standard deviation. The most appropriate effect size measure in this regard is *Hedge's g* and there are many online effect size calculators that can be used to calculate the value for 'g' if you have the mean, standard deviation and sample size for both groups. However, and for convenience, we have added a simple Effect Size Calculator on our companion website for use with the worked examples in this chapter and the next. There are also full instructions accompanying the Calculator on the website. If we use these values (Intervention group: mean = 63.022, sd = 8.654, n = 20; Control group: mean = 58.777, sd = 9.657, n = 20) then we will get the following estimated effect size and associated 95% confidence interval (using the bias correction factor) from the calculator:

$$g = +0.45 \ (95\% \ CI: -0.17, +1.08)$$

We now have all the figures that we need to report the main findings of this particular trial. One way of doing this is shown in Table 4.1.

Table 4.1 Findings of the effects of an after-schools reading programme*

Outcome	Intervention Group Mean (sd)	n	Control Group Mean (sd)	n	Effect Size, Hedge's g (95% CI)**
Reading Score	63.0 (8.7)	20	58.8 (9.7)	20	+.45 [−.17, 1.08]

*Adjusted post-test mean scores reported, controlling for differences between groups at pre-test

**With bias correction factor applied

Analysis of Sub-Group Effects

What we have done so far is to show how to use linear regression to analyse data from an RCT and to derive the main findings to report. Typically in relation to trials, there is an interest not just in the overall effects of a particular programme or intervention but also in whether that programme/intervention is possibly having differential effects for particular sub-groups of participants. In our current example, there may be reason for thinking that the after-schools reading programme may be having a greater effect for boys than girls. In this sense, rather than assuming that all children in the intervention group will experience a similar boost at post-test compared to those in the control group, it could be that the programme is designed in such a way that it is particularly attractive to boys. As such we could find that the average boost for boys may be different to the average boost for girls. If we have reason to believe this then this type of additional sub-group analysis as it is often called would be justified and pre-specified in the protocol for the trial.

To analyse such sub-group effects we simply extend the linear regression model that we have been working with to include two additional independent variables: a variable representing the grouping variable we are interested in (in this case the dummy variable we have called *boy*, coded '1' for boys and '0' for girls); and a variable representing the interaction effect between the variables 'intervention' and 'boy'. This variable (what we have called *intvn_boy* and calculated by multiplying 'intervention' by 'boy') is generated using the **Transform → Compute Variable ...** facility in SPSS. In the resultant window that opens up, select the variable boy and place it in the 'Numeric Expression:' window, use the calculator buttons to add a multiply operation ('*') and then select intervention and place it in the window as well. This should result in the function you need: 'boy*intervention'. Finally, type in the name that you want the new variable to be called in the 'Target Variable:' window (in this case 'intvn_boy') and then click 'OK'.

In essence, this enhanced regression model with *boy* and *intvn_boy* added creates four lines of best fit for: boys in the intervention group; boys in the control group; girls in the intervention group; and girls in the control group. Just as above, what the model then allows us to do is compare each line of best fit to see if the differences are statistically significant. All of this is best illustrated by considering the output from such a regression model. In SPSS, and once you have ensured that you have reset the 'split file' command, you should choose: **Analyze → Regression → Linear ...** from the top menu and then select the variable *posttest* as the dependent variable and the variables *Zpretest, intervention, boy* and *intvn_boy* as the four independent variables. Click 'OK' and you will obtain the output shown in Output 4.4.

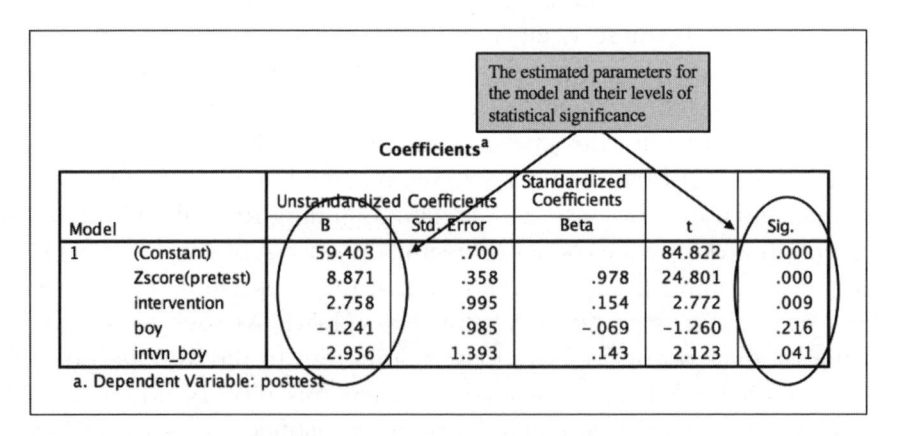

Coefficients[a]

Model		Unstandardized Coefficients B	Std. Error	Standardized Coefficients Beta	t	Sig.
1	(Constant)	59.403	.700		84.822	.000
	Zscore(pretest)	8.871	.358	.978	24.801	.000
	intervention	2.758	.995	.154	2.772	.009
	boy	-1.241	.985	-.069	-1.260	.216
	intvn_boy	2.956	1.393	.143	2.123	.041

a. Dependent Variable: posttest

The estimated parameters for the model and their levels of statistical significance

Output 4.4

As before, the best way to help interpret what is going on in this model is to write it out as an equation and then to enter values to compare what happens for different sub-groups. With this in mind, the main equation is as follows:

Fundamentals of analysing RCT data   93

predicted post-test score = 59.4 + 8.9*(z_pretest) + 2.8*(intervention)
− 1.2*(boy) +3.0*(intervention*boy)

Also, and just as we did previously, we can enter the value '0' for *Zpretest* as we are wanting to explore what the model tells us about the effects of the intervention and of gender on the average child at pre-test. This, in turn, means that we can effectively ignore the '8.9*(Zpretest)' term in the equation. Beyond this, we need to enter values for *boy*, *intervention* and *intvn_boy* to derive our four lines of best fit as follows:

Boys in Intervention Group ('boy' = '1', Intervention = '1'):
predicted post-test score = 59.4 + 2.8*(1) − 1.2*(1) + 3.0*(1*1)
= 59.4 + 2.8 − 1.2 + 3.0 = **64.0**

Boys in Control Group ('boy' = '1', Intervention = '0'):
predicted post-test score = 59.4 + 2.8*(0) − 1.2*(1) + 3.0*(0*1)
= 59.4 + 0 − 1.2 + 0 = **58.2**

Girls in Intervention Group ('boy' = '0', Intervention = '1'):
predicted post-test score = 59.4 + 2.8*(1) − 1.2*(0) + 3.0*(1*0)
= 59.4 + 2.8 − 0 + 0 = **62.2**

Girls in Control Group ('boy' = '0', Intervention = '0'):
predicted post-test score = 59.4 + 2.8*(0) − 1.2*(0) + 3.0*(0*0)
= 59.4 + 0 − 0 + 0 = **59.4**

In working through the above we have effectively calculated the adjusted post-test mean scores for each of the sub-groups. Also, and in doing so, we can see how the model actually works. Thus, in this case:

- the *constant* represents the adjusted post-test mean score for girls in the control group;
- the coefficient for *intervention* represents the average effect for all children (boys and girls) of being in the intervention group compared to the control group;
- the coefficient for *boy* represents the average difference of boys from girls;
- the coefficient for *intervention*boy* represents the added boost for boys specifically due to being in the intervention group compared to girls in the intervention group.

When undertaking sub-group analyses of this type, our main focus in relation to the actual model is this last coefficient representing the interaction effect (between *intervention* and *boy* in this case). From the output (see Output 4.4) we can see that this term is statistically significant (p = 0.041) and this tells us that we have sufficient evidence to report this effect. If this term was not statistically significant (i.e. if the value was above 0.05) then we would simply report in our findings that we conducted a sub-group analysis but found no evidence that the reading programme was having differential effects for boys and girls.

However, and in this case, the interaction effect is statistically significant and so we can proceed to report the findings. We have already calculated the adjusted mean post-test scores for all four sub-groups above. In addition, and as before, we need to calculate the standard deviations and sample sizes for each of the four groups and we do this using the Split File facility in SPSS as before, but this time placing the two variables *intervention* and *boy* in the 'Groups Based on:' window. Now that we have the means, standard deviations and sample sizes for each sub-group, we can also calculate two effect sizes: one comparing boys in the intervention and control groups and one comparing girls in the intervention and control groups. As before, we do this using the Effect Size Calculator on our companion website. Once this is all done, the findings can be reported in full, as illustrated in Table 4.2. As can be seen, the reading programme does seem to have a larger effect for boys (g = .59) compared to girls (g = .28). It should be noted that whilst the statistical model has provided us with sufficient evidence that there is likely to be a difference in the effects of the programme for boys and girls, the confidence intervals for the effect sizes for both groups are very wide and both include zero. This is due to the very small sizes of the sub-samples involved in this particular case. Thus, although we have evidence that boys are benefitting more from the programme than girls, we need to report and discuss the effect sizes with caution; explaining that they are indicative only and carry a relatively large margin of error.

Table 4.2 Findings of the effects of an after-schools reading programme*

Outcome	Intervention Group Mean (sd)	n	Control Group Mean (sd)	n	Effect Size, Hedge's g (95% CI)**
Reading Score					
Boys	64.0 (10.5)	10	58.2 (7.8)	10	.60 [–.30, 1.50]
Girls	62.2 (6.8)	10	59.4 (11.5)	10	.28 [–.60, 1.16]

*Adjusted post-test mean scores reported, controlling for differences between groups at pre-test

**With bias correction factor applied

Real-Life Example: Analysis of RCT Evaluation of 'Doodle Den'

In this final section, we will pull all of this together and replicate the analysis of a real-life trial of an after-school literacy programme – Doodle Den – that we ran. The programme and the methods used in the trial are described in detail in an article we published in the *International Journal of Educational Research*, entitled 'A randomised control trial evaluation of a literacy after-school programme for struggling beginning readers', and available in open access format to view online (Biggart et al., 2013). Doodle Den was targeted at struggling beginning readers aged 5–6 in an area of significant socio-economic disadvantage and involved the children attending three after-school sessions per week that each lasted one-and-a-half hours. The programme ran for 36 weeks and was delivered by two staff – a qualified teacher and a qualified youth worker or childcare professional. Doodle Den is a structured programme. Each session begins with a snack and sign-in routine, followed by a variety of literacy educational activities before concluding with a 'fun' element based on a literacy theme.

The children were referred by their teachers from eight different schools. The total number of children referred (n = 623) were then randomly allocated, on an individual basis, to the intervention (n = 311) or control (n = 310) groups. There was some attrition, with a proportion of children either not completing the pre-test or post-test and with 237 in the intervention group and 227 in the control group eventually completing both pre-test and post-tests (76% and 73% respectively). The complete dataset, with a detailed summary guide of the variables, has been archived on the Irish Social Science Data Archive (ISSDA) website and can be downloaded in an SPSS format from www.ucd.ie/issda/data/doodleden/. For convenience a reduced version of the dataset is also available on the companion website at https://study.sagepub.com/connelly.

For this analysis, we will take the main primary outcome for the study – children's overall literacy ability as measured through the Drumcondra Primary Reading Test. The three key variables in the dataset are labelled *CPre_Literacy_ability* and *CPost-Literacy_ability* and *Group* respectively. Group is coded '0' for the control group and '1' for the intervention group. Before we run the main analysis, we can get a feel for the data by just calculating summary statistics for both groups at pre-test and post-test. One way to do this would be to use the **Data → Split File …** command and to select the option 'Organise output by groups' and place *Group* in the window 'Groups Based on:' and then click 'OK'. Having done this, we just need to select: **Analyze → Descriptive Statistics → Descriptives …** and place the two variables

CPre_Literacy_ability and *CPost_Literacy_ability* in the 'Variable(s):' window and then click 'OK'. The resultant output is shown in Output 4.5. It can be seen that the two groups are quite similar at pre-test although there is a slight difference in their mean scores: .36 (sd = .18) for the control group and .39 (sd = .17) for the intervention group. As can also be seen, those in the intervention group do seem to have made greater progress at post-test (an increase of .35) compared to the control group (increase of .29).

However, to determine whether this is a statistically significant difference, and thus whether we can claim that we have robust evidence of the effectiveness of Doodle Den, we need to run the basic linear regression model we outlined earlier. However, before we run the main regression, you will recall that we need to transform the pre-test variable into its equivalent standardised score (z score). Prior to doing this, you should ensure that you have reset the 'split file' command. Once done, and as

Intervention group = Control *An increase of .2914 from pre-test to post-test*

Descriptive Statistics[a]

	N	Minimum	Maximum	Mean	Std. Deviation
Child pre-test: Literacy ability score	238	.00	.90	.3552	.17507
Child post-test: Literacy ability score	241	.10	1.00	.6466	.24476
Valid N (listwise)	193				

a. Intervention group = Control

Intervention group = Intervention *An increase of .3497 from pre-test to post-test*

Descriptive Statistics[a]

	N	Minimum	Maximum	Mean	Std. Deviation
Child pre-test: Literacy ability score	235	.07	.97	.3850	.17017
Child post-test: Literacy ability score	237	.17	1.00	.7347	.22599
Valid N (listwise)	187				

a. Intervention group = Intervention

Output 4.5

Fundamentals of analysing RCT data

before, we transform the variable by selecting: **Analyze → Descriptive Statistics → Descriptives** ... and putting the variable *CPre_Literacy_ability* into the 'Variable(s):' window and also select the option of 'Save standardized values as variables'. Click the 'OK' button and you will see that SPSS has created a new variable labelled *ZCPre_Literacy_ability*. With this in place we can now run the main regression model using: **Analyze → Regression → Linear** ... and selecting the variable *CPost_Literacy_ability* as the dependent variable and the variables *ZCPre_Literacy_ability* and *Group* as the two independent variables. Click 'OK' and you will obtain the key output shown in Output 4.6.

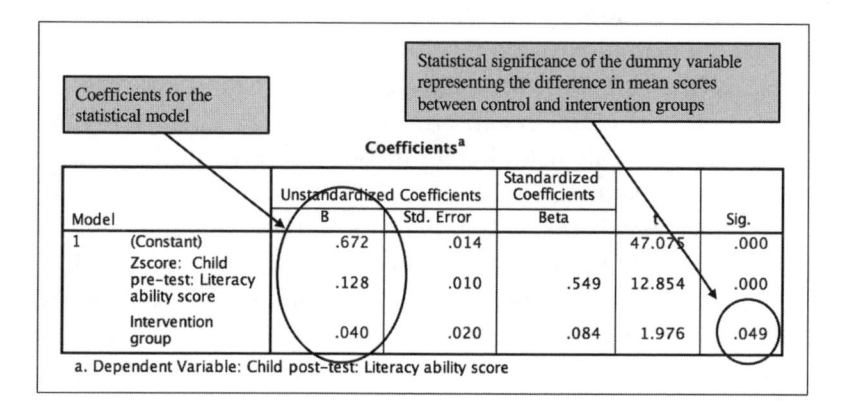

Coefficients[a]

Coefficients for the statistical model

Statistical significance of the dummy variable representing the difference in mean scores between control and intervention groups

Model		Unstandardized Coefficients B	Std. Error	Standardized Coefficients Beta	t	Sig.
1	(Constant)	.672	.014		47.075	.000
	Zscore: Child pre-test: Literacy ability score	.128	.010	.549	12.854	.000
	Intervention group	.040	.020	.084	1.976	.049

a. Dependent Variable: Child post-test: Literacy ability score

Output 4.6

Just to reinforce the approach to interpreting the output, we can write out this model as a simple equation:

$$\text{predicted post-test score} = 0.672 + 0.040*(\text{intervention}) + 0.128*(\text{pre-test score})$$

As we are going to use the model to estimate what the predicted post-test mean scores are for the average child in the intervention and control schools, we can replace the pre-test score with '0' to represent the average child (remembering that, because this has been standardised, the average child will have a score of '0') and we can then put in '0' and '1' respectively to represent the control and intervention group children. Doing this we get:

Control Group:

$$\text{predicted post-test score} = 0.672 + 0.040*(0) + 0.128*(0) = \mathbf{0.672}$$

Intervention Group:

predicted post-test score = 0.672 + 0.040*(1) + 0.128*(0) = **0.712**

Alongside these adjusted post-test mean scores, we also need their associated standard deviations and sample sizes. However, this is where we will encounter a problem due to missing data. What we want is to ensure that the standard deviations and sample sizes are only calculated based on the children whose data were included in the model (i.e. those that had pre-test and post-test data). To do this, we need to find a way of creating a filter variable to use that is coded '0' for having missing data and '1' for having full data and thus included in the model. One way to do this is to use the **Analyze → Regression → Linear ...** procedure to create a new variable representing the unstandardised residuals estimated from the model. These are the values that are derived from the model using each child's actual pre-test score, group membership and post-test score. The key point here is that SPSS will only calculate this for those children who have no missing data and are thus included in the model. To create this variable, we need to run the same regression model again but, this time, after selecting the relevant variables and before clicking 'OK', click on the 'Save...' button and select 'Unstandardized' from the list of options under the 'Residuals' list top right. Click 'Continue' and then, in the main window, click 'OK'. Alongside the main output we have already discussed, you will also notice that a new variable has been created at the end of your dataset named *RES_1*.

If you have a look at the variable itself in Data View, you will see that the value for *RES_1* for the first child in the data is '0.01765'. To understand where this came from, have a look across the dataset to see their pre-test score and group membership. In this case, you find that they have a score of '1.90640' for *ZCPre_Literacy_ability* and '0' for *Group*, meaning that they are in the control group. If we add these values into the formula we created for the model we get:

predicted post-test score = 0.672 + 0.040*(0) + 0.128*(1.906) = **0.916**

The residual value (0.01765) is simply the difference between this predicted score and the child's actual post-test score (0.93333), allowing for rounding errors.

For the present purposes, however, we are not interested in the actual residual values but simply whether a value has been calculated or not. We can therefore re-code this variable so that it is just coded '1' if there is a predicted value (and thus the child has full data and is included in the model) and '0' if there are missing data (thus indicating that there were missing data for the child and hence they were not included in the model).

To do this select **Transform → Recode into Same Variables ...** choose PRE_1 and place it into the 'Variables:' window and click 'Old and New Values'. In the second window that opens up, select 'System-missing' from the list of options on the left for 'Old Value'. On the right-hand side for 'New Value' select 'Value:' and type in '0' and then click on the button 'Add'. Next, select 'All other values' from the left-hand side and then select 'Value' on the right-hand-side and type in '1'. Click the 'Add' button again and in the 'Old —> New:' window you should have the commands:

SYSMIS —> 0

ELSE —> 1

Click 'Continue' and then 'OK' and you will see that the variable *RES_1* has now been transformed so that it just consists of the values '0' or '1'. Finally, we can use this variable to filter out children who did not contribute to the model before we then calculate the standard deviations and sample sizes for the control and intervention groups. To set it as a filter, select **Data → Select Cases ...** choose 'If condition is satisfied' and then click on the 'If...' button. In the second window that opens up, choose *RES_1* and place it in the top window. Use the calculator buttons to then select '=' and '1' so that the window has the expression: 'RES_1 = 1' and then click 'Continue' and finally 'OK'. With the filter set, use the **Data → Split File ...** command and select the option 'Organise output by groups' and place *Group* in the window 'Groups Based on:' and then click 'OK'. Having done this, and finally, we can select **Analyze → Descriptive Statistics → Descriptives ...** and place the variable *CPost_Literacy_ability* in the 'Variable(s):' window and then click 'OK'. The resultant output is shown in Output 4.7. This, in turn, gives us the rest of the data we need so that:

Control group: mean = 0.672, sd = 0.243, n = 193

Intervention group: mean = 0.712, sd = 0.231, n = 187

We can now enter these values into the Effect Size Calculator, as before, to get the effect size and its associated 95% confidence interval: g = 0.17 [-0.03, 0.37]. All we have left to do now is to present the data in a table as shown in Table 4.3.

Beyond these main effects we can also reproduce the sub-group analyses. In this particular trial there was an interest in whether the programme had differential effects for boys and girls. To test this we need to extend the above regression model to add in a dummy variable for gender and then an interaction effect for gender*intervention. In this case we can see that the variable Gender is currently coded '1' for boys and '2' for girls. We therefore

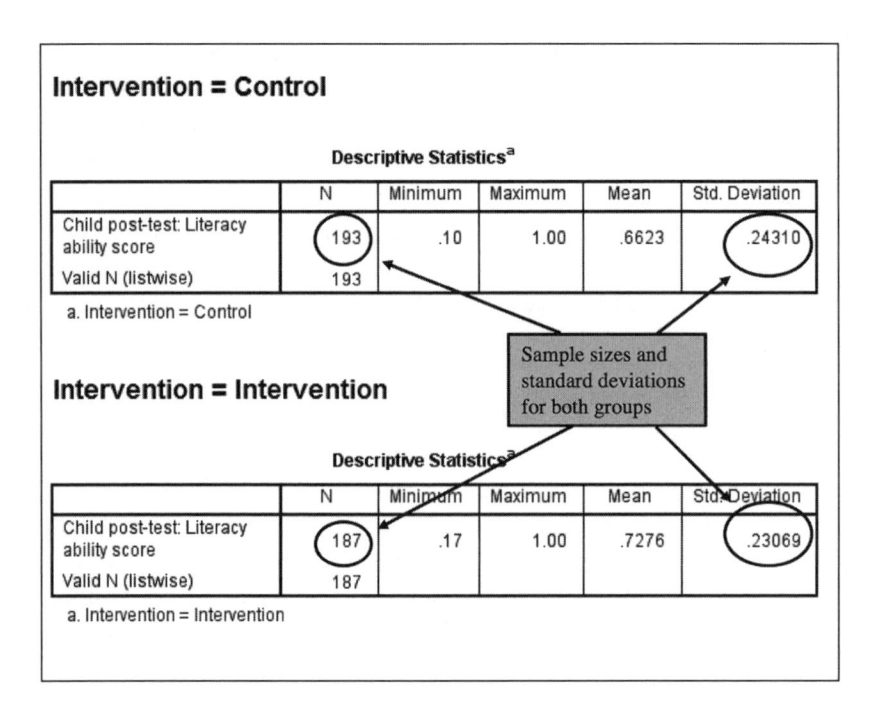

Using randomised controlled trials in education

Intervention = Control

Descriptive Statistics[a]

	N	Minimum	Maximum	Mean	Std. Deviation
Child post-test: Literacy ability score	193	.10	1.00	.6623	.24310
Valid N (listwise)	193				

a. Intervention = Control

Intervention = Intervention

Descriptive Statistics[a]

	N	Minimum	Maximum	Mean	Std. Deviation
Child post-test: Literacy ability score	187	.17	1.00	.7276	.23069
Valid N (listwise)	187				

a. Intervention = Intervention

Sample sizes and standard deviations for both groups

Output 4.7

Table 4.3 The effects of Doodle Den on children's overall literacy ability*

	Intervention Group		Control Group		Effect Size, Hedge's
Outcome	Mean (sd)	n	Mean (sd)	n	g (95% CI)**
Literacy Ability	0.71 (0.23)	187	0.67 (0.24)	193	+0.17 [−0.03, 0.37]

*Adjusted post-test mean scores reported, controlling for differences between groups at pre-test

**With bias correction factor applied

need to use **Transform → Recode into Same Variables ...** to recode this so that boys are coded '1' and girls coded '0'. In the second window that opens, select the option 'Value:' in the left-hand column and type in '2'. In the right-hand column select 'Value:' and type in '0'. Click the 'Add' button. As boys are already coded '1' then we do not need to do anything else. As such, click 'Continue' and then 'OK'. To aid interpretation of the model, it is probably worth also changing the name of the variable from 'Gender' to 'Boy' and the label values so that 'Girl' is coded '0' rather than '2'. As we are doing this, let's go the whole way and change the name 'Group' to 'Intervention' as well. This all reduces the risk of making mistakes when interpreting more complex models that include interaction terms.

With all this done, we can then create the interaction term by using the **Transform → Compute Variable …** facility in SPSS. In the window that opens up, select the variable *Boy* and place it in the 'Numeric Expression:' window, use the calculator buttons to add a multiply operation ('*') and then select *Intervention* and place it in the window as well. This should result in the function you need: 'Intervention*Boy'. Finally, type in the name that you want the new variable to be called in the 'Target Variable:' window (in this case 'intvn_Boy') and then click 'OK'. Finally, we can run the regression using **Analyze → Regression → Linear …** from the top menu and then select the variable *CPost_Literacy_ability* as the dependent variable and the variables *ZCPre_Literacy_ability, intervention, Boy* and *Intvn_Boy* as the four independent variables. Click 'OK' and you will obtain the output shown in Output 4.8. Interestingly, and in this case, the interaction effect term in the model is not statistically significant (p = 0.265). We therefore have no evidence to suggest that there is a difference in the effects of the intervention on boys and girls in relation to this particular outcome. As such, we would not go any further in terms of calculating adjusted post-test mean scores and separate effect sizes for boys and girls. Doing this would encourage the reader to believe that there may be gender differences when our findings are telling us that there is no evidence of such. Rather, we would just report that, for this outcome, we undertook a sub-group analysis but found no evidence of differential effects for the programme in relation to gender.

As another example, we will also examine another outcome that was considered by the trial – whether Doodle Den had a positive effect in

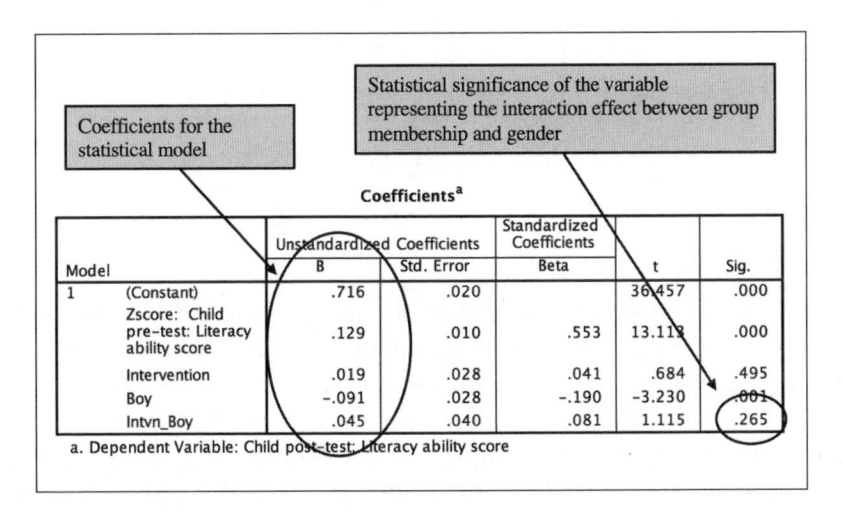

Coefficients[a]

Model		Unstandardized Coefficients B	Std. Error	Standardized Coefficients Beta	t	Sig.
1	(Constant)	.716	.020		36.457	.000
	Zscore: Child pre-test: Literacy ability score	.129	.010	.553	13.113	.000
	Intervention	.019	.028	.041	.684	.495
	Boy	-.091	.028	-.190	-3.230	.001
	Intvn_Boy	.045	.040	.081	1.115	.265

a. Dependent Variable: Child post-test: Literacy ability score

Coefficients for the statistical model

Statistical significance of the variable representing the interaction effect between group membership and gender

Output 4.8

102 Using randomised controlled trials in education

relation to reducing behavioural problems amongst the children, rated by the teachers using an attention deficit hyperactivity disorder scale. The relevant variables in the dataset for this measure at pre-test and post-test respectively are: *TPre_ADHD_behaviours* and *TPost_ADHD_behaviours*. We will assume by this stage that you know how to run the analysis for both the main effect and to explore gender differences within this. However, it is worth just reminding you to create and use the standardised scores for the pre-test variable. The output for both models is shown in Output 4.9.

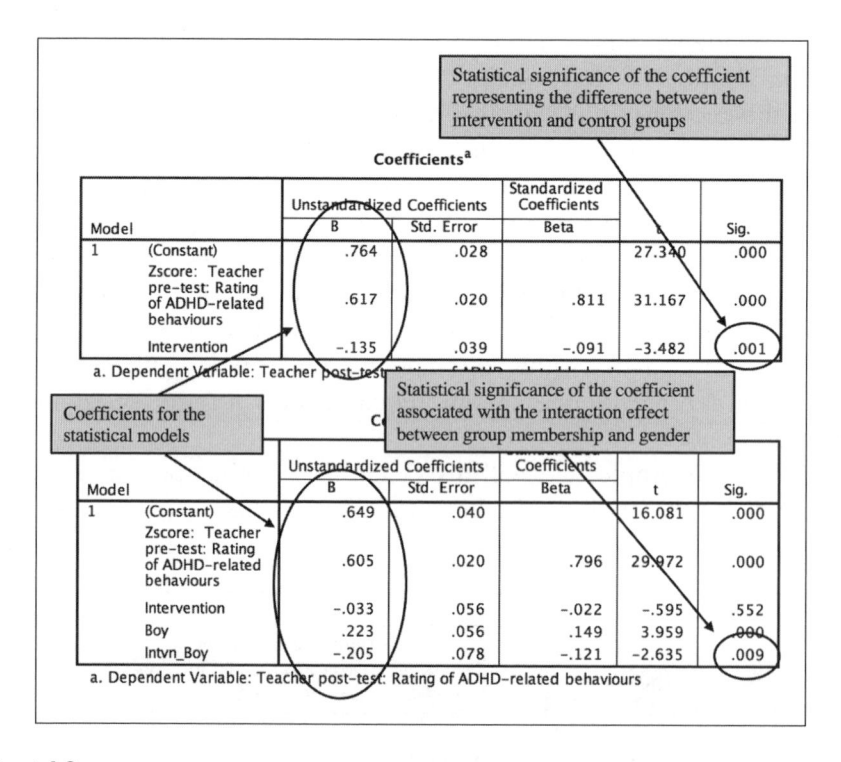

Coefficients[a]

Model		Unstandardized Coefficients B	Std. Error	Standardized Coefficients Beta	t	Sig.
1	(Constant)	.764	.028		27.340	.000
	Zscore: Teacher pre-test: Rating of ADHD-related behaviours	.617	.020	.811	31.167	.000
	Intervention	-.135	.039	-.091	-3.482	.001

a. Dependent Variable: Teacher post-test Rating of ADHD-related behaviours

Statistical significance of the coefficient representing the difference between the intervention and control groups

Coefficients for the statistical models

Statistical significance of the coefficient associated with the interaction effect between group membership and gender

Coefficients[a]

Model		Unstandardized Coefficients B	Std. Error	Standardized Coefficients Beta	t	Sig.
1	(Constant)	.649	.040		16.081	.000
	Zscore: Teacher pre-test: Rating of ADHD-related behaviours	.605	.020	.796	29.972	.000
	Intervention	-.033	.056	-.022	-.595	.552
	Boy	.223	.056	.149	3.959	.000
	Intvn_Boy	-.205	.078	-.121	-2.635	.009

a. Dependent Variable: Teacher post-test Rating of ADHD-related behaviours

Output 4.9

As can be seen, there is evidence that the programme has had the effect of reducing problem behaviours amongst the children. The adjusted mean scores in this instance can be read off from the first model as 0.764 for the control group and 0.629 for the intervention group. Thus, and as the coefficient for intervention tells us, those in the intervention group have a mean score that is −0.135 lower on average that those in the control group and this is statistically significant as we can also see (p = 0.001). Following the

Table 4.4 The effects of Doodle Den on children's behavioural problems*

Outcome	Intervention Group Mean (sd)	n	Control Group Mean (sd)	n	Effect Size, Hedge's g (95% CI)**
Behavioural Problems	0.63 (0.66)	253	0.76 (0.82)	235	−.18 [−.36, −0.00]

*Adjusted post-test mean scores reported, controlling for differences between groups at pre-test

**With bias correction factor applied

same procedures as last time, we can calculate the associated standard deviations and sample sizes and also the effect size to get the findings as summarised in Table 4.4. As can be seen, the programme has an estimated effect of d = −.18 in reducing children's problem behaviour.

Interestingly, and in relation to the second model representing our subgroup analysis for gender, it can be seen that the coefficient associated with the interaction term between gender and group membership is also statistically significant (p = 0.009), indicating that there is also evidence that the programme is having a differential effect for boys and girls. Again following the same procedures as outlined earlier, we can write out the model as an equation and then use this to calculate the adjusted post-test mean scores for each group as follows:

Main Model

predicted post-test score = .649 + .605*(pre-test score) − .033*(intervention) + .223*(boy) − .205*(intervention*boy)

Boys in Intervention Group ('boy' = '1', Intervention = '1'):

predicted post-test score = .649 + .605*(0) − .033*(1) + .223*(1) − .205*(1)

= .649 + 0 − .033 + .223 − .205 = **.634**

Boys in Control Group ('boy' = '1', Intervention = '0'):

predicted post-test score = .649 + .605*(0) − .033*(0) + .223*(1) − .205*(0)

= .649 + 0 − 0 + .223 − 0 = **.872**

Girls in Intervention Group ('boy' = '0', Intervention = '1'):

predicted post-test score = .649 + .605*(0) − .033*(1) + .223*(0) − .205*(0)

= .649 + 0 − .033 + 0 − 0 = **.616**

Girls in Control Group ('boy' = '0', Intervention = '0'):

predicted post-test score = .649 + .605*(0) − .033*(0) + .223*(0) − .205*(0)

= .649 + 0 − 0 + 0 − 0 = **.649**

Having derived the adjusted mean scores, we can then calculate their associated standard deviations and sample sizes using the methods described earlier that begin with creating and applying a filter variable, splitting the file by *Boy* and *Intervention* and then generating descriptive statistics for the four groups above. The Effect Size Calculator can then be used, finally, to calculate the effect sizes for boys and girls and their associated 95% confidence intervals. The results are all summarised in Table 4.5. As can be seen, there is very little effect for girls, and this is non-significant going by the confidence interval. In contrast, there is a notable positive effect for boys (d = −.30). Moreover, with interaction effects such as this, it is sometimes useful to illustrate this with a simple clustered bar chart. This can often highlight very clearly the nature of the differential effects across groups as shown, in this case, by Figure 4.6.

Table 4.5 Findings of the effects of Doodle Den on children's problem behaviour, by gender*

Outcome	Intervention Group Mean (sd)	n	Control Group Mean (sd)	n	Effect Size, Cohen's d (95% CI)**
Problem Behaviour					
Boys	.63 (.72)	129	.87 (.86)	119	−.30 [−.55, −.05]
Girls	.62 (.55)	119	.65 (.72)	111	−.05 [−.31, .21]

*Adjusted post-test mean scores reported, controlling for differences between groups at pre-test

**With bias correction factor applied

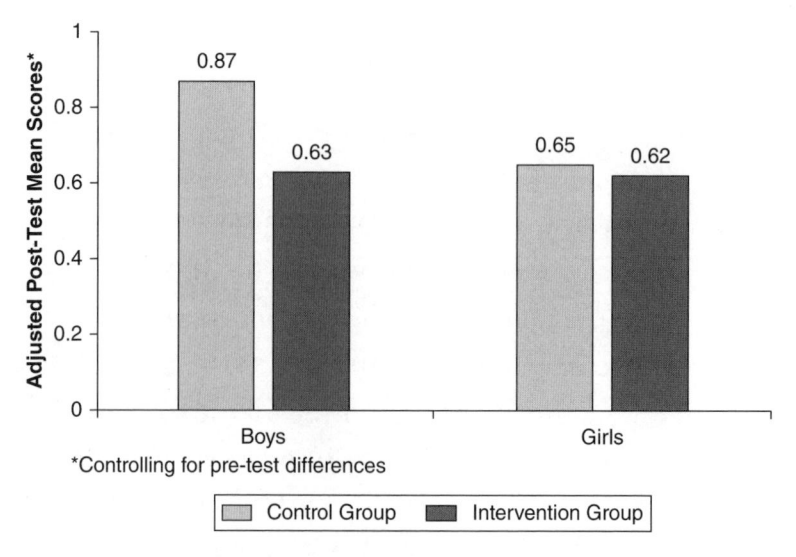

Figure 4.6 The effects of Doodle Den on children's behaviour problems, by gender

In all of our examples of sub-group analysis so far, we have focused on gender differences that involve the use of a simple dummy variable. However, it is also quite possible to do a sub-group analysis in relation to scale variables as well. As a final example we will stay with this dataset but revert back to the literacy outcome variable used earlier – *CPost-Literacy ability*. In the dataset there is a variable *CPre_age_mths* that records the age of the child in months. It is broadly normally distributed with a mean of 67.6 (sd = 4.4). It could be hypothesised that a programme like this may be more effective for younger children compared to older children. To test whether this is the case we can simply follow the same process as above in terms of creating an intervention variable, in this case based on *Intervention*CPre_age_mths*, and then adding this along with the variable *CPre_age_mths* into the model. If we do this, we will obtain the output shown in Output 4.10. In this case, and as can be seen, the coefficient representing the interaction effect in the model is not statistically significant (p = 0.844), indicating that there is no evidence to suggest that Doodle Den is having differential effects for children of different ages. However, if we did find evidence of such an effect then we will need to find a way of clearly reporting and illustrating this and we will show how this can be done in the next chapter.

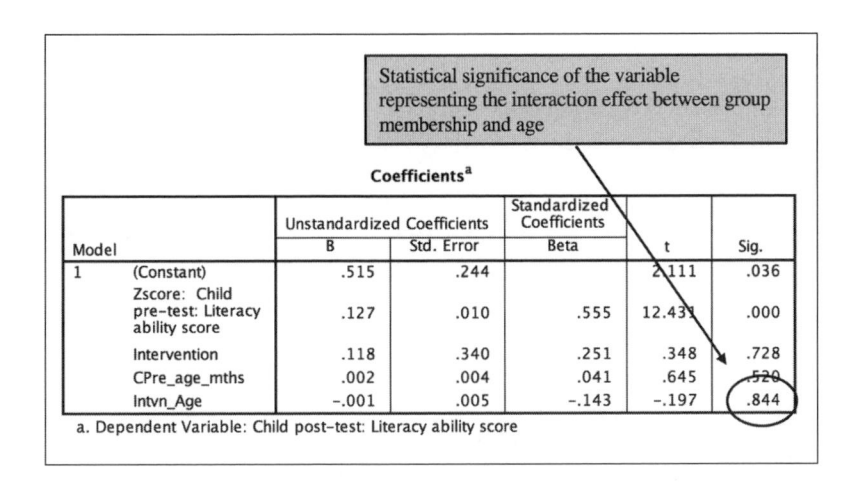

Coefficients[a]

Model		Unstandardized Coefficients B	Std. Error	Standardized Coefficients Beta	t	Sig.
1	(Constant)	.515	.244		2.111	.036
	Zscore: Child pre–test: Literacy ability score	.127	.010	.555	12.431	.000
	Intervention	.118	.340	.251	.348	.728
	CPre_age_mths	.002	.004	.041	.645	.520
	Intvn_Age	-.001	.005	-.143	-.197	.844

a. Dependent Variable: Child post–test: Literacy ability score

Statistical significance of the variable representing the interaction effect between group membership and age

Output 4.10

Conclusions

In this chapter we have covered all of the essential steps involved in the analysis of data from an RCT. It should be clear by now why we initially spent so much time focusing on the theory and interpretation of linear regression models. Whilst any particular trial may involve an examination of the effect of a programme or intervention on a number of outcomes, the analysis of the main effects and of any sub-group differences we may be interested in will always be the same. Of course, things can get a little more complicated in terms of the types of outcome variable we are dealing with and also where we need to account in the analysis for the clustered nature of our data. However, and as will be seen in the following chapter, whatever the situation, the basic approach to the analysis of our trial data remains the same and simply involves extending the approach to statistical modelling described above.

Further Reading

Linear Regression

- *Statistical Modelling for Social Researchers*, by R. Tarling (Routledge, 2009, Ch. 4).
- *Understanding Social Statistics*, by J. Fielding and N. Gilbert (Sage, 2006, Ch. 12).
- *Discovering Statistics Using SPSS for Windows*, by Andy Field (Sage, 2009, Ch. 7).

Websites

For all datasets used in this chapter and to access the Effect Size Calculator, please visit the book's companion website at: https://study.sagepub.com/connelly.

5

Dealing with the Analysis of More Complex RCT Designs

Introduction

If we are dealing with a simple RCT design, where participants have been randomised individually to the control and intervention groups and where we have outcomes measured as scale variables, then we have already covered all of the essential aspects to how we analyse the trial data in the last chapter. However, things are not always this simple. On the one hand, we may well have some outcomes that are binary in nature rather than scale. An example of this would be for interventions aimed at encouraging students to continue on into higher education. The outcome measure here could just be whether they eventually enrolled on a degree programme at a higher education institute (coded '1') or not (coded '0').

On the other hand, we may have trials where participants cannot be randomly allocated on an individual basis to an intervention or control group. As noted in Chapter 3, this will often be the case for educational programmes, for example, that are delivered on a whole-class or even whole-school basis. For practical reasons, it is often just not possible to disrupt the organisation of schools to re-arrange students on the basis of random selection. In such circumstances, we tend to recruit a number of schools and then randomly allocate the schools, as a whole, to the intervention or control groups rather than the individual students. Indeed this approach – called a *cluster* randomised controlled trial – is by far the most common in education precisely because most interventions and programmes are delivered on this basis.

In both circumstances, whether we are dealing with binary outcomes and/or with a cluster RCT, the use of linear regression in the way covered in the previous chapter would be inappropriate for reasons we will explain shortly. However, the good news is that this does not mean that we have to learn entirely new approaches to analysing these different types of data. Rather, we simply need to extend the basic approach to linear regression covered in the last chapter to situations where our dependent variable is binary and/or where our data are naturally clustered. This chapter will work through how we do this in both cases. We will then conclude with a few general points that should be borne in mind when undertaking the analysis of trial data.

Analysing Trial Data with Binary Outcomes

Before we focus directly on the analysis of data from a trial that has binary outcomes, we will take a quick step back to explain the overall approach adopted to analysing such data using a technique known as binary logistic regression. Once we have run through the basic principles of this method, we will then demonstrate how it is applied to the analysis of a trial involving a binary outcome. The example we will use here is from a small trial we conducted that sought to assess the effectiveness of a book-gifting programme delivered through health visitors during their standard visits to parents with a two-year-old child (see O'Hare and Connolly, 2014). The programme, Bookstart+, has been developed by Booktrust and involves the health visitor giving a pack of books and associated reading materials provided in a bag to the parent during their visit. These books are intended to be used to read to the young child, with the aim of beginning to develop paired reading habits between the parent and child and, ultimately, to begin to inspire a love of books in the children and their families. Alongside presenting the pack to the parents, the health visitors during their visit also talk through the pack with the parents to encourage them to share the books, stories and rhymes with their two-year-old child.

More details on the programme and on the findings of the trial are reported elsewhere (O'Hare and Connolly, 2014). It involved 462 families in total who were individually randomly allocated to either the intervention or control group. The trial itself focused on three outcomes, all measured through a parental questionnaire: the parents' own attitudes to reading; the parents' attitudes to sharing and reading books with their child; and the family's use of the local library. This latter measure reflected an aim of the programme to encourage more use of local libraries and where possible local libraries agreed to host local events for parents and young children.

In the trial, we used a number of items to develop a scale measure for each of these three outcomes. However, and for the purposes of illustration, we will take just one item related to the final outcome on library use based on the answer to the question 'Have you, for yourself or on behalf of a child, borrowed a book or other material from a local library in the last three months?' The answer to this question was coded '1' for yes and '0' for no. We will now use this variable to explain binary logistic regression and illustrate its application to the analysis of trial data using binary outcomes.

Binary Logistic Regression

Binary logistic regression is one of a family of statistical models called *generalised linear models* that have sought to develop ways of generalising from the ordinary linear regression model we covered in the last chapter to deal with dependent variables that are not scale or continuous in nature. Each of these models involves transforming the dependent variable in some way prior to the analysis so that we can then undertake a linear regression. On the positive side, SPSS does all the work in transforming the dependent variable for us, so we do not need to worry about this. Moreover, we then build our statistical model by adding in dependent and independent variables in the same way as we have done before. However, and the slight downside to this, is that because the dependent variable has been transformed then we cannot interpret the coefficients in the model so directly as we did with ordinary linear regression. Rather, and as we will now see, there are a couple of additional steps involved in the interpretation of the statistical models we produce.

To understand all of this, and the way that dependent variables are transformed for binary logistic regression, let us take the variable for library use introduced above. It can be found in the dataset called **booktrust.sav** on this book's companion website. We will begin by just focusing on the extent of library use at pre-test, as measured by the variable *librarypre*. Using **Analyze → Descriptive Statistics → Frequencies ...** we can select the variable and place it in the 'Variable(s):' window and click 'OK'. This gives us the summary data shown in Output 5.1. We can see that we have data for 340 parents in total, and of these 114 stated that they had visited a library within the last three months (33.5%).

Now, rather than just reporting the percentage of parents using their local library over this period, we can transform this statistic to report the probability that a parent from our sample will have visited the library in this period. The probability is given by the number of parents who visited the library divided by the total number of parents. In this case we therefore have 114/340 = 0.35. Probabilities will always have a value between 0 and 1; with 0 indicating that there is no chance at all that the event will happen and 1 indicating that it will definitely happen. We can also calculate the probability of a parent not visiting the library in the same way, this time by dividing the number of parents who did not visit the library by the total number of parents to give 226/340 = 0.65. Here we can see a basic rule of probability when we are dealing with just two outcomes: that if the probability of one outcome occurring is p, then the probability of the other outcome occurring is simply $1 - p$. Thus, and in this case, the probability of visiting the library is 0.35 and so the probability of not visiting the library is $1 - 0.35 = 0.65$.

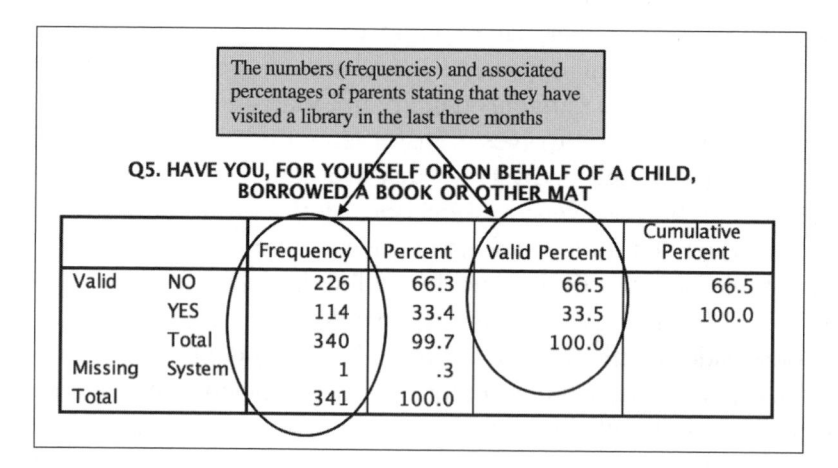

The numbers (frequencies) and associated percentages of parents stating that they have visited a library in the last three months

Q5. HAVE YOU, FOR YOURSELF OR ON BEHALF OF A CHILD, BORROWED A BOOK OR OTHER MAT

		Frequency	Percent	Valid Percent	Cumulative Percent
Valid	NO	226	66.3	66.5	66.5
	YES	114	33.4	33.5	100.0
	Total	340	99.7	100.0	
Missing	System	1	.3		
Total		341	100.0		

Output 5.1

So far we have calculated the probability of a parent using their local library (0.35) but we can transform this statistic further by presenting it in the form of odds. Odds are calculated by the following formula:

$$\text{odds} = p / (1 - p)$$

In our present example, the odds of a parent visiting their local library are then calculated by dividing the probability that they will visit their library by the probability that they will not. In this case the odds are therefore $0.35/0.65 = 0.538$ or not far off 0.5 or 1/2. In classic odds language we would thus state that these reflect 'odds of 1 to 2 in favour of visiting the library'. In other words, these odds suggest that for every person likely to visit the library there are roughly two others who will not (i.e. the odds of '1 to 2'). The use of odds is at the heart of binary logistic regression.

However, rather than binary logistic regression working with the dependent variable expressed as odds, it transforms these odds by taking their natural logarithm so that the transformed dependent variable we are dealing with is actually the log of the odds (or 'log-odds'). In this case it would be log(0.538) = −0.620.

By this point you may well be struggling to understand this or at least to see its relevance. However, please do bear with us as you will soon see how it all begins to fit together. The key point to understand about binary logistic regression models is that they are used to predict the log-odds of particular individuals achieving a certain outcome. This will become much clearer if we run through an example using our dataset and then show how we interpret the findings. Hence let us use binary logistic regression to see if there is a difference between parents in relation to their chances of visiting a library depending on whether their child is a boy or a girl. In more technical terms, what we will be doing is using the regression model to predict the log-odds of a parent with a girl visiting the library and the log-odds of a parent with a boy doing the same. Although some of this will be new to you, you will also be reassured to see that many aspects of our approach are similar to how we dealt with ordinary linear regression models in the last chapter.

To run a simple binary logistic regression, select **Analyze → Regression → Binary Logistic ...** and then place the variable *library-pre* into the 'Dependent:' window and the one independent variable we are interested in this time, *boy*, into the 'Covariates:' window. Click 'OK' and you will find the table shown in Output 5.2 at the end of the output that SPSS produces.

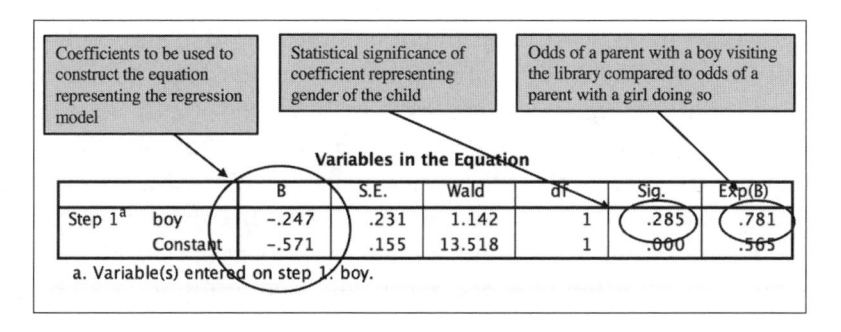

Variables in the Equation

		B	S.E.	Wald	df	Sig.	Exp(B)
Step 1[a]	boy	−.247	.231	1.142	1	.285	.781
	Constant	−.571	.155	13.518	1	.000	.565

a. Variable(s) entered on step 1: boy.

- Coefficients to be used to construct the equation representing the regression model
- Statistical significance of coefficient representing gender of the child
- Odds of a parent with a boy visiting the library compared to odds of a parent with a girl doing so

Output 5.2

In one way, the model is similar to what we covered in the last chapter with ordinary linear regression. Indeed we can begin our interpretation exactly as we would do if it were linear regression, by using the coefficients to write the model out as an equation. However, and as we do, remember that the dependent variable is now the log-odds of visiting a library:

predicted log-odds of visiting library = −0.571 − 0.247*(boy)

We can also use the statistical significance of each term in the model to determine whether there is evidence that each variable is associated with the dependent variable. In this case, and in relation to the variable *boy*, we can see that it is not statistically significant (p = 0.285) and so we can conclude already from this model that there is no evidence to suggest that a parent's decision to visit and use their local library is associated with whether their child is a boy or girl. As we will see shortly, the extension of models like this, by adding further independent variables and interaction terms, is also done in the same way as we would do for ordinary linear regression.

However, and beyond this, there are two important differences in how we interpret this model compared to those produced through ordinary linear regression. First, we can see in Output 5.2 a new column headed 'Exp(B)'. This column represents the values created when taking the exponential of each coefficient in the model (shown in the second column headed 'B'). It is important to remember that we are dealing with a dependent variable that represents the log-odds of a parent visiting a local library. Mathematically, taking the exponential of a number does the exact opposite of taking its logarithm. As such, once we have taken the exponential of the coefficient for *boy*, we actually have a useful statistic that indicates the odds-ratio of parents with boys visiting a library compared to girls. Thus, and for example, if Exp(B) for the variable *boy* had been '2.000' then this would have been interpreted as indicating that the odds of parents with boys visiting a local library were twice as high as the odds of parents with girls doing the same. As it is, however, it can be seen from Output 5.2 that Exp(B) is 0.781. As this figure is less than one then it indicates that the balance is the other way: that the odds of a parent with a boy visiting their local library are less than (i.e. 0.781 times less than) that of the odds of a parent with a girl visiting their local library. However, we already know that this figure is not statistically significant and so we should not read too much into this finding.

Beyond this, the other main difference in the interpretation of the findings from binary logistic regression compared to ordinary linear regression is in relation to how we make sense of the coefficients. As we are dealing with a transformed dependent variable then we cannot directly interpret the coefficients in the model. All we can draw from the actual coefficients in the model is that if the coefficient is positive then it represents a positive effect or difference for that independent variable and if it is negative then it represents a negative effect. Beyond this, the larger the figure, the larger the effect. Thus, in this case, we can see that the coefficient for boys is '−0.247' and so this indicates that the odds of parents visiting their local library will be lower or reduced if the child is a boy.

Rather than interpreting the coefficients directly, our main approach is to use the model to estimate the log-odds for particular groups and then to transfer these back into a more easily understandable measure (in this case the predicted probability of each group of parents visiting their local library). This takes a couple of steps but they are not difficult if you follow them carefully. To illustrate this let us take the current example and work out the log-odds for parents with boys and parents with girls respectively:

$$\text{predicted log-odds of visiting library} = -0.571 - 0.247*(boy)$$

Parents with boys (boy = '1'):

$$\text{predicted log-odds of visiting library} = -0.571 - 0.247*(1)$$
$$= -0.571 - 0.247 = -\mathbf{0.818}$$

Parents with girls (boy = '0'):

$$\text{predicted log-odds of visiting library} = -0.571 - 0.247*(0)$$
$$= -0.571 - 0 = -\mathbf{0.571}$$

These predicted log-odds can be transformed by taking the exponential of each to give us the odds of each group of parents. We can then re-arrange the formula for calculating odds from probabilities to calculate the probabilities from the odds. Doing all this in one step, we can use the following formula:

$$\text{predicted probability} = \frac{\exp(\text{log-odds})}{1 + \exp(\text{log-odds})}$$

Thus, for parents with boys and girls we get:

$$\text{predicted probability (boys)} = \frac{\exp(-0.818)}{1 + \exp(-0.818)} = \frac{0.441}{(1 + 0.441)} = \mathbf{0.306}$$

$$\text{predicted probability (girls)} = \frac{\exp(-0.571)}{1 + \exp(-0.571)} = \frac{0.565}{(1 + 0.565)} = \mathbf{0.361}$$

And so, finally, we can deduce from our statistical model that the probability of parents with girls visiting their local library over the last three months is a little higher (0.361) compared to parents with boys (0.306), however this difference is not statistically significant (p = 0.285). These probabilities can easily be converted into predicted percentages by just multiplying them by 100 so that we get 36.1% for parents with girls and 30.6% for those with boys. Of course, and with just one independent variable, this is just a very elaborate way of calculating what we could have done with a simple frequency table using **Analyze → Descriptive Statistics → Crosstabs …** . By placing the variable *librarypre* into the 'Row(s):' field, and boy into the 'Column(s):' field, and selecting the Column Percentages option using the 'Cells …' button, we get the output shown in Output 5.3. As can be seen, the percentages match those we estimated with our binary logistic regression model. However, the use of binary logistic regression models suddenly becomes very useful when we are considering more than one independent variable, as we shall now see.

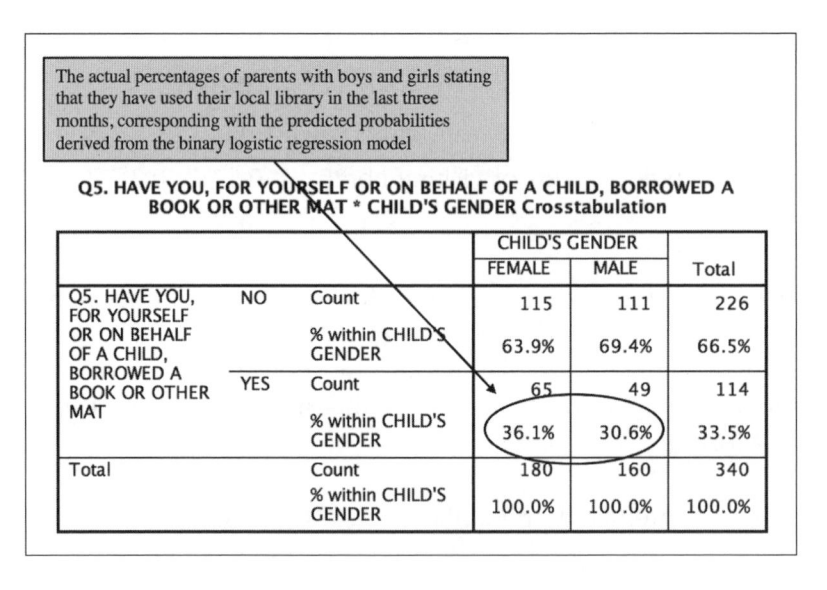

The actual percentages of parents with boys and girls stating that they have used their local library in the last three months, corresponding with the predicted probabilities derived from the binary logistic regression model

Q5. HAVE YOU, FOR YOURSELF OR ON BEHALF OF A CHILD, BORROWED A BOOK OR OTHER MAT * CHILD'S GENDER Crosstabulation

			CHILD'S GENDER FEMALE	CHILD'S GENDER MALE	Total
Q5. HAVE YOU, FOR YOURSELF OR ON BEHALF OF A CHILD, BORROWED A BOOK OR OTHER MAT	NO	Count	115	111	226
		% within CHILD'S GENDER	63.9%	69.4%	66.5%
	YES	Count	65	49	114
		% within CHILD'S GENDER	36.1%	30.6%	33.5%
Total		Count	180	160	340
		% within CHILD'S GENDER	100.0%	100.0%	100.0%

Output 5.3

Applying Binary Logistic Regression to Trial Data

How we specify the binary logistic regression model for the analysis of trial data is exactly the same as how we did it for ordinary linear regression in the previous chapter. As such, we set the post-test variable as the dependent variable and we add in two independent variables: one representing the pre-test variable and a dummy variable representing group membership. However, and remember from the last chapter, that rather than adding in the actual pre-test variable, we add in its standardised score instead for ease of interpretation of the resultant model. Even where we have binary pre-test variables, as in this case, we can still calculate and use their standardised scores. For our present trial data, therefore, once you have created the variable representing the standardised score at pre-test, select **Analyze → Regression → Binary Logistic ...** and place the variable *librarypost* into the 'Dependent:' field, *Zlibrarypre* and *intervention* into the 'Covariates:' field, and then click 'OK'. The key output of interest to us is reproduced in Output 5.4.

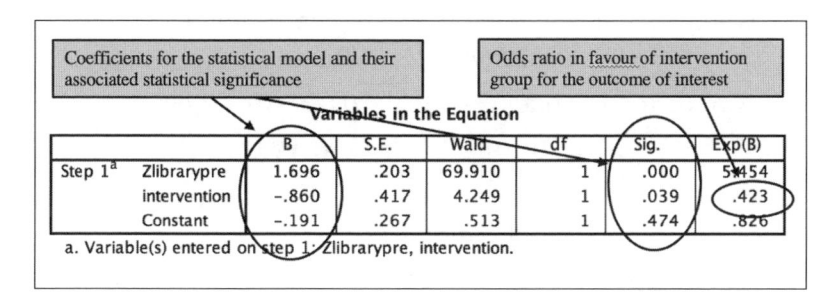

Coefficients for the statistical model and their associated statistical significance

Odds ratio in favour of intervention group for the outcome of interest

Variables in the Equation

		B	S.E.	Wald	df	Sig.	Exp(B)
Step 1[a]	Zlibrarypre	1.696	.203	69.910	1	.000	5.454
	intervention	-.860	.417	4.249	1	.039	.423
	Constant	-.191	.267	.513	1	.474	.826

a. Variable(s) entered on step 1: Zlibrarypre, intervention.

Output 5.4

Just as with ordinary linear regression, the first thing we can see is that the difference at post-test in relation to parents visiting their local library between intervention and control groups is statistically significant (p = 0.039). We can therefore already conclude that there is evidence that the Bookstart+ programme is having an effect in relation to this outcome. However, and from visual inspection of the output, we can also see that the coefficient for *intervention* is negative, suggesting that being in the intervention group reduces the likelihood of parents using their local library. This is confirmed by the Exp(B) for *intervention* that has a value of 0.423. As explained earlier, this is the odds ratio comparing the odds of parents visiting their local library if they are in the intervention group compared to the control group. In this case, for parents who took part in Bookstart+, their odds of using the local library have reduced by more than a half compared to the control group (i.e. their odds at post-test are only 0.423 times that of the control group parents). We should remember that because we also have *Zlibrarypre* entered into the model, these differences are those calculated once we have controlled for any pre-test differences in library usage between the intervention and control groups.

Our next step in the analysis, just as we would do with ordinary linear regression, is to use the model to calculate the adjusted post-test averages for both groups. However, and in this case, we are working with percentages rather than mean scores. Also, and as we have already seen, we are initially dealing with the predicted log-odds of parents in both groups using their local libraries at post-test so we just need to do a little extra work to convert these into more directly meaningful results for the reader. We thus begin as usual by constructing our equation representing the model and then substituting in the values for the variable *intervention* to derive the predicted log-odds for both groups at post-test:

$$\text{predicted log-odds} = -0.191 - 0.860*(intervention) + 1.696*(Zlibrarypre)$$

Average parents in control group (*intervention* = '0' and *Zlibrarypre* = '0'):

$$\text{predicted log-odds} = -0.191 - 0.860*(0) + 1.696*(0)$$
$$= -0.191 + 0 + 0 = -\mathbf{0.191}$$

Average parents in intervention group (*intervention* = '1' and *Zlibrarypre* = '0'):

$$\text{predicted log-odds} = -0.191 - 0.860*(1) + 1.696*(0)$$
$$= -0.191 - 0.860 + 0 = -\mathbf{1.051}$$

And with these log-odds, we can derived the predicted post-test probabilities of parents using their local library, once we have controlled for pre-test differences:

$$\text{predicted probability (control)} = \frac{\exp(-0.191)}{1 + \exp(-0.191)} = \mathbf{0.452}$$

$$\text{predicted probability (intervention)} = \frac{\exp(-1.051)}{1 + \exp(-1.051)} = \mathbf{0.259}$$

We therefore have our first key findings: that the adjusted post-test percentages of parents who state they have used their local libraries in the last three months are 45.2% for the control group and just 25.9% for the intervention group. The only other information we need to be able to report these findings fully are the sample sizes for both groups and then a measure of the effect size of this difference. For the sample sizes, and as before, we should only report the numbers of participants who had both pre-test and post-test data and thus contributed to this statistical model. To do this, we can just use the 'Save …' button when creating our binary logistic

Analysis of more complex RCT designs 117

regression model and select 'Unstandardised Residuals'. This creates a new variable called *RES_1* that will only have a value if we have data for all of the dependent and independent variables in the model. For clarity, we can rename this variable *filter*. As before, we can then just turn this variable into one that is coded '1' if the participant has all the data and '0' if there are some missing data and thus they were not included in the model. We do this using **Transform → Recode into Same Variables ...** and then select *filter* and place it in the 'Variables:' field before clicking on the 'Old and New Values' button. As we did in the last chapter, we then add in the two conditions into the 'Old —> New:' window:

SYSMIS —> 0

ELSE —> 1

Once we click 'Continue' and then 'OK' in the main window, we will have our *filter* variable ready for analysis. We then use **Data → Select Cases ...** to choose the option 'If condition is satisfied', click on the 'If' button and then add in the expression 'filter = 1' in the top window, and then click 'Continue' and then 'OK' in the main window. We can now calculate our sample sizes by just using **Analyze → Descriptive Statistics → Frequencies ...** and select intervention and place it in the 'Variable(s):' field before clicking 'OK'. As shown in Output 5.5, the actual size of our sample once we have omitted those with missing data is 107 for the control group and 95 for the intervention group.

INTERVENTION OR CONTROL

Final sample sizes to report, once 'select cases' is used to remove participants with missing data

		Frequency	Percent	Valid Percent	Cumulative Percent
Valid	CONTROL	107	53.0	53.0	53.0
	INTERVENTION	95	47.0	47.0	100.0
	Total	202	100.0	100.0	

Output 5.5

Finally, to obtain the effect size and its associated 95% confidence interval we return to the Effect Size Calculator on our companion website. This time, however, as we are working with different data we would tend to use a different measure of effect size. For data like these the most common effect size measure is the odds-ratio that we have already been introduced to. Using the calculator, just input the proportion for the intervention group

118 Using randomised controlled trials in education

and its sample size (0.259 and 95 respectively) and the same for the control group (0.452 and 107 respectively) and you will get the following odds-ratio and its 95% confidence interval: 0.424 [0.233, 0.769]. We now have all the information we need from the analysis of the trial to report the findings as shown in Table 5.1. The evidence would suggest, therefore, that the book-gifting programme has actually had the effect of reducing parents' use of their local library in the short term. This finding is discussed in more detail and the implications considered in the main report of the trial (see O'Hare and Connolly, 2014).

Table 5.1 Findings of the effects of Bookstart+ on families' use of their local library*

Outcome	Intervention Group %	Intervention Group n	Control Group %	Control Group n	Effect Size, Odds Ratio (95% CI)
Proportion of Parents Reporting that they Used their Local Library within the Last 3 Months	25.9	95	45.2	107	+.424 [−.233, .769]

*Adjusted post-test percentages, controlling for differences between groups at pre-test

Just as with ordinary linear regression in the last chapter, we can also extend this basic model to explore sub-group effects. In this case we will see whether there is any evidence to suggest that the programme has had differential effects on parents depending on whether they have boys or girls. To do this, we need to create an interaction effect using **Transform → Compute Variable ...** calculated by multiplying the two variables *intervention* and *boy*. In the window that opens up, we can type in the name of the new variable we wish to create (we can call it 'intvn_boy') in the 'Target Variable:' field and the numeric expression 'intervention*boy' in the 'Numeric Expression:' field and then click 'OK'. After this we can use **Analyze → Regression → Binary Logistic ...** to create our statistical model. As before, place the variable *librarypost* into the 'Dependent:' field and then the variables *Zlibrarypre*, *intervention*, *boy* and *intvn_boy* into the 'Covariates:' field and then click 'OK'. The resultant model is shown in Output 5.6.

It can be seen that the coefficient for the interaction term intervention*boy is statistically significant (p = .026) so there is evidence to suggest that the programme does have a differential effect on parents depending on whether they have boys or girls. When we have models including interaction terms it is difficult to interpret the model just by looking at the coefficients, notwithstanding the fact that these are also all related to the log-odds transformed dependent variable. As such, the best method for

Analysis of more complex RCT designs

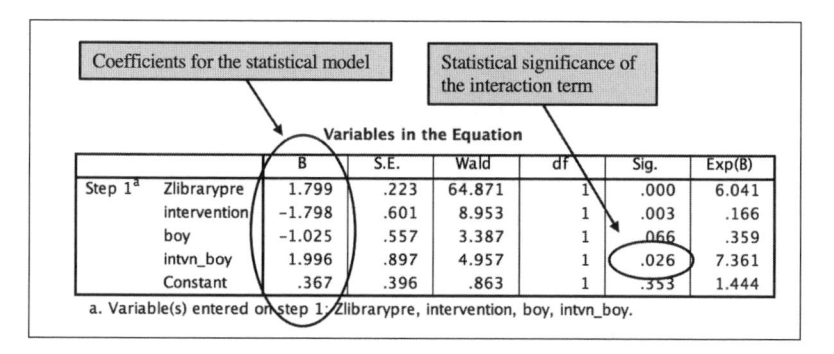

Variables in the Equation

		B	S.E.	Wald	df	Sig.	Exp(B)
Step 1[a]	Zlibrarypre	1.799	.223	64.871	1	.000	6.041
	intervention	-1.798	.601	8.953	1	.003	.166
	boy	-1.025	.557	3.387	1	.066	.359
	intvn_boy	1.996	.897	4.957	1	.026	7.361
	Constant	.367	.396	.863	1	.353	1.444

a. Variable(s) entered on step 1: Zlibrarypre, intervention, boy, intvn_boy.

Coefficients for the statistical model

Statistical significance of the interaction term

Output 5.6

interpreting the model is to write it out as a formula and then use this to calculate the predicted post-test percentages for the four groups. The model itself is:

$$\text{Predicted post-test log-odds} = 0.367 + 1.799*(Zlibrarypre) - 1.798*(intervention) - 1.025*(boy) + 1.996*(intvn\_boy)$$

Adding in respective values, as done previously, we get the following:

Control group boys (*Zlibrarypre* = '0'; *intervention* = '0'; *boy* = '1'; *intvn_boy* = '0')

$$\text{predicted post-test log-odds} = 0.367 + 1.799*(0) - 1.798*(0) - 1.025*(1) + 1.996*(0)$$
$$= 0.367 + 0 - 0 - 1.025 + 0 = \mathbf{-0.658}$$

Control group girls (*Zlibrarypre* = '0'; *intervention* = '0'; *boy* = '0'; *intvn_boy* = '0')

$$\text{predicted post-test log-odds} = 0.367 + 1.799*(0) - 1.798*(0) - 1.025*(0) + 1.996*(0)$$
$$= 0.367 + 0 - 0 - 0 + 0 = \mathbf{0.367}$$

Intervention group boys (*Zlibrarypre* = '0'; *intervention* = '1'; *boy* = '1'; *intvn_boy* = '1')

$$\text{predicted post-test log-odds} = 0.367 + 1.799*(0) - 1.798*(1) - 1.025*(1) + 1.996*(1)$$
$$= 0.367 + 0 - 1.798 - 1.025 + 1.996 = \mathbf{-0.460}$$

Intervention group girls (*Zlibrarypre* = '0'; *intervention* = '1'; *boy* = '0'; *intvn_boy* = '0')

$$\text{predicted post-test log-odds} = 0.367 + 1.799*(0) - 1.798*(1)$$
$$- 1.025*(1) + 1.996*(1)$$
$$= 0.367 + 0 - 1.798 - 0 + 0 = -\mathbf{1.431}$$

As before, we can now use the formula outlined earlier to transform the predicted log-odds into predicted proportions, giving us:

Control group boys: 0.341

Control group girls: 0.591

Intervention group boys: 0.387

Intervention group girls: 0.193

Our next step is to calculate the sample sizes for each group. To do this we need to create a filter variable again by clicking on the 'Save …' button when creating our binary logistic regression model and selecting 'Unstandardised Residuals'. After running the regression model, this creates a new variable called *RES_1* that we can rename as *filter2* and that will only have a value if we have data for all of the dependent and independent variables in the model. As before, we can then use **Transform → Recode into Same Variables …** : just turn this variable into one that is coded '1' if the participant has all data and '0' if there are some missing data and thus they were not included in the model. Once done we can use **Data → Select Cases …** to select cases if 'filter2 = 1'. With this all done, we can derive our sample sizes by using **Analyze → Descriptive Statistics → Crosstabs …** and placing intervention in 'Row(s)' and boy in 'Column(s)' before clicking 'OK'. As shown in Output 5.7, the actual total size of our sample once we have omitted those with missing data is 202 and we can see the respective sizes for each of the four sub-groups.

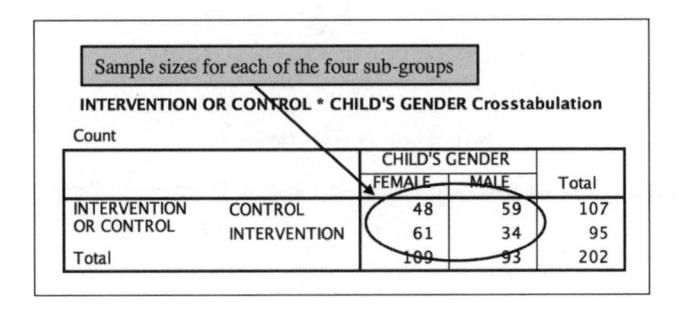

Sample sizes for each of the four sub-groups

INTERVENTION OR CONTROL * CHILD'S GENDER Crosstabulation

Count

		CHILD'S GENDER FEMALE	CHILD'S GENDER MALE	Total
INTERVENTION OR CONTROL	CONTROL	48	59	107
	INTERVENTION	61	34	95
Total		109	93	202

Output 5.7

Finally, with our respective proportions and associated sample sizes we can use the Effect Size Calculator to compute the two effect sizes and their associated 95% confidence intervals for boys and girls respectively. Pulling all this together, we can report the findings as shown in Table 5.2. It can be seen that the Bookstart+ programme appears to have slightly increased the percentage of parents with boys visiting their local library (from 34.1% in the control group to 38.7% in the intervention group). However, this needs to be treated with caution as the confidence interval for the effect size crosses the threshold at '1.000', indicating that it includes in its range values below the threshold (that would suggest the programme has reduced library usage) as well as values above the threshold (suggesting it has increased library usage). The picture for parents with girls is clearer, however, with a notable drop in library usage for parents using their local library (from 59.1% in control group to just 19.3% in intervention group) and the confidence for the associated effect size of 0.166 falls securely below the threshold of '1.000'.

Table 5.2 Findings of the effects of Bookstart+ on families' use of their local library, by gender of child*

Outcome: Proportion of Parents Reporting that they Used their Local Library within the Last 3 Months	Intervention Group %	n	Control Group %	n	Effect Size, Odds Ratio (95% CI)
Parents with Boys	38.7%	34	34.1%	59	1.220 [0.509, 2.927]
Parents with Girls	19.3%	61	59.1%	48	0.166 [0.070, 0.390]

*Adjusted post-test percentages, controlling for differences between groups at pre-test

Analysing Cluster Randomised Controlled Trials

The final main issue that we need to cover is how to analyse data generated through cluster randomised controlled trials. As we have already noted, many educational interventions and programmes take place on a whole-class or even a whole-school basis. As such, it is not always possible to randomly allocate individual students to the intervention or control groups. In these circumstances we would typically tend to recruit a number of schools to the trial and then randomly allocate these to either the intervention or control group. Once allocated, the programme is then delivered to the relevant classes in the schools in the intervention group whereas the classes in the control group schools just carry on as normal.

Some programmes are aimed at the whole school or possibly a number of year groups within a school. As such, we would have a trial where there are a number of schools allocated to the intervention and control groups and then, within this, where we have a number of classes in each of the schools participating in the trial. In other cases, a programme might be aimed at a particular year group and schools are asked to randomly pick just one class from that year group to take part in the trial. And also, just to complicate matters further, there will be some trials where a number of schools are recruited and then, rather than randomly allocating the schools to control and intervention conditions, the classes within each school are randomly allocated to either deliver the programme or intervention or to act as the control group. At the end of the chapter we will say a little more about how to handle differing scenarios like this. However, and for now, we will focus on the main approach to be used in analysing such data as this will be the same, regardless of the 'tweaks' we may need to make to this to reflect the particular set-up of schools and classes and their allocation to control and intervention groups. For the purposes of what follows, therefore, we will focus on a situation where we have a trial involving a number of schools (or preschools in this instance) and where there is just one class per preschool taking part in the trial. As such, and because we are only dealing with one class per school, we then essentially have a two-level model with children clustered within a number of classes, which is a common set-up for cluster RCTs. Should the design have included two or more classes in each school then we would have had a three-level model (i.e. children clustered within classes clustered within schools).

As before, we need to begin with a broader discussion regarding how to handle such data and, in particular, some of the key issues to note with the statistical technique we use in these cases – called multilevel modelling or hierarchical linear modelling – before then demonstrating how it is applied to the analysis of cluster RCTs.

Multilevel Modelling

It was not long ago that multilevel modelling (MLM) was regarded as a specialist statistical technique that was the preserve of only a select handful of serious statisticians. However, with advances in software it has become considerably more accessible as a method. Also, and critically, for those who have developed a good grasp of linear regression techniques as we have covered in this and the previous chapters, then they will find that it is actually just a simple step from what they have been doing already to undertaking multilevel modelling.

Analysis of more complex RCT designs   123

Multilevel modelling is a technique that represents an extension of linear regression to cases where our data are hierarchically organised. This is actually a very common scenario in education where we are typically not just dealing with a sample of children who can all be considered as separate individuals but where we tend to have children clustered together in classes that are then clustered together in schools. Of course, we need not stop there. We typically have schools clustered together within education authorities and education authorities within counties and so on.

The key point about all of this is that we can no longer treat each child as being separate and independent from one another, which is a fundamental assumption that we need to make in order to use the types of regression models we have been working with so far. Rather, there is likely to be some correlation between the characteristics of children in the same classes (whether these are education, social, attitudinal and so on) either because they tend to come from the same local neighbourhoods and/or because of their shared experiences as a class. In other words, children who share the same class will tend to be a little more similar to one another compared to if they were all completely independent of one another and all from different classes. The main consequence of this is that the variation between children, in whatever outcome we are interested in measuring, is likely to be a little less in samples where the children are clustered together compared to samples where all the children are completely independent of one another.

There will be times where ignoring the hierarchical nature of the data will result in fundamentally misleading results. For example, we might find a correlation between two variables only to see it disappear once we adopt a technique that can account for the clustering of the data. In such circumstances this could indicate that the original correlation is simply a result of the mediating effects of the clustering of subjects (within classes or neighbourhoods or whatever) and that, once we control for the effects of this clustering, there is no longer any relationship between the two variables concerned. However, and more routinely, the main consequence of ignoring clustering is that it reduces the standard errors of the estimates we produce through our analysis. The most important consequence here is that this, in turn, results in an increased likelihood of us generating findings that appear to be statistically significant when they should not be (known in statistics as committing a 'Type I error').

To understand this, consider the two scenarios in Figure 5.1. In both cases we are comparing the means of two groups of children involved in an RCT. We can see that, in both scenarios, the mean scores for both groups are the same and so the raw differences in mean scores between the two

124 Using randomised controlled trials in education

groups are also the same. However, in Scenario A the level of variation within each group is larger than that for Scenario B. As such there is much more overlap in scores for Scenario A than for Scenario B. The key point from this is that if we were to do an independent samples t-test to assess the statistical significance of the differences in mean scores between both groups, the statistical significance will be higher in Scenario B, where there is much less overlap between the samples and therefore a greater likelihood that the difference between the two groups is likely to reflect a real difference. In contrast, the statistical significance in Scenario A will be lower, and depending on the sample sizes, may not even be statistically significant. This is because there is much more overlap between the two samples and thus more of a chance that the two samples might actually be from the same population and that the difference in mean scores might just be due to random variation.

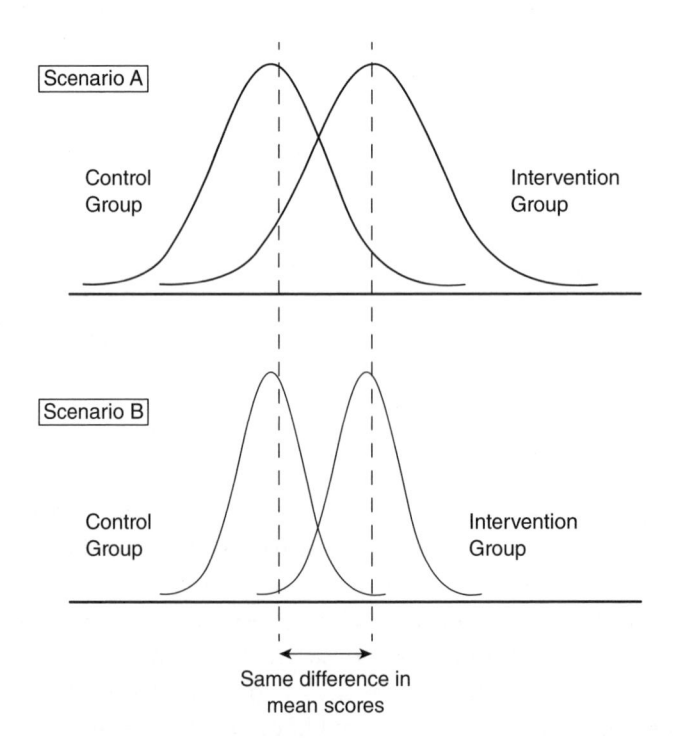

Figure 5.1 Comparing two samples with the same mean scores but differing levels of variation

When applying this to cluster RCTs, what we may often see is that the estimated mean scores between the control group and intervention group are broadly the same whether we account for the clustering or not.

Analysis of more complex RCT designs 125

However, by not accounting for the clustering of the data we will tend to be working with misleadingly reduced variations (i.e. Scenario B) that will, in turn, make it more likely that our findings will be statistically significant when they may not be. Also, and because our measure of effect size (Hedge's g) involves dividing the difference in mean scores by the pooled standard deviation for the sample as a whole, then reduced variation (and thus reduced standard deviations) will result in inflated and misleading estimates of effect size.

To illustrate all of this further, let us consider the dataset **mifc.sav**. This is taken from a cluster randomised controlled trial involving 74 preschools in Northern Ireland and the border counties of the Republic of Ireland. The preschools were randomly allocated to either a control group or intervention group and the latter delivered the *Media Initiative for Children: Respecting Difference* programme for one school year. The programme is based around short one-minute media messages broadcast on regional television that involve cartoon characters in a playground. Each message is based on a simple storyline that typically involves an example of exclusion and then the characters learning that it is better to be inclusive. The media messages are supported by a comprehensive curriculum and set of resources for use in preschools that focus on building core social and emotional skills in young children (aged three to four), raising awareness and celebrating diversity, promoting respect for differences and modelling out more inclusive behaviours for the young children. The programme is described in more detail in the full report on the trial, along with the full findings from the trial (see Connolly et al., 2010).

For the current dataset, we will focus on just two outcomes. The first is children's ability to recognise emotions in others, based upon asking them to recognise and name emotional expressions in eight scenarios presented to them. The resultant measure is a scale variable ranging from 0 to 8, with a high score indicating greater ability to recognise and label emotions. The second outcome relates to children's ability to recognise instances of potential exclusion. It involves showing them a photograph of a playground scene where one child is standing apart from others. The children are asked to describe what they can see and are then prompted for further information. The resultant variable is a binary variable coded '1' if they notice and make reference to the child on their own, and '0' otherwise. In addition, we have included a measure representing programme fidelity. This is a scale variable representing the degree to which the programme was delivered according to its manual. It has been standardised with a mean score of zero and standard deviation of one.

For the main analysis we will use the specialist software package MLwiN designed specifically by the Centre for Multilevel Modelling at the University of Bristol. The software is free to download and use by academics and students in UK universities. For those outside the UK, single licences can also be purchased, including discounted prices for students, from the Centre for Multilevel Modelling's website. For further details see www.bristol.ac.uk/cmm/. Whilst we will run through the following analyses using MLwiN, you will still be able to follow and understand the theory behind it so that you can run such an analysis with other appropriate software.

Although MLwiN includes facilities for handling and manipulating data, it is easier for most people to run the initial parts of their analysis in SPSS and then to prepare and save the dataset ready for conducting the multilevel modelling elements in MLwiN. With this in mind, we have done three things with the **mifc.sav** dataset in preparation for the main analysis. The first is to create a variable we have named *cons* that is just a constant with the value '1' for all cases and a variable named *DENOM* that is also a constant that we need for the binary logistic regression models. This is needed for MLwiN to allow us to add a constant into our models (that, as we have seen, is done automatically in SPSS). In addition, it can be seen that we have created new variables representing the standardised scores for the pre-test variables and we have also calculated and added an interaction effect for intervention*boy. Finally, we have added in two variables to represent individual children (*idchild*) and each preschool setting (*idsetting*). Before we can open the dataset in MLwiN we have to save it in one of the formats that MLwiN will recognise. On this occasion we will save it as a Stata ('.dta') file. To do this choose **File → Save As ...** from the main menu in SPSS and then from the 'Save as type:' drop-down menu choose the option 'Stata Version 8 SE (*.dta)' and then click 'Save'.

When you first open MLwiN you will see a large empty interface window with a grey background and a drop-down menu system running across the top. MLwiN is a Windows-based system and all of the windows that you open up will appear within this main interface window. Initially, choose **File → Open worksheet** and then use the folder system to find the file you have just saved and select it. If you cannot see your file, make sure you have chosen 'Stata dataset (*.dta)' from the 'Supported file types' drop-down menu to the right of where the file name will appear. Click 'OK' and you should see a new 'Names' window appear within MLwiN listing the variables in the dataset as shown in Figure 5.2.

The main window we will be using is the Equations window that can be opened up by selecting **Model → Equations** from the main menu. This opens up the 'Equations' window as also illustrated in Figure 5.2. At any

Analysis of more complex RCT designs 127

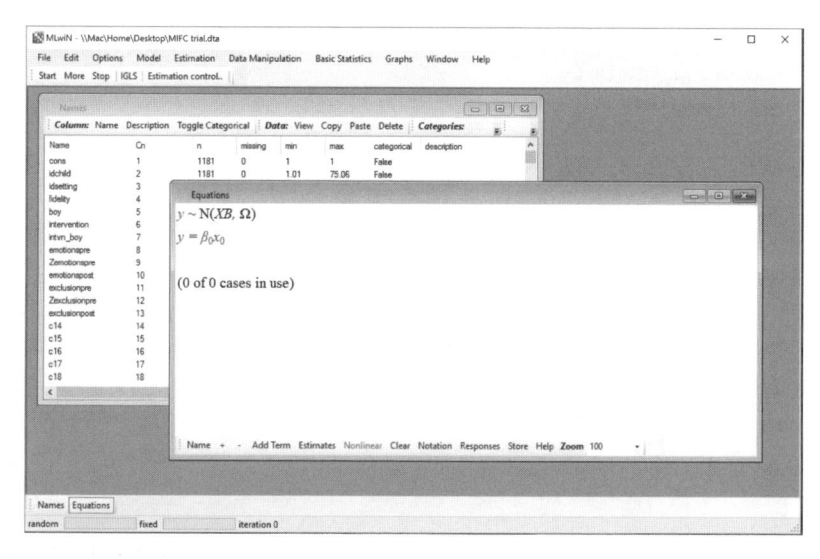

Figure 5.2 Opening and using the equations window in MLwiN

time, if things become too busy you can close windows within MLwiN that are not needed. In relation to the Equations window, it first appears in the format shown in Figure 5.2. You will see that the second line shows the beginning of a model that we need to build, just as we have been doing up until this point with ordinary linear and binary logistic regression. For this model you will also see that the dependent variable, currently depicted by 'y', is coloured red, indicating that it has yet to be defined. Also, on the right-hand side of the equation, the first term 'B_0x_0' is also red, again indicating that this needs to be specified. Above this equation line, we see that MLwiN is assuming that the dependent variable is a scale variable that is normally distributed. This is what we want for now, as we are dealing with a scale variable. However, and later on, we will see how things can be changed to indicate that our variable is binary.

To define the dependent variable, click on 'y' and a small dialogue box will appear as shown in Figure 5.3. For this dialogue box, use the first drop-down menu to select *emotionspost* and then the second drop-down menu to specify that the data have two levels. Within this, use the remaining drop-down menus to tell MLwiN that the higher level (level 2) is represented by the variable *idsetting* and the lower level (level 1) is represented by *idchild* as shown in Figure 5.3 and then click the 'done' button to finish.

Next, we need to specify what independent variables should be included in the model. To do this, click on the term 'B_0x_0' in red to open up the dialogue box shown in Figure 5.4. Initially, we will need to add in a constant

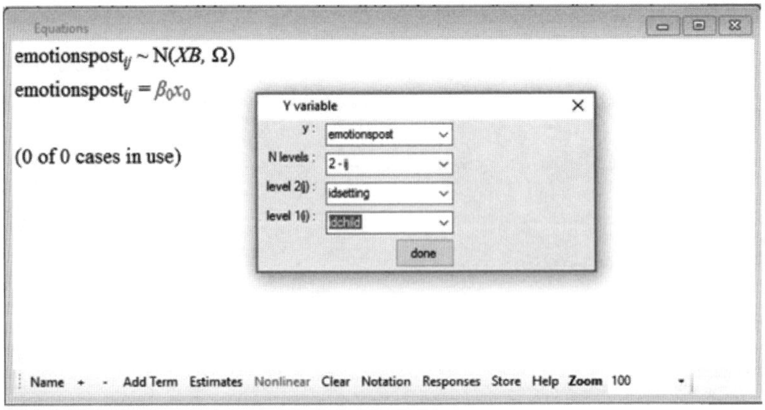

Figure 5.3 Defining a dependant variable in MLwiN

so use the drop-down menu to select the variable *cons*. We will also need to specify that this is a two-level model and so you should also select the options 'j(idsetting)' and 'i(idchild)' as shown in Figure 5.4 and then click the 'Done' button. Finally, and to display the model in the format we want, click twice on the name 'Estimates' at the bottom of this window until the model is displayed in the format shown in Output 5.8. Initially, however, the model will not have any estimated values in it. Rather, the numbers will be coloured blue with values '000(000)'. This indicates that the model has yet to be run and estimated. To do this, click on the option 'Start' that you will find just below the main menu running across the top of the main MLwiN interface window. Once you have done this, you should have the estimated model shown in Output 5.8. The numbers should also be coloured green indicating that the model has been estimated successfully.

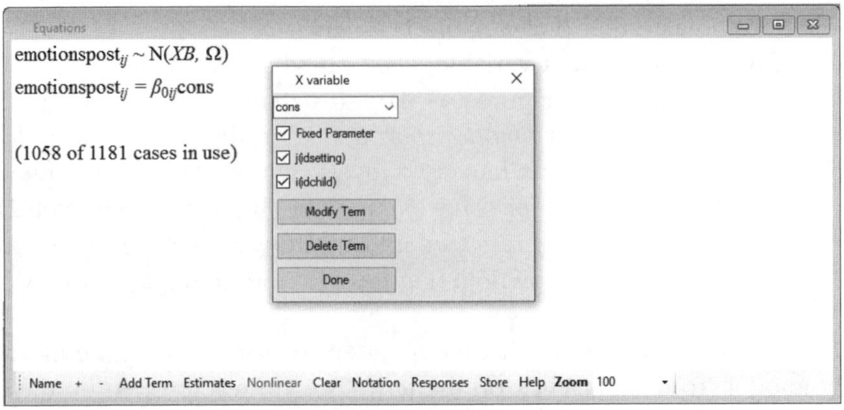

Figure 5.4 How to specify independent variables in MLwiN

Analysis of more complex RCT designs 129

```
Equations
emotionspost_ij ~ N(XB, Ω)
emotionspost_ij = β_0ij cons
β_0ij = 6.918(0.059) + u_0j + e_0ij

[u_0j] ~ N(0, Ω_u) : Ω_u = [0.122(0.040)]

[e_0ij] ~ N(0, Ω_e) : Ω_e = [1.540(0.069)]

-2*loglikelihood(IGLS Deviance) = 3511.071(1058 of 1181 cases in use)

Name + - Add Term Estimates Nonlinear Clear Notation Responses Store Help Zoom 100
```

Output 5.8

The format shown in Output 5.8 is the main format that is used by MLwiN and one that we will simply adapt and extend as we enter additional independent variables shortly for our main analyses of trial data. For now, though, there are five points to note about this output. The first is that the figure '6.918' is the estimated figure for the constant. When you have a model like this with just a constant and no other independent variables (sometimes called the 'null model') then this constant simply represents the mean score for the dependent variable *emotionspost*. If you were to calculate the mean of this variable in SPSS you will notice that it is slightly different from this. This is because the figure shown in Output 5.8 has been adjusted to take into account the clustered nature of the data.

Second, the other figure in parentheses besides this figure of 6.918 – '(0.059)' – represents the standard error for this estimate of the coefficient for the constant. As a general rule of thumb, and particularly useful when first eyeballing findings like this, is that you can determine whether a coefficient is statistically significant if its absolute value is more than twice that of its standard error. In this case, the standard error is 0.059 and thus 2 × 0.059 = 0.118. We can see in this case that the estimate value for the constant (6.918) is much greater than 0.118 and so we can conclude that the constant is statistically significant.

Third, we can see that the main model is shown in the second line: 'emotionspost$_{ij}$ = B$_{0j}$cons' and this is just telling us that our model is of the form: 'post-test score' = B*constant. However, the value for the constant is actually then shown on the third line and it can be seen that it is represented by the equation: 'B$_{0j}$ = 6.918(0.059) + u$_{0j}$ + e$_{0ij}$'. This is similar to the full specification of a regression model that we encountered in the previous chapter where we included an error term so that the actual model includes the best estimate for the dependent variable (i.e. 6.918) but then an error term, which will be different for each individual, depicting the difference between the estimate and the actual value for that person. However, and in this case, notice how there are two error terms that separate out: the error in relation to the difference between the individual child and the mean score for their preschool (e_{0ij}); and then the difference between the mean score for their preschool and the overall estimated mean score of 6.918 (u_{0j}).

Fourth, and in the model, each child has a unique number (depicted by 'i') and each preschool has its own unique number (depicted by 'j'). We can see from the equation in the second line that the dependent variable is listed as 'emotionspost$_{ij}$'. This indicates that there is a separate value for each child in each school (i.e. the ith child in the jth school). Similarly, the error term 'e' is written as 'e_{0ij}'. The '0' indicates that it is associated with the coefficient B_0 whereas the 'ij' indicates that there is also a separate value for each child in each school. However, the other error term 'u' is written as 'u_{0j}'. This indicates that there is just one value for each school and hence it will be the same for all children within a particular school.

Fifth, and finally, the variation for the variable *emotionspost* is shown in the final two figures for Ω_u and Ω_e respectively. What the multilevel model has done is to take the overall variation for the dependent variable and separate it out in terms of the variation between schools and then the variation between individual children. As can be seen, and by reference to their standard errors, both estimated variations are statistically significant as their values are clearly higher than two times their standard errors. There are two important points we can deduce from these figures. The first is that there is evidence that some of the variation in *emotionspost* is associated with differences between preschools. Having stated this, however, we need to be careful not to assume that this is therefore evidence that differences between preschools have a direct effect on children's ability to recognise emotions. This could be the case and, if so, would indicate that some preschools are more effective than others in developing this skill among young children. However, and alternatively, it could be that there is no difference in the effectiveness of preschools and, actually, this setting-level variation is simply a reflection of the differences between preschools in terms of differences in catchment areas (i.e. some schools located in largely affluent, middle-class areas; others in economically deprived inner city areas; others in mixed rural areas; and so on). To help us interpret what this variation represents, we can add in additional variables to represent socio-economic background, rural/urban distinctions and so on, and see whether this setting-level variation changes. The second key point to draw from these figures is that we can use these to calculate the proportion of variation that is associated with setting-level factors and individual-level factors. In this sense, the total variation is simply calculated as 0.122 + 1.540 = 1.662. The proportion of this associated with variations between settings is therefore given by 0.122/1.662 = 0.073 or 7.3%, also known as the 'variance partition coefficient'.

Applying Multilevel Modelling to the Analysis of Cluster RCTs with Scale Outcomes

With all this in mind, we can now turn to applying multilevel modelling to the analysis of cluster RCT data. We will run the main analysis to see whether there is evidence that the programme is having a positive effect on the children's ability to recognise emotions. As we covered in the previous chapter, this involves setting *emotionspost* as the dependent variable and then adding *Zemotionspre* (the pre-test score but standardised) and *intervention* as independent variables. Initially, and for the purposes of comparison, it is worth running this model with SPSS as an ordinary linear regression and ignoring the clustered nature of the data. The resultant output from SPSS is shown in Output 5.9. As can be seen, the statistical significance of the intervention coefficient indicates that the programme would appear to be having a positive effect.

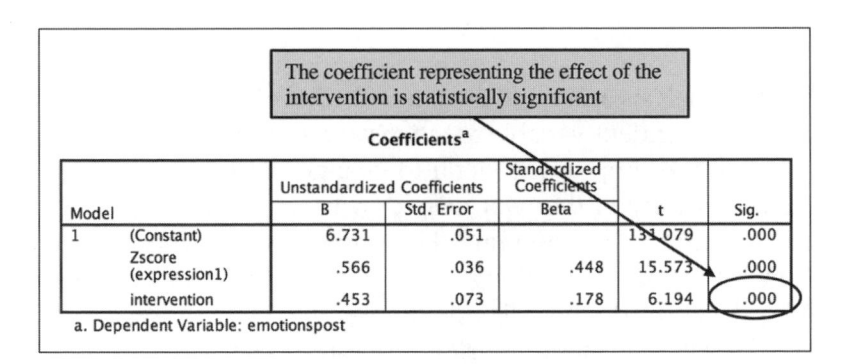

Coefficients[a]

The coefficient representing the effect of the intervention is statistically significant

Model		Unstandardized Coefficients B	Std. Error	Standardized Coefficients Beta	t	Sig.
1	(Constant)	6.731	.051		131.079	.000
	Zscore (expression1)	.566	.036	.448	15.573	.000
	intervention	.453	.073	.178	6.194	.000

a. Dependent Variable: emotionspost

Output 5.9

To help increase our familiarity with MLwiN, let us briefly look at how we would recreate this (single level) model. Starting where we left off with Output 5.8, the first thing we need to do is to change the model from two levels to one. To do this, we click on the name of the dependent variable and, in the dialogue box that opens up, use the drop-down menu for 'N Levels:' to choose '1 – j' and then click 'Done'. Next, we need to add in our

132   Using randomised controlled trials in education

additional two independent variables alongside the existing *cons* variable. To do this, click on 'Add Term' at the bottom of the 'Equations' window, using the drop-down menu in the dialogue box, select *Zemotionspre* and then just click 'Done'. Next, just repeat the process to add in the variable *intervention*. You should see from the equation that the model is now specified. However, all the figures will be blue, indicating that they need to be estimated. The last stage in the process, as before, is to click the 'Start' button at the top of the main interface window, directly below the top row of menu items. Once done, you should have the output shown in Output 5.10. Reassuringly, you can see that the estimated coefficients and their standard errors are the same as in the model generated through SPSS.

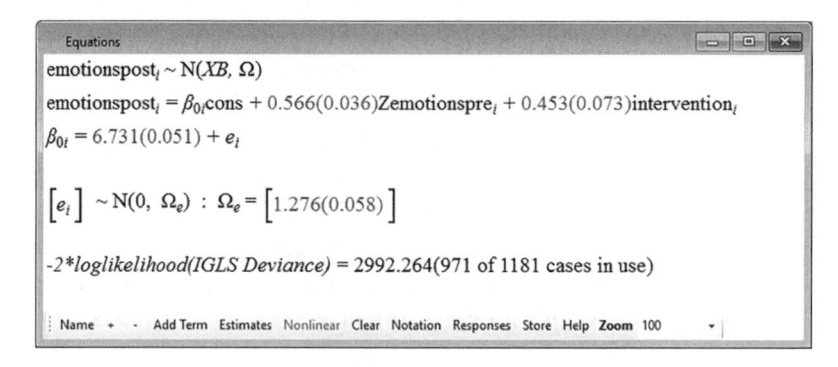

Equations

emotionspost$_i$ ~ N(XB, Ω)

emotionspost$_i$ = β_{0i}cons + 0.566(0.036)Zemotionspre$_i$ + 0.453(0.073)intervention$_i$

β_{0i} = 6.731(0.051) + e_i

$[e_i]$ ~ N(0, Ω$_e$) : Ω$_e$ = $[1.276(0.058)]$

-2*loglikelihood(IGLS Deviance) = 2992.264(971 of 1181 cases in use)

Name + - Add Term Estimates Nonlinear Clear Notation Responses Store Help Zoom 100

Output 5.10

To re-run the analysis as a multilevel model, all we need to do is click once more on the dependent variable *emotionspost* and in the dialogue box that opens up, use the drop-down menu to change the number of levels to '2 – ij' and also specify in the next drop-down menu that appears for 'Level 2(j)' that the variable representing the second level is *idsetting*, and then click 'Done'. The only other thing to do is to add in an error term ('u') for the settings level. To do this, click on the variable *cons* and select 'idsetting' and click 'Done'. The model is now properly specified so we can finally click the 'Start' button again to estimate the parameters. The resultant output is shown in Output 5.11.

As we can see from this the main model as it is set out – as an equation – should be very familiar to us. The only additional detail is that the model has now separated out the remaining variance by individual and setting levels as shown. Our focus, though, is the main model and we can see that the coefficient for intervention has remained broadly the same as it was for the single level model (now 0.432, compared to 0.453 for the single level model). However, and as we would expect, the standard error for this

Analysis of more complex RCT designs 133

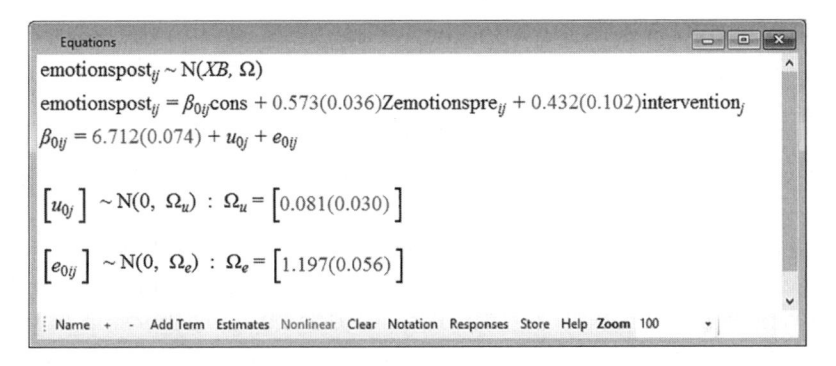

```
Equations
emotionspostᵢⱼ ~ N(XB, Ω)
emotionspostᵢⱼ = β₀ᵢⱼcons + 0.573(0.036)Zemotionspreᵢⱼ + 0.432(0.102)interventionⱼ
β₀ᵢⱼ = 6.712(0.074) + u₀ⱼ + e₀ᵢⱼ

[u₀ⱼ] ~ N(0, Ωᵤ) :  Ωᵤ = [0.081(0.030)]

[e₀ᵢⱼ] ~ N(0, Ωₑ) :  Ωₑ = [1.197(0.056)]

Name  +  -  Add Term  Estimates  Nonlinear  Clear  Notation  Responses  Store  Help  Zoom  100
```

Output 5.11

estimate has increased from 0.073 for the single level model to 0.102 for this multilevel model.

It will be remembered from the previous chapter that we can use the coefficients in the model from Output 5.11 to estimate the adjusted post-test mean score for the control group (in this case, the value of the constant, 6.712) and for the intervention group (6.712 + 0.432 = 7.144). In relation to the other information we need, namely the associated standard deviations and sample sizes for both estimated means, there are four steps to calculating these. This may feel a little convoluted but it is not complicated so long as you follow the steps carefully. For those with good experience of MLwiN, or are able to use other statistical packages such as Stata, this whole process can be a lot simpler. However, we are including these additional steps on the assumption that you only have experience of SPSS and are being introduced to MLwiN for the first time.

The first step involves going back to the SPSS dataset and running the above model but as a single-level ordinary linear regression using **Analyze → Regression Linear ...**, selecting the relevant variables (*emotionspost* as the dependent variable and *Zemptionspre* and *intervention* as the independent variables) but also clicking on the 'Save...' button and selecting 'Unstandardized Residuals'. As covered in the last chapter, when the model has been run we can see a new variable at the end of the dataset called *RES_1*. To help clarify matters, we will rename this variable as *filter*. Finally, we just need to **Transform → Recode into Same Variables ...**, select the variable filter, click on the 'Old and New Values' button and create the two expressions covered in the last chapter ('SYSMIS —> 0' and 'ELSE —> 1') and click 'Continue' and then 'OK'.

The second step involves creating two datasets – one that just includes all children with no missing data from the control group and the other that does the same for the intervention group. To do this, use **Data → Select**

Cases ... and then select 'If condition is satisfied', and in the top window input the expression 'intervention = 1 & filter = 1' and click 'Continue' to return to the main Select Cases window. In the main Select Cases window, under 'Output', choose 'Copy selected cases to a new dataset', and in the field for 'Dataset name:' call in 'intervention_group'. Once done click 'OK' and you will see that SPSS has opened up a new window with a new dataset called 'intervention_group'. Click on this window and then choose **File → Save As ...** and save the dataset with the name 'intervention_group' and as file type 'Stata Version 8 SE (*dta)'. Once done, repeat this step but using the expression 'intervention = 0 & filter = 1' to create a dataset you can call 'control_group', and ensure you save this also as a Stata file.

The third step is then to open each of these datasets, in turn, in MLwiN and run a simple two-level model (*idchild* as level 1 and *idsetting* as level 2) with our post-test outcome variable as the dependent variable (in this case *emotionspost*) and with just *cons* as the one independent variable. You should obtain the output shown in Output 5.12 that is from the intervention_group dataset. The two pieces of information we want from this are the sample size that is listed in the last line (481) and the standard error of the estimate of the mean score for the intervention group that we get from the model (in this case 0.079). Repeating this process for the control group dataset we get a sample size of 490 and standard error of 0.080.

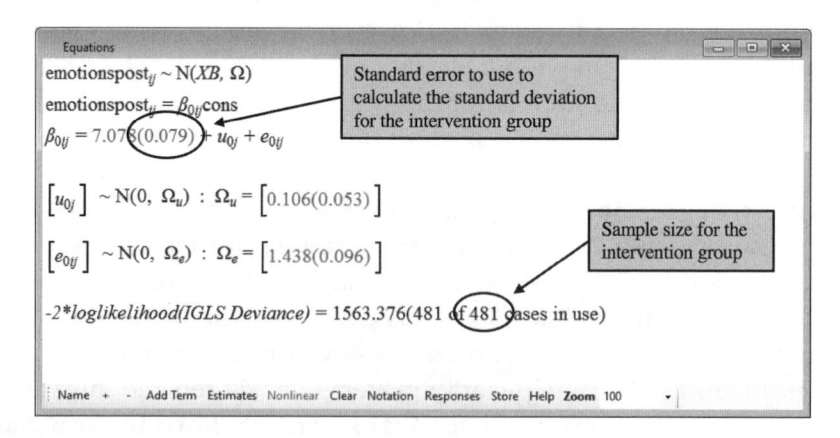

Equations

emotionspost$_{ij}$ ~ N(XB, Ω)

emotionspost$_{ij}$ = β_{0ij}cons

β_{0ij} = 7.078(0.079) + u_{0j} + e_{0ij}

Standard error to use to calculate the standard deviation for the intervention group

$[u_{0j}]$ ~ N(0, Ω$_u$) : Ω$_u$ = $[0.106(0.053)]$

$[e_{0ij}]$ ~ N(0, Ω$_e$) : Ω$_e$ = $[1.438(0.096)]$

Sample size for the intervention group

-2*loglikelihood(IGLS Deviance) = 1563.376(481 of 481 cases in use)

Name + - Add Term Estimates Nonlinear Clear Notation Responses Store Help Zoom 100

Output 5.12

The final step is to use the standard errors to calculate the standard deviation for both datasets. We do this by using the following formula:

Standard deviation = standard error × square root of sample size

Thus, for our two groups we get:

SD (Control Group) = 0.080 × sqrt(490) = 0.080 × 22.136 = 1.771

SD (Intervention Group) = 0.079 × sqrt(481) = 0.079 × 21.932 = 1.733

We now, finally, have all the information we need for both groups to use the online Effect Size Calculator to calculate the effect size and its associated 95% confidence interval. The findings are summarised in Table 5.3, which also compares these with the findings we could generate from SPSS if analysing the data with a single level ordinary linear regression model, thus ignoring the effects of clustering (see Output 5.9). It can be seen from Table 5.3 that analysing the data using a multilevel model and hence taking the clustering into account does not have any notable influence on the adjusted post-test mean scores estimated for both groups. However, it does have an effect on their associated standard deviations, increasing the size of the standard deviations for both groups. This, in turn, has a knock-on effect on the estimated effect size that is influenced by the standard deviations. Most importantly, we can see that the main consequence of not taking the clustering of the data into account in the analysis is to produce an estimated effect size that is higher than it should be (d = 0.36 rather than d = 0.25 when analysing the data appropriately).

Table 5.3 Findings of the effects of the Media Initiative for Children: Respecting Difference programme on young children's ability to recognise emotions, by analysis type*

Analysis Type	Intervention Group Mean (sd)	n	Control Group Mean (sd)	n	Effect Size, Cohen's d (95% CI)
Multilevel Model	7.14 (1.73)	481	6.71 (1.77)	490	0.25 [0.12, 0.37]
Single Level Model	7.18 (1.24)	481	6.73 (1.29)	490	0.36 [0.23, 0.48]

*Adjusted post-test mean scores reported, controlling for differences between groups at pre-test

Of course we can extend this basic model in MLwiN to undertake subgroup analyses. To do this, we just continue with the model we had in Output 5.12 and use the 'Add Term' button at the bottom of the Equations window to include the additional variables *boy* and *intvn_boy*. The resultant model is shown in Output 5.13. On this occasion, we can see from the standard error for the main interaction term *intvn_boy* that it is not statistically significant (i.e. 2 × 0.143 = 0.286, which is larger than the absolute value for the coefficient of 0.238). Whilst MLwiN does not show the statistical significance for each coefficient, it can be calculated by selecting from the menu across the top of the main interface window: **Model → Intervals and tests**. This opens up the window shown in Figure 5.5. Select 'fixed # of functions' at the bottom of the window, and in the list of terms that appear type in '1' against *intvn_boy* and then click 'Calc'. The results are shown in the window and, as can be seen, the statistical significance of this term is p = 0.095.

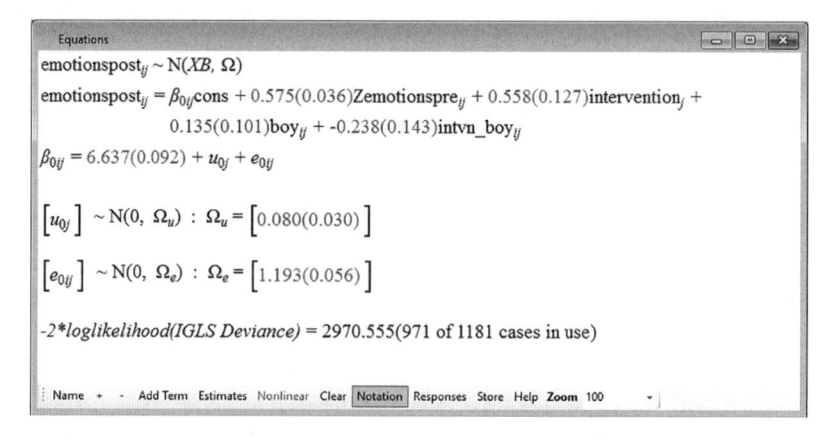

Equations

emotionspost$_{ij}$ ~ N(XB, Ω)

emotionspost$_{ij}$ = β_{0ij}cons + 0.575(0.036)Zemotionspre$_{ij}$ + 0.558(0.127)intervention$_j$ + 0.135(0.101)boy$_{ij}$ + -0.238(0.143)intvn_boy$_{ij}$

β_{0ij} = 6.637(0.092) + u_{0j} + e_{0ij}

$[u_{0j}]$ ~ N(0, Ω$_u$) : Ω$_u$ = $[0.080(0.030)]$

$[e_{0ij}]$ ~ N(0, Ω$_e$) : Ω$_e$ = $[1.193(0.056)]$

-2*loglikelihood(IGLS Deviance) = 2970.555(971 of 1181 cases in use)

Output 5.13

Intervals and tests

	#1
fixed : cons	0.000
fixed : Zemotionspre	0.000
fixed : intervention	0.000
fixed : boy	0.000
▶ fixed : intvn_boy	1.000
constant(k)	0.000
function result(f)	-0.238
f-k	-0.238
chi sq. (f-k)=0. (1df)	2.788
+/- 95% sep.	0.280
+/- 95% joint	0.280
p-value	0.095

joint chi sq test(1df) = 2.788 (p=0.095)

○ random ● fixed # of functions 1

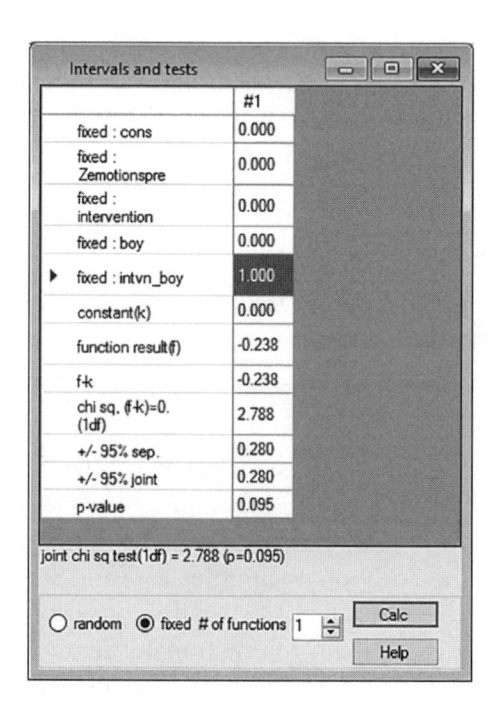

Figure 5.5 Calculating the statistical significance for each coefficient in MLwiN

If this interaction term was statistically significant then this would have provided evidence that the effectiveness of the programme was different for boys and girls. We could then have proceeded, just as in the last chapter, to write out this extended model and use it to estimate the adjusted post-test scores for boys and girls in the control and intervention groups respectively. Also, and as set out in the last example above, we would create a filter term in SPSS and use **Data → Select Cases ...** to generate four datasets for the four sub-groups, using the expression: 'boy = 1 & intervention = 1 & filter = 1' (which would, in this instance, be the group of boys in the intervention group). As shown above, we would then use these four datasets to calculate the standard errors and sample sizes for each and then, from this, their standard deviations and, ultimately, the effect sizes for boys and girls respectively.

Applying Multilevel Modelling to the Analysis of Cluster RCTs with Binary Outcomes

For the next example, we will demonstrate how to use MLwiN to run a multilevel binary logistic model, this time for the outcome representing whether the young children demonstrated any awareness of exclusion in the playground (coded '1') or not (coded '0') from a photograph they were shown. To do this, in the main Equations window, we need to tell MLwiN that we now wish to estimate a binary logistic regression. To do this we click on the term 'N(XB, Ω)', and in the dialogue box that appears select 'Binomial' and 'Logit' and click 'Done'. Click on 'y' or the current dependent variable if you still have outputs showing from the previous model, and select *exclusionpost* and ensure that you have two levels selected as before. Add in the two key independent variables *Zexclusionpre* and *intervention*

Equations

exclusionpost$_{ij}$ ~ Binomial(DENOM$_{ij}$, π_{ij})

logit(π_{ij}) = β_{0j}cons + 0.142(0.083)Zexclusionpre$_{ij}$ + 0.862(0.325)intervention$_j$

β_{0j} = -2.752(0.251) + u_{0j}

$[u_{0j}]$ ~ N(0, Ω_u) : Ω_u = $[0.930(0.293)]$

var(exclusionpost$_{ij}$|π_{ij}) = π_{ij}(1 - π_{ij})/DENOM$_{ij}$

(1140 of 1181 cases in use)

Output 5.14

and click on *cons* to check that all three options are selected, i.e. 'Fixed Parameter', 'j(idsetting)' and 'i(idchild)'. Finally, click the 'Start' button to estimate the model. You should generate the output shown in Output 5.14.

As can be seen from the standard error for the intervention coefficient, it is clearly statistically significant. If you wish, you can use the **Model → Intervals and tests** option to find that it is actually p = 0.008. Just as shown earlier, we can use this model to estimate the predicted log-odds for the intervention and control groups:

Predicted log-odds (control) = −2.752 + 0.142*(0) + 0.862*(0) = **−2.752**

Predicted log-odds (intervention) = −2.752 + 0.142*(0) + 0.862*(1) = **−1.890**

These predicted log-odds, in turn, can be converted into predicted percentages:

Predicted percentage (control) = exp(−2.752)/[1+exp(−2.752)] = 0.060

Predicted percentage (intervention) = exp(−1.890)/[1+exp(−1.890)] = 0.131

As can be seen, for preschool children in the control group, only 6.0% were able to demonstrate an awareness of exclusion at post-test and this compared to 13.1% in the intervention group. Alongside these adjusted post-test percentages, we also need to report the sample sizes for both groups. These can be calculated directly from SPSS using the procedure with a filter variable covered previously. Doing this, you will find that the number of children who contributed to this model (i.e. with no missing data) is 567 for the intervention group and 573 for the control group.

Finally, we need to calculate an effect size and its associated 95% confidence interval. The problem in this case is that if we just enter the above percentages and sample sizes into the Effect Size Calculator, we will get the correct odds-ratio (2.36) but a misleading confidence interval (1.54, 3.60) as we have not taken into account the clustering of the data. In this instance, and to obtain a proper estimate of the confidence interval, we need to calculate and use what are referred to as the effective sample sizes for both groups. These will be smaller than the actual sample sizes and give us some idea of how the statistical power of the trial has been reduced due to the effects of clustering. We can calculate the effective sample sizes using what is known as the 'design effect' for the trial. For example, if the design effect is 2.0 then we would divide the actual sample sizes by 2.0 to get the effective sample sizes. In this case, the design effect is telling us that the effects of clustering are equivalent to reducing the actual sample size by half.

There are three steps to calculating the effective sample sizes. First, we need to estimate the intra-cluster (or intra-class) correlation coefficient (ICC), which is a measure of how similar children are in each preschool setting. To calculate this, we run a multilevel binary logistic regression in MLwiN with the post-test variable as the dependent variable and just a constant added as the independent variable. In this case we obtain the model shown in Output 5.15. We use the value for the variance, Ω_u (which can also be represented by σ^2_u) to derive an approximate estimate for the ICC using the following formula:

$$ICC = \sigma^2_u / (\sigma^2_u + 3.29)$$

In our present example, therefore, this gives us $0.937(0.937 + 3.29) = 0.222$.

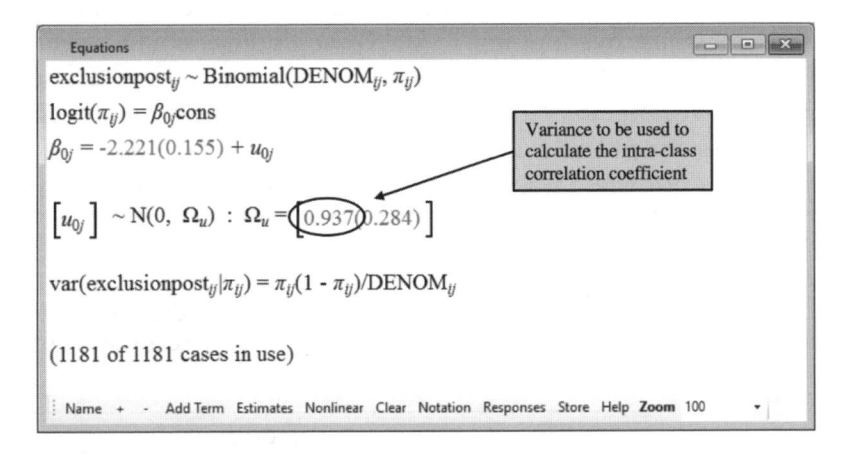

```
Equations
exclusionpost_ij ~ Binomial(DENOM_ij, π_ij)
logit(π_ij) = β_0j cons
β_0j = -2.221(0.155) + u_0j

[u_0j] ~ N(0, Ω_u) : Ω_u = (0.937(0.284))

var(exclusionpost_ij|π_ij) = π_ij(1 - π_ij)/DENOM_ij

(1181 of 1181 cases in use)
```

Variance to be used to calculate the intra-class correlation coefficient

Output 5.15

The second step is to use this estimated ICC to calculate the design effect for the trial. This is calculated using the following formula

$$\text{Design effect} = 1 + (M - 1)*ICC$$

where M is the average cluster size. In our present trial we have already calculated the actual sample sizes as 567 for the intervention group and 573 for the control group, giving an overall sample size for children with no missing data of 1140. For this trial there were 74 preschool settings and so the average size of each cluster is $1140/74 = 15.41$. This, in turn, gives us a design effect as follows:

$$\text{Design effect} = 1 + (15.41 - 1)*0.222$$
$$= 1 + 14.41*0.222$$
$$= 1 + 3.20$$
$$= 4.20$$

The third and final step is to use this design effect to calculate our effective sample sizes. In our case, the effective sample size for the intervention group is 567/4.20 = 135. Similarly, the effective sample size for the control group is 573/4.20 = 136.

With the adjusted post-test percentages and their effective sample sizes, we can use the online Effect Size Calculator as before to calculate the odds-ratio and its 95% confidence interval. Doing this gives us: 2.36 (0.99, 5.62). As can be seen, although the effect size estimate is not altered by the use of effective samples, we can see that the confidence interval has increased and is just overlapping 1.000. These findings could be reported formally as shown in Table 5.4. As can be seen, the effects of the programme are to more than double the odds of children being able to recognise instances of exclusion (increasing the odds by a factor of 2.36). Notice how the estimated ICC and effective sample sizes are also reported in the notes.

Table 5.4 Findings of the effects of the Media Initiative for Children: Respecting Difference programme on preschool children's ability to recognise instances of exclusion*

Outcome	Intervention Group %	n	Control Group %	n	Effect Size, Odds Ratio (95% CI)**
Proportion of Preschool Children Identifying Exclusion	13.1%	567	6.0%	573	2.36 [0.99, 5.62]

*Adjusted post-test percentages, controlling for differences between groups at pre-test
** Estimated ICC = 0.222. Odds-ratio calculated using effective sample sizes of 135 (control) and 136 (intervention)

Assessing the Effects of Programme Fidelity

Finally, we will take a brief look at how to assess whether fidelity to the programme is associated with outcomes. In this instance, we are only concerned with analysing the data for the intervention group. We can therefore use **Data → Select Cases ...** in SPSS to create a sample including just intervention group children as we have done before. After saving it in Stata format we can open it in MLwiN to run the model shown in Output 5.16.

It will be seen in this model that we have the post-test score as the dependent variable (*emotionspost*) and two independent variables: the pre-test score (*Zemotionspre*) and the measure of fidelity to the programme described earlier (*fidelity*). We obviously do not have the dummy variable intervention in the model as we are only dealing with intervention group children. This is the model we use each time to ascertain if there is any evidence that variations in levels of fidelity are associated with variations in outcomes. Our focus is whether the coefficient for the variable fidelity is statistically significant or not. In this case, it can be seen from the standard error that it is clearly not significant. What this tells us is that there is no association between the preschool settings' fidelity to the programme and the outcomes achieved in relation to the young children's ability to recognise emotions in this case, once pre-test differences are accounted for.

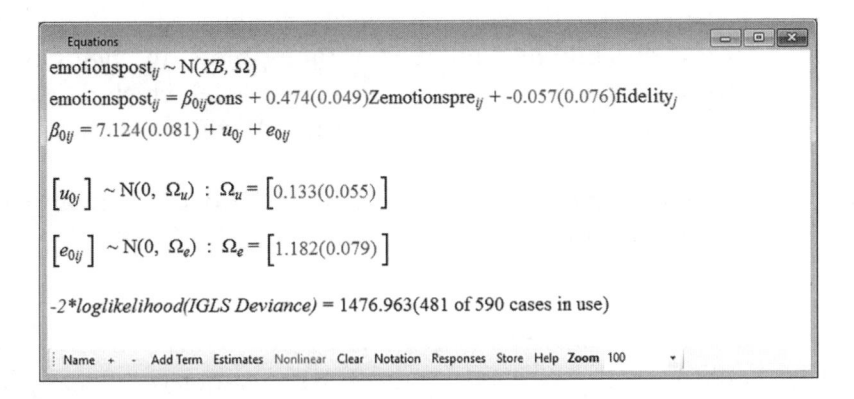

```
Equations
emotionspost_ij ~ N(XB, Ω)
emotionspost_ij = β_0ij cons + 0.474(0.049)Zemotionspre_ij + -0.057(0.076)fidelity_j
β_0ij = 7.124(0.081) + u_0j + e_0ij

[u_0j] ~ N(0, Ω_u) : Ω_u = [0.133(0.055)]

[e_0ij] ~ N(0, Ω_e) : Ω_e = [1.182(0.079)]

-2*loglikelihood(IGLS Deviance) = 1476.963(481 of 590 cases in use)

Name  +  -   Add Term  Estimates  Nonlinear  Clear  Notation  Responses  Store  Help  Zoom  100
```

Output 5.16

Conclusions

This chapter has shown how to deal with the two most common adaptations to the classic RCT design, namely how to approach the analysis of trials that use binary outcomes and also how to deal with data from cluster randomised controlled trials. Whilst there is considerable variation in trials in relation to the outcomes they use and their actual design, it has been seen that the overall approach to the analysis of trial data remains the same. Through the development of generalised linear models and advances in multilevel modelling, we have considerable flexibility to be able to analyse any type of trial design that might arise. Most trials in education will use scale outcome measures, with some including one or more binary outcome measures. However, should we need to deal with ordinal outcome measures or other types of outcome measure, possibly based upon counts of how many times something occurs in a given time period (i.e. following a Poisson distribution), then there are generalised linear models to deal with these.

Similarly, whilst we covered data from a cluster randomised controlled trial that was organised in two levels (young children clustered within preschool settings), these multilevel models can easily be extended to include three or more levels in cases where, for example, we have children located within classes located within schools. We can also use such multilevel models to account for multisite trial designs where there might be 40 schools but, within each school, the children are randomly allocated to the control or intervention groups, or where each school has a number of classes participating in a trial and, within this, the classes in each school are randomly allocated to the control or intervention groups. Also, multilevel models are a particularly powerful technique for analysing repeated measures designs where we might collect data on each child at a number of time points. In such circumstances, we would have each observation as one level, clustered within children (second level) who may be clustered within classes (third level) and so on.

Beyond this, and in conclusion, there are five brief but important points to stress regarding our overall approach to the analysis of trials.

Intention to Treat Analysis

All trials should have a published protocol that sets out very clearly and comprehensively the design of the trial, including who is to be recruited and how they are to be randomly allocated to control and intervention groups. It is not uncommon that individuals drop out of a trial, or do not comply fully with the programme or intervention, or even cross over from the control group to an intervention group or vice versa. Instances like this essentially break the principle of random assignment to groups and if not accounted for are likely to lead to the introduction of bias into the trial and the comparisons between groups. It is with this in mind that participants should always be analysed on an *intention to treat* basis. This essentially means that even if individuals have dropped out of the trial, or failed to follow the programme properly, or have actually moved across from one group to another, they should all still be included in the dataset and all analysed on the basis of what group they had originally been allocated to.

Missing Data

For the purposes of this and the previous chapter, we have essentially dealt with missing data by deleting cases on a list-wise basis. In other words, if an individual has a pre-test score missing or a post-test score missing for a particular outcome then they are deleted from that analysis. In some respects missing data provide a particular challenge to the full application of an intention to treat analysis. However, if participants have withdrawn and refuse to cooperate further then there is little that can be done and list-wise deletion will essentially lead to them being excluded from the analysis. One way to address this, which is becoming widely accepted, is through the use of a technique known as multiple imputation. Unfortunately it is beyond the scope of this present book to cover this particular approach. However, it involves using the data that we do have to estimate and fill in missing values. It imputes data like this for several datasets (hence the term multiple imputation) and then the analysis that is undertaken is applied to all imputed samples and these are used to generate mean estimates. It is possible to conduct all of the analysis of a trial using multiple imputation from the outset or, alternatively, you can focus just on the observed data (thus dealing with missing data through list-wise deletion) but then conduct a sensitivity analysis by re-running the analysis again using multiple imputation to assess whether there is any evidence that your original analysis may be biased.

Assumptions and Conditions

The purpose of this book has been to demonstrate, practically, how statistical models can be applied to the analysis of trial data. This is not a general statistics textbook and we have not had the space to cover each of the techniques discussed in these last two chapters fully. However, it is very important that you familiarise yourself properly with each of these techniques. Most importantly, each technique is based upon a number of assumptions regarding the data and it is important for you to check these before running your main analyses. One assumption for ordinary linear regression, for example, is that we are dealing with a sample where each case is independent from one another. When discussing the theory behind multilevel modelling earlier in this chapter, we saw the real consequences that can arise for our analysis and resultant findings when we ignore this with a sample that is actually organised in clusters.

Similarly, some techniques have particular conditions that need to be met before it is appropriate for these to be used. We would not, for example, use ordinary linear regression for a dependent variable that is binary. Similarly, we should not add in an ordinal variable into a regression model unless we have converted it first into a series of dummy variables. For multilevel modelling, a critical issue is that we need a sufficient number of higher level clusters (typically schools in our case) to be able to generate reliable estimates for the variances in our models. What constitutes a 'sufficient number' is open to debate. Few people would question a trial with 40 or more schools and a trial with at least 30 schools would tend to be acceptable. However, multilevel modelling has been successfully applied to the analysis of trials with as few as 20 schools and there has been some research involving simulation to suggest that multilevel models are sufficiently robust to be used with just 10 or less higher level units, if your concern is mainly just to correct for the effects of clustering (Maas and Hox, 2005).

Overall, therefore, it is important that you do not use this book as your main source of information or learning for the particular statistical techniques and models covered. If you are unfamiliar with regression or multilevel modelling then it is important that you take some time to read about and understand these techniques more fully so that you can apply them properly.

Dealing with non-randomised controlled trials

There will be occasions where it is simply not possible to undertake a fully randomised controlled trial and/or where an intervention has already started and it is important to undertaken some evaluation of its effectiveness, even if it means simply recruiting a control group that is as matched as possible to the group participating in the programme. Having said this, we would argue that such cases should be rare and that, in most instances, it is quite possible to set up and run an RCT. Rather than practical considerations being the main obstacle, it is often the lack of commitment and/or planning that gets in the way. However, we do accept that there will be occasions when there will be data from a non-randomised controlled trial to analyse. In such circumstances, and assuming you still have pre-test and post-test measures and a control and intervention group, then the approach to the analysis is exactly as set out in this and the last chapter. One possible difference, given that your two groups are not randomly allocated and thus there are likely to be biases that have been introduced, is to mitigate these as far as possible by controlling for additional covariates. Thus, alongside adding in the pre-test score as an independent variable in each model, you could add in other measures that you believe may be associated with your outcome variables and where your intervention and control groups may differ in their characteristics. For example, this could include a measure of socio-economic deprivation or ethnicity or specific attitudes or previous experiences. In such circumstances, you just need to follow the same procedures as covered in these two chapters but also include these additional covariates as independent variables. In each case it is important to remember to standardise all of these variables before adding them to the models so that you can interpret these exactly as set out above.

Analysis plans

Finally, a critical issue in the analysis of trials is to be open and completely transparent in your approach. This is why publishing a protocol at the outset is so important in order that you protect yourself against charges of bias, selective reporting, opportunism or cherry-picking results. Within this, it is essential that you outline in detail, and from the outset in your protocol, how you intend to approach the analysis of the trial data. This is where you would set out which statistical models you will employ for which outcomes, whether you will be using multilevel models or not and what specific sub-group analyses you intend to undertake. All of your decisions need to be carefully justified at the beginning. Alongside explaining such matters as how you will estimate your standard deviations for use in calculating effect sizes, it is particularly important to be very clear and to provide a strong justification for any sub-group analyses you wish to undertake. Running a large number of post-hoc sub-group analyses with no prior justification will attract criticisms of you engaging in a 'fishing exercise' which will undermine the robustness of your findings.

Further Reading

Binary Logistics Regression
- *Statistical Modelling for Social Researchers*, by R. Tarling (Routledge, 2009, Ch. 5).
- *Advanced Quantitative Data Analysis*, by D. Cramer (Open University Press, 2003, Ch. 9).
- *Discovering Statistics Using SPSS*, by Andy Field (Sage, 2009, Ch. 8).

Multilevel Modelling

- LEMMA (Learning Environment for Multilevel Methodology and Applications), Centre for Multilevel Modelling, University of Bristol: www.bristol.ac.uk/cmm/learning/online-course/
- *Statistical Modelling for Social Researchers*, by R. Tarling (Routledge, 2009, Ch. 6).
- *Discovering Statistics Using SPSS*, by Andy Field (Sage, 2009, Ch. 19).

Websites

For all datasets used in this chapter and to access the Effect Size Calculator, please visit the book's companion website at: https://study.sagepub.com/connolly.

6

How to Report RCTs and Synthesise Evidence from Different Trials

Introduction

This chapter will focus on how to write up and report the findings of randomised trials. Taking the CONSORT statement as the guide, the chapter sets out clearly the information that needs to be reported and in what format. The chapter also provides the reader with an appreciation of how the findings of individual RCTs are used in the synthesis of research evidence through the use of systematic reviews and meta-analysis. In all of this, the chapter stresses the need to be tentative in interpreting the findings and in the claims that are made from these.

Reporting results from RCTs

Trials that are inadequately conducted and inaccurately or incompletely reported can generate misleading (biased) results by artificially augmenting the outcomes and consequently having a detrimental impact on decision-making. Compared to trials in health, trials in education tend to be particularly poorly reported. Torgerson et al. (2005) compared the quality of trial reports in healthcare and education (between 1990 and 2003) and concluded that the reports of healthcare trials were of a higher quality than education trials but also published in higher quality journals. Furthermore, of the 84 education trials included in their review, none concealed allocation or reported a rationale for the sample size and only one trial reported confidence intervals.

As the number of trials in education increases, it is therefore essential that we exercise great care when writing up our trials for publication, whether it is a final report for the organisation that funded the research or an article for a peer-reviewed academic journal. It is with this in mind that we should strive to write in a style that is accessible for novice and familiar readers alike, ensuring that we are clear, transparent and honest in all aspects of our reporting. It is also important to acknowledge who has funded and supported the study so that any relevant conflicts of interest are stated and the independence (or otherwise) of the research team is clear.

The CONSORT statement (Consolidated Standards of Reporting Trials) was developed to try to minimise the risk described above and improve the transparency and reporting of trials by providing researchers with an 'evidence-based, minimum set of recommendations for reporting randomized trials' (www.consort-statement.org). The statement consists of a 25-item checklist and flow diagram, which details the progress of participants through the trial. CONSORT also makes provision for different types of trial and has developed extensions to the statement, which provide additional criteria and guidance for reporting, for example: cluster RCTs and trials in the area of psychological and social science (Montgomery et al., 2013). The CONSORT statement is widely endorsed by over 400 academic journals and is revised and updated on an ongoing basis.

CONSORT focuses on issues specifically related to the reporting of the internal and external validity of a trial and is not intended as a measure of quality assessment. For this reason, it is not an exhaustive list of what you should cover in a report of the RCT you have just conducted. There is other important information that should also be included that is not necessarily within the remit of CONSORT, for example: details of ethical approval, participant consent procedures and other data that were collected alongside the trial such as cost-effectiveness data or process-related data. As well as providing a comprehensive guide to reporting RCTs, the checklist provided by CONSORT can serve as a useful reference point at the initial design phase of a trial.

CONSORT guidelines were originally developed to improve the reporting of medical trials and, over the years, extensions to the guidelines have been developed to support the reporting of special types of RCTs, for example: cluster trials, pragmatic trials or N-of-1 trials (for a full list see www.consort-statement.org/extensions). An extension for the reporting of psychological and social interventions is currently being developed to address the lack of rigour in the reporting of such trials (e.g. Torgerson et al., 2005) as well as the limited available guidelines (Montgomery et al., 2013).

Trial registration and protocol publication

Before the first participant is recruited it is an essential requirement of CONSORT that a trial protocol is made publicly available either in an academic journal, through a trial registry website or hosted on another, easily accessible website or location. Details relating to how and where readers can access the trial protocol should be included in the final report.

The protocol should describe the proposed rationale, methodology and analysis of the full trial. It should closely mirror the information that is reported in the final write-up of the study and acts as a road map for the researcher during the implementation of the trial. It allows the reader to judge if there were any deviations in the conduct of the trial between the publication of the protocol and completion of the final report. All deviations to what is contained in the protocol should be clearly highlighted in the final write-up of the study alongside the accompanying reasons for any changes.

The act of making a trial protocol permanently and publicly available guards against the risk that any trial data might be swept under the carpet and not made publicly available (publication bias) or indeed that certain, perhaps unfavourable outcomes are not reported (selective outcome reporting). It also reduces the likelihood of unnecessary duplication and can facilitate identifying gaps in relation to areas where trials are needed.

If you choose to register your trial, there are several registries for clinical trials and those that are recognised by the World Health Organisation can be found on their website (www.who.int/ictrp/network/primary/en). A relevant registry for trials in education and social sciences is the ISRCTN (International Standard Registered Clinical/Social Study Number: www.isrctn.com) and once your trial is registered you are provided with a unique identification number, which should be quoted on all documentation relating to the trial. This registry does charge a one-off fee so it is important that the fee is included in any funding application.

What follows is an outline of the CONSORT reporting requirements for each section of your report.

Title and abstract

The title and abstract of any report are crucial in terms of providing the necessary information that readers need to establish the relevance of a study and decide whether they should read the entire report or not. For this reason the title should always contain the word 'randomised' and if the trial is clustered then the title should include 'cluster' as well as 'randomised'. The abstract should be a structured summary of the trial design, methods, results and conclusions. CONSORT provides detailed guidance on the precise nature of the information that should be included in abstracts (including conference abstracts) under each of these headings (www.consort.org).

Introduction and hypotheses

The introduction section of the report aims to provide the reader with a review of the relevant research as well as a rationale for the proposed study. It is very important that your trial is located within the context of previous research and often a good starting point is a review of the relevant systematic reviews in the area, many of which are housed in the Cochrane Library (www.thecochranelibrary.com) and the Campbell Collaboration Library (https://campbellcollaboration.org/library). It is important that you provide a justification for your research – if the answer to the question you are about to pose is already known (or can be answered through a systematic review) then you might well be at risk of exposing potential participants to unnecessary research procedures (see the discussion on ethics and the principle of equipoise in Chapter 3). Thus, you should start with a general discussion of the issue at hand and as your introduction becomes more focused it should logically lead the reader through the relevant issues, including a discussion of the relevant theoretical debates within which the study is located. An important component of the introduction section is a description of *how* the programme is thought to work and the conceptual framework that underpins the intervention being tested. This theory of change relates specifically to the development of the programme's logic model, described in greater detail in Chapter 2. The introduction should conclude with a statement of the study's hypotheses so that it is clear to the reader what original contribution the study will make to what is already known.

Methodology

Design: The type of trial needs to be explicitly stated. Whilst many RCT designs have two parallel conditions (treatment and control) there are also alternative trial designs that are common in education including cluster, multi-arm parallel and crossover trials. It is here that you should also describe the allocation ratio between groups (most trials are 1:1) and the unit of randomisation, i.e. whether individual participants or the clusters (e.g. year group, school or local education authority) were allocated to intervention and control groups. If the trial you are reporting is clustered, ensure that you describe the cluster.

Recruitment and eligibility criteria: A full description of the methods of recruitment and the eligibility criteria used to select participants (or clusters) should be provided in order to help the reader determine the applicability and generalisability of the study and its results. For this reason, eligibility criteria are directly related to the external validity of a trial. Participants should be fully recruited to the trial before randomisation takes place. Similarly related to a trial's generalisability is the location of the settings and where the data were collected. Such information might include the country, city, number of settings and their socio-economic context.

Description of the intervention and control conditions: The intervention should be described in enough detail that it can be replicated, including for example: the content of the programme being evaluated, frequency of delivery, who delivers it (for example, peers, teachers, trained volunteers), what training is required to implement the programme. Typically, the control group receive what is described as 'business as usual'; however, it is important to describe what 'business as usual' actually entails. If it is normal classroom activity, as is the case in many educational RCTs, then this can vary considerably between regions and particularly between countries. This variation in control condition has implications for the generalisability of trial results and might make it more difficult to draw comparisons about the effectiveness of a programme that has been evaluated in different jurisdictions or countries. Ultimately, this information aids interpretation of the results and enables the reader to more fully understand what the comparison group has been exposed to.

Pre-specify outcomes and measures: The outcomes that you hypothesise the intervention will change need to be pre-specified in advance of the start of the trial, along with how you plan to measure these outcomes. You should identify the most important outcome as your primary outcome; the remaining outcomes will be secondary outcomes. It is preferable to have only one primary outcome to limit the risk of multiple testing, however it is possible to have two or three co-primary outcomes if you have a very good reason for doing so, but no more than this. If you are measuring your outcomes over several time points, then you also need to pre-specify which time-point is of primary interest.

It is important that the measures you use to assess your outcomes are appropriate, valid and reliable tools so that they provide the least biased estimate possible. All measures (and their associated properties) should be described in full so that others can subsequently use the same outcomes. Often it is easier to present the relevant information in a table format, identifying primary and secondary outcomes within this. See Table 6.1 as an example.

Table 6.1 Reading outcomes measured in the randomised controlled trial evaluation of the Time to Read volunteer mentoring programme

		Internal consistency (Cronbach's alpha)	
Outcome	Measure	Reported in other studies	Achieved in this sample
Primary outcome			
Reading ability	The Group Reading Test II, ages 6–14 (Group Reading Test II, 1997)	.94 – .96 (Group Reading Test II, 1997)	Not estimated
Secondary outcomes			
Self esteem	The Global Self Worth scale of The Self Perception Profile for Children (Harter, 1985)	.53 – .77 (Shevlin et al., 2003)	.72 – .80
Enjoyment of education	The 'liking school' subscale of Pell and Jarvis's (2001) attitudinal scale	.65 (Pell and Jarvis, 2001)	.70 – .73
Aspirations for the future	The Expectations/Aspirations measure (Loeber et al., 1991)	.78 – .87 (Kersteter, 2004)	.54 – .64

Source: Miller and Connolly (2012)

For clustered trials make sure that you specify which outcomes are measured at the level of the individual and which outcomes are measured at the level of the cluster. Sometimes only the statistically significant results are reported, introducing a serious reporting bias, which is problematic. Pre-specifying the primary and secondary outcomes and measures in the trial protocol can alleviate the risk of this happening, but it is equally important that authors document and clearly report any changes that they make to the outcomes and measures (or their designation as primary and secondary) during the course of the trial, including the reasons for doing so.

Sample size: A trial needs to have enough participants that it has a high probability (power) of detecting any differences in outcomes between groups should they exist. Larger samples will be needed to detect smaller effects and you will need to provide the reader with all the information (assumptions) you used in your power calculation. Chapter 3 provides more information on how to conduct a sample size calculation and the software that is available to help you do so. However, the information you will need to include in your report is:

- the effect size you planned to be able to detect. This is based on what other similar RCTs have reported and is a best estimate of the 'true' population effect;
- the significance level (alpha) used – usually 0.05 in education trials;

- statistical power to be achieved – conventionally 80%;
- the proportion of variation likely to be explained by covariates included in the model.

Importantly, this information describes the parameters that were used in your initial (pre-study) power calculation and is not changed to reflect parameter estimates from your own data just collected.

Additional information will be required for cluster randomised trials, such as cluster size and the intra-class correlation (ICC), which describes how similar the members of a given cluster are to each other (this will be different for each outcome so use the ICC associated with the primary outcome in your power calculation). The results of the power calculation, i.e. number of clusters or number of individuals required in the intervention and control groups, should then be reported. If any allowance has been made for attrition, then this should be reported too. Reporting the intended size of the trial allows the reader to judge whether or not this was achieved. In reality, many trials are underpowered, which limits our ability to draw reliable conclusions regarding the effectiveness of an intervention. CONSORT argue that calculating the achieved power of a study (after it has been conducted) is a redundant exercise because the confidence intervals around the estimated effects provide an indication of power at this point.

Interim analyses: If your trial is being conducted over a long period of time then you may plan to have several data collection points. In medical trials these data can be analysed to determine whether the intervention is working particularly well or badly for one group and as such the trial might be stopped if the data strongly suggest this to be the case. This is rarely applicable in education; however, the issue pertaining to multiple data points is an important one. The more data points and interim analyses there are, the higher the risk of a Type I error occurring (associated with multiple testing) and finding a false positive. For this reason any interim analyses should be pre-specified in the protocol and the Bonferroni correction should be applied so that a more stringent p-value is used for these tests. Reporting interim analyses can inadvertently and falsely raise hopes that the intervention is more effective than the final analysis will bear out to be the case, so care needs to be exercised when planning how interim data should be analysed and reported.

Randomisation: You will need to report the precise method of randomisation that was used to allocate participants (or clusters) to groups. Simple randomisation is the most straightforward and least predictable method of allocation but if the sample sizes are quite small then there is a risk that the intervention and control groups might be unbalanced. For this reason you can opt to use restricted, blocked or stratified random allocation (see Chapter 3 for further detail of these methods of allocation). An alternative method of allocation that is often used in education trials is minimisation. It is effective in creating two groups that are balanced across the characteristics you deem to be most important, especially when sample sizes are small, as can be the case in clustered trials. The statistical software used (e.g. Minim in the case of minimisation, see: www-users.york.ac.uk/~mb55/guide/minim.htm) should be described as well as all relevant details pertaining to the allocation process, e.g. characteristics used in the blocking, stratification or minimisation procedures (including the ratio of allocation, usually 1:1 but other ratios are possible). It is important that the allocation process cannot be corrupted or the sequence predicted by whomever it might be that is recruiting participants. For this reason it is good practice that an independent person or organisation generates the allocation sequence and that you report who enrolled participants in the trial, who generated the allocation sequence, and who communicated the outcome of the allocation to participants. To try and avoid participants or clusters dropping out of the trial because they are unhappy with the group they have been allocated to, it is preferable that allocation should be conducted only *after* the participant/cluster has fully consented to take part in the study. If the trial is clustered then details relating to how individuals within clusters were sampled are also required.

Blinding: To minimise the risk of bias it is necessary to report *who* was blinded to the allocation of participants or clusters. In education trials it is generally not possible to blind participants but it is frequently possible to ensure that the individuals who are collecting the data (the outcome assessors) are blind to condition. How this blinding is achieved and the situations in which it might have been breached (and why) should be described.

Analysis: The proposed method of analysis and whether or not it is intention to treat (ITT) should be pre-specified and described in enough detail that someone familiar with such analytical approaches can replicate it. Details of the statistical models that were used, as well as covariates (including those used in the allocation process), should be pre-specified and reported. Sub-group analyses (using an interaction term) should also be pre-specified and because they are often underpowered should be interpreted with caution.

Results

Participant flow through the trial: CONSORT strongly recommend that a flow diagram is used to report enrolment, randomisation, treatment allocation, follow-up and analysis of participants or clusters. The recommended format is illustrated in Figure 6.1 and you will see that the reasons for non-participation, withdrawal and attrition are documented within this. It is therefore essential that detailed and accurate withdrawal and attrition records be kept as the trial is rolled out, so that you have the relevant information to report once the trial is completed. This information enables the readers to ascertain whether an intention to treat analysis was undertaken (i.e. all those randomised were also analysed) and the reasons why any participant or cluster is lost to follow-up after randomisation. It is relevant to the assessment of the trial's generalisability and allows us to see whether there has been differential attrition between the intervention and control groups, which might introduce bias, particularly if the reasons for attrition are related to the outcomes being measured. The dates of recruitment and follow-up should be reported in order to provide context for the study as well as provide some indication of how long recruitment might take for this type of trial.

Comparing groups at baseline: The characteristics of the intervention and control groups in relation to both demographic and pre-test outcome measures should be compared at baseline so that the groups' similarity can be

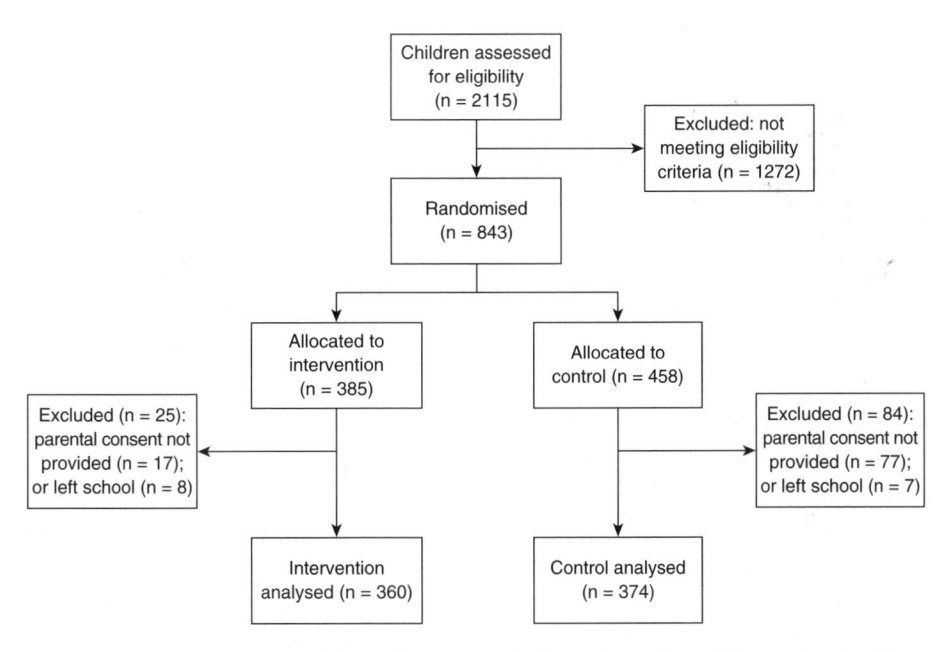

Figure 6.1 Flow diagram of the selection and allocation of participants in the Time to Read volunteer mentoring trial

Source: Miller and Connolly (2012)

assessed. Appropriate measures of central tendency and spread should be provided for each characteristic and outcome. As the randomisation process eliminates selection bias, any pre-test differences between groups will be due to chance. Consequently, significance tests between the groups at baseline are not necessary and can be misleading. Even so, this does not necessarily mean that the two groups are equivalent.

Group comparisons at pre-test (sometimes also referred to as baseline) are best described in a table format, providing further information relating to the generalisability of the trial and the relevance of its results – an example of reporting group differences in outcomes at pre-test is provided in Table 6.2.

Table 6.2   Pre-test means and standard deviations across all outcomes measured in the Time to Read volunteer mentoring trial (Miller and Connolly, 2012)

Outcome	Min. & Max.	Pre-test Intervention Mean (SD)	Pre-test Control Mean (SD)	Pre-test Total Mean (SD)
Reading ability	10 – 25	91.55 (4.71)	92.44 (4.79)	92.03 (4.77)
Self-esteem	9 – 45	18.53 (4.24)	18.62 (4.29)	18.58 (4.27)
Enjoyment of education	6 – 24	33.74 (7.36)	34.00 (6.67)	33.88 (6.99)
Aspirations for the future	7 – 24	22.41 (2.46)	22.68 (2.31)	22.56 (2.38)

Reporting summary results: All planned analyses – including all outcomes and all time points – should be reported, regardless of whether they are statistically significant or not. This includes the number of cases included in the analysis (for each group) as well as whether the analysis is intention to treat or on-treatment.

An intention to treat (ITT) analysis means that all randomised cases are included in the analysis regardless of whether they received the intervention or not, or indeed whether they withdrew from the programme or not. If a trial adopts an ITT approach, even if participants withdraw from the programme, outcome data should still be collected for the duration of the trial. The advantage of this approach is that it allows for generalisability, preserves the sample size and provides a more realistic estimate of the effect, taking into account 'real world' scenarios in which some participants do not comply with the programme or indeed drop out altogether (Gupta, 2011). An on-treatment analysis (also known as a per-protocol analysis) means that cases are analysed according to whether they received the intervention as intended. The advantage of this approach is that it allows the researcher to understand how the programme might work in an ideal world; however, by ignoring the data from participants who did not complete, or withdrew entirely from the programme, we risk over estimating the intervention effect and for only a sub-sample of participants.

The following information should be reported for each outcome: the group mean and standard deviation for intervention and control, the difference between the groups – i.e. the effect size and the confidence intervals associated with this difference – and the number of participants included in the analysis. 'P values' are also commonly reported alongside this, however they should not be reported in isolation – this is discussed in more detail below. Table 6.3 provides an example of how trial results should be summarised.

Table 6.3 Example of reporting main effects using the results from the Time to Read tutoring evaluation (adapted from Miller and Connolly, 2012)

Outcome	Min. & Max.	Intervention (n = 360) Mean (SD)	Control (n = 374) Mean (SD)	Effect Size	Sig.	95% CI
Future Aspirations	10 – 25	22.45 (2.45)	22.63 (2.40)	+0.17	0.03	[0.015, 0.328]
Enjoyment of Learning	9 – 45	33.79 (7.48)	33.83 (6.83)	–0.09	0.14	[–0.215, 0.031]
Self-Esteem	6 – 24	18.57 (4.18)	18.73 (4.27)	–0.04	0.54	[–1.874, 0.098]
Locus of Control	7 – 24	15.14 (2.99)	14.66 (3.25)	–0.05	0.70	[–0.314, 0.211]
Reading Score	81 – 99	91.64 (4.67)	92.51 (4.77)	<–0.01	0.98	[–0.233, 0.229]

Different types of effect size measures: The magnitude of the difference between group means can be expressed using a measure of effect size. There are many different types of effect measures and the one that you choose will depend upon the level of measurement of your outcome variable. In education trials outcomes tend to be measured on a continuous scale; for example, a test or attitude score. For continuous data the absolute difference in means between the control and intervention groups can be used, however it is more helpful to express this value as a *standardised* mean difference (SMD), for example Cohen's d or Hedges' g, so that it can be understood and interpreted in the context of other studies reporting effects from using other scales. The SMD is calculated by taking the difference in means between groups and dividing it by the standard deviation of the sample (Higgins and Green, 2008) thus expressing the mean difference in units of a standard deviation. For dichotomous data you need to use a ratio effect such as an odds ratio or risk ratio. Ratio effects tend to be more commonly reported in medical trials where the outcome is dichotomous; for example, alive or dead, disease recurrence or no recurrence. However, dichotomous outcomes are also used in education trials, for example: achieving five or more A* to C grades at GCSE, or not. Table 6.4 provides a list of the frequently used measures of effect, which are also described in more detail in the next section.

Table 6.4 The most commonly used measures of effect

Level of measurement	Effect measure	Notes
Continuous outcomes	Difference in means	This is the absolute difference in group means.
	Standardised mean difference	Difference in group means divided by the sample standard deviation.
	Cohen's d	As SMD but SD is calculated as the pooled SD of the two groups.
	Hedges' g	As SMD but pooled SD is calculated using a slightly different formula to Cohen's d to incorporate an adjustment to remove bias.
Dichotomous (binary) outcomes	Odds ratio (OR)	Ratio of the odds of an event occurring. A OR of 1 means that there is no difference in odds between the intervention and control groups. An OR of 5 means that the odds of the event occurring in the intervention group are five times greater than the odds of the event occurring in the control group.
		'Risk' is not the same as 'odds' and OR is not equivalent to RR, so be careful when interpreting either of these ratios. Convert OR to RR for easier interpretation.
	Risk ratio (RR)	The relative risk of an event occurring in each of the two groups. Thus a RR of 5 in favour of the intervention group means that the intervention group is five times more likely to experience the event in question compared to the control group.
Ordinal outcomes	Proportional odds ratios	Uncommonly used.
Time-to-event outcomes	Hazard ratio	Also known as survival data.

Interpreting effect sizes: The estimated effect of the intervention, the effect size, should be reported alongside the uncertainty (precision) of the estimate, using confidence intervals – typically at the 95% level. A 95% confidence interval means that we can be 95% confident that our CI includes the population mean. It is typically reported after an effect size in square brackets as we have been doing throughout this book. This level of reporting is a requirement associated with the CONSORT statement but it is also a position endorsed by the APA (American Psychological Association, 2010), whose guidelines clearly state that discussion and interpretation of results should be based on both 'point and interval estimates' (p. 34).

Effect sizes and confidence intervals are important because looking solely at the statistical significance of a result can be misleading – 'p values' imply certainty (importance versus unimportance) whereas the CI surrounding an effect size demonstrates uncertainty – the precision, or lack thereof – in our effect size estimate. If we look at the estimated impact of the Time to Read programme on *aspirations for the future* (Table 6.3) we can see that there is an SMD of 0.17 between the control and intervention groups at post-test, in favour of the intervention group. This difference is statistically significant (p = .03) and the lower and upper 95% confidence limits are 0.015 and 0.328, respectively. So whilst the statistically significant result is important, it is also important to note that the estimated range in which the 'true' effect of the intervention might lie is very wide and thus very imprecise, i.e. the 'true' effect might be anything as small as 0.015 or as large as 0.328. This additional information illustrates that a statistically significant finding can belie a very imprecise estimate of the impact of an intervention.

Point estimates and precision are essential alongside hypothesis significance testing. While an effect size tells us something important about the *magnitude* of the difference between the intervention and control group on the outcome of interest, reporting 'p values' in isolation provides an incomplete picture of the results. It is best practice to report exact 'p values' rather than simply a relative value more or less than α. This approach also provides the reader with more information than simply reporting that p<0.05 or 0.01. Too frequently researchers concentrate on whether an effect is statistically significant or not, rather than on the size of the effect. If we focus simply on whether or not we should reject the null hypothesis then we risk missing the most important part of our findings: an estimation of the magnitude of any effect and its precision. A clearer focus on estimation and precision will mean fewer studies are consigned to the file drawer that might otherwise be classed as 'not statistically significant'. It is with this in mind that we need to be careful about the language we use when reporting our results.

Interpretation of the effect size estimate is a judgement that is to be made by the researcher. It means saying something about the practical significance, rather than the statistical significance of a result, which might be viewed as a more objective judgement. It does mean however that readers can decide for themselves whether or not this judgement is reasonable – the results, such as they are, remain unchanged. Depending on the readership, some effect size measures might need more explanation than others, so it is important to provide a sufficient description of the effect size as well as simply the value.

We should report our results in a way that a lay reader can understand it because *how* results are reported matters in terms of what message readers take away. The impact an intervention can have needs to be easily understood by teachers and others who will incorporate the research into policy or practice, not just researchers. Reporting effect sizes and confidence intervals, ensuring our discussion revolves around these concepts (practical significance) rather than simply p values (statistical significance), will maintain our focus on estimation rather than the falsely dichotomous world of statistically significant (implying important and publishable) or not statistically significant, which (wrongly) implies lack of importance and a higher likelihood of being consigned to the file drawer. Equally important is reporting the results in a language that can be easily understood. For example, to aid the interpretation of effect sizes in reports arising from education trials that they fund, the Education Endowment Foundation (educationendowmentfoundation.org.uk) convert effect sizes into 'months' progress' such that an effect size of 0.02 is equivalent to one month's progress and an effect size of 0.45 is equivalent to about six month's progress (Higgins et al., 2012). Similarly, for the Time to Read trial, we expressed effect sizes as percentiles whereby an effect size of 0.17 was approximately equivalent to moving a child from the 50th percentile to the 58th percentile in the class.

Cohen's reference values in education studies: In education and the social sciences there tends to be much more variation in scores associated with the outcomes that we measure (such as test scores, attitudes or behaviour) than would typically be observed in the biological or medical sciences. This greater level of variation means that we observe larger standard deviations and because of this observed effects are often smaller than those reported in the biological/medical sciences. Thus, in education a Cohen's d effect size in the region of 0.2 can be very meaningful whereby going by Cohen's reference values – which are now more than twenty years old – this would otherwise be classified as small. Ensure that when you are determining the practical significance of an effect size that you look at other similar research so that you can locate your findings within the context of the wider relevant literature. We need to use (and develop if necessary) reference values that are meaningful for our particular area.

Sub-group analyses: It is important to distinguish between planned analyses and exploratory analyses. To avoid any bias that could be attributed to selective reporting, ensure that you report all your pre-specified analyses and clearly state which analyses, if any, are exploratory. As with the main analyses described above, the sub-group analyses should be similarly reported using both point and interval estimates alongside p values.

Discussion

The discussion should start with a summary of the results. It is important that the findings are located within the wider context of existing research (refer to any relevant systematic reviews) and you should be clear about both the theoretical and practical contribution that the study makes to the area. It should faithfully address the shortcomings and limitations of the trial and acknowledge any potential sources of bias that might be influencing the results. The practical implications of the results should also be discussed, bearing in mind the tension between practical and statistical significance. It is easy for researchers' conclusions to go beyond that which is supported by the data, so be circumspect whilst also remembering that many studies are underpowered and thus the risk of making a Type 2 error (accepting the null hypothesis when it is in fact false) is high. We need to keep in mind that 'no evidence of an effect' is *not* the same as 'evidence of no effect'.

External validity and generalisability were referred to frequently in the methodological discussion above and it is here that this argument is pulled together so that it is clear to the reader how generalisable these results actually are. In which contexts, with which populations, can the intervention be implemented and achieve the same effect?

Synthesising evidence from different trials

Being able to gather together RCTs that have evaluated the same type of intervention allows us to combine effect and precision estimates to gain a much clearer view of what the weight of evidence tells us about the effectiveness of that intervention, rather than simply one study. For this reason, replication is important within the social sciences and when these studies are combined facilitates evidence-based decision-making.

Typically, reviews of research literature are based on a narrative description of a convenience sample of studies. There is frequently no clarity regarding why particular studies have been included in the review – or indeed excluded – and the conclusions of the author are frequently made on a 'vote-counting' basis, i.e. how many studies were statistically significant compared to the number that were not.

It is easy to see where bias might creep into this type of review and so a more systematic and methodologically rigorous approach is required if we are to draw reliable, robust conclusions regarding where the weight of evidence actually lies. There are very specific sources of bias that might impact our ability to draw a conclusion we can trust from the research literature. It is unfortunately the case that those studies with positive results are, overall, more likely to be published than studies that report a negative or no effect (*publication bias*). Similarly those same studies with positive results tend to be published faster, cited more frequently and easier to find (*dissemination bias*). We mentioned before about the risks associated with selective outcome reporting of our own results, but it is also a risk for those published studies that report mixed results: it is the statistically significant results that are more widely reported (*outcome reporting bias*) with the non-significant results tending to be largely overlooked. When gathering together studies that might be included in a narrative literature review there is an unsurprising tendency to search for and include studies that support what we already believe (*confirmation bias*), however this potentially omits an entire portion of the literature from our review that might otherwise support an alternative or contrasting position (*selection bias*).

There are a number of organisations (relevant to education) that support, produce and curate systematic reviews including the Cochrane Collaboration (www.cochrane.org), the Campbell Collaboration (www.campbellcollaboration.org) and the EPPI Centre (eppi.ioe.ac.uk). These all have libraries of reviews that they have produced and both are easily and freely searchable. The organisations support review authors and provide considerable expertise, rigour and peer review in relation to conducting systematic reviews, as well as keeping them updated. Similar to the CONSORT statement for reporting RCTs, the PRISMA statement provides guidance related to the transparent and rigorous reporting of systematic reviews (Liberati et al., 2009) and is a good reference point even at the planning stage of your review.

Characteristics of a systematic review

A systematic review (also called a research synthesis) is a particular type of literature review that aims to produce a complete and unbiased report of the weight of evidence in relation to a particular research question (in this case the effectiveness of a programme or intervention). It is considered to be a study in itself where the cases (and unit of analyses) are individual studies rather than individual people. For this reason the same approach, structure and rigour are applied to a systematic review as are applied to primary research. Before starting the review, the review research question needs to be formulated and the methodological and statistical procedures that the review will follow should be published in a protocol that is typically peer reviewed to ensure the planned review meets the highest methodological standards. The publication of the protocol also ensures that the completed review adheres to the proposed methods and analyses and is honestly reported.

Authors of systematic reviews make a concerted effort to search, find and include all relevant research, whether that research is published or not. Thus, clear criteria are essential to determine which studies are eligible for inclusion. These criteria will relate to all aspects of a study, including: the relevance of the area it is investigating (including the type of intervention that is being evaluated); the type of participants that are sampled; the methodological approach taken; the outcomes that have been identified and how they have been measured. This information then informs the search strategy that should be developed in consultation with an expert trial search coordinator so that an explicit, detailed search strategy can be written and the appropriate databases are identified. The Pearl Harvesting Methodological Framework is a method of information retrieval that is gaining in popularity and worth considering if you are thinking about designing a search strategy (Sandieson, 2006; Sandieson et al., 2010). Sources of grey literature – research that is not formally published and includes reports or doctoral theses for example – should also be searched. Reviews aim to include *only* studies that are methodologically rigorous, i.e. studies that will provide the most reliable and valid estimate of the effect (or relationship) in question. Frequently this means that only well-conducted randomised controlled trials are included in reviews although sometimes quasi-experimental studies are included too, especially if there are few RCTs that have been conducted in the area under investigation.

Once potentially eligible studies have been located through the searches, they need to be screened for eligibility, which means that certain information needs to be systematically extracted and coded from each one. It is crucial that the inclusion and exclusion criteria are applied consistently across all studies. To ensure consistency, a special form (sometimes called a data extraction tool) is often used and this is especially helpful to ensure inter-rater reliability, as more than one author should be screening studies. The type of data that should be extracted from included studies will comprise means, standard deviations and sample sizes within each group for each outcome. It is these data that are included in a meta-analysis (as long as there are a sufficient number of studies) to provide a quantitative summary of the cumulated research findings. Meta-analysis is the statistical method that is used to combine data from studies (described in more detail below) and allows us to determine the magnitude of the relationship under investigation. Data relating to the methodological quality of studies are also extracted at the same time to ensure that included studies are robust as well as relevant.

There are criticisms of systematic reviews however. It is sometimes argued that the inclusion criteria (e.g. related to topic, methodology, or outcomes) can be too stringent, which means the review has a very narrow focus that might not be relevant or interesting to everyone. Typically, systematic reviews only include RCTs or quasi-experimental designs. This precludes the inclusion of other types of evidence, such as studies with a qualitative approach, although there are review methods that facilitate the inclusion and synthesis of other types of research (Higgins and Green, 2008). Equally it has been argued that combining several less than perfect studies will not result in a more reliable estimate of the population effect. Finally, a criticism often levelled at quantitative researchers more generally, but which also applies here, is that outcomes are not always linked to theory and it is important that theory development is not neglected in favour of understanding the statistical patterns within the data.

Meta-analysis

The purpose of a meta-analysis is to estimate – across a number of studies – the mean effect of an intervention and to also understand whether and how the effect size reported in these individual studies varies around the mean. A meta-analysis combines the results from all the studies we have identified from the searching and screening processes described above and allows us to distinguish genuine patterns in the data from chance variation. It is the statistics reported in the individual included studies that are used as data in the meta-analysis. There are situations however when a meta-analysis might not be appropriate and these can include circumstances in which there are too few studies, if the study methods and characteristics vary widely so 'like' is not being compared with 'like', or if the studies are not asking the same question, i.e. the hypotheses vary.

The simplest way to combine statistical tests is to use a vote-counting method whereby the results of several studies are combined on the basis of the direction of the relationship and whether or not it is statistically significant, e.g. significant positive findings, significant negative findings, non-significant findings. However, this method is very imprecise and provides no information relating to the magnitude of the effect or the strength of the relationship under investigation. For this reason, more sophisticated methods, e.g. meta-analysis are described below.

Variation between study results

There are two main reasons why studies with the same hypothesis might generate different findings. The first of these is sampling variability whereby sample means vary from the population mean purely by chance fluctuations. The second of these is study variability, i.e. studies are conducted differently and this variation is in addition to the sampling variability. There are statistical tests that can help determine whether or not the variance between studies is too large to be explained by sampling error alone (described in more detail below).

Data preparation

Before combining the data from several studies into a meta-analysis it is necessary to check that a number of assumptions are met. Firstly, the results that are used in a meta-analysis must all test the same comparison/relationship. Secondly, the individual tests that go into the analysis must be independent of each other, and finally you should be confident that the primary researchers made valid assumptions when they conducted their tests, e.g. samples are independent, normally distributed and of equal variance. It is often the case that evaluations do not report an effect size and it is necessary to use whatever statistical information is available in the report to calculate an effect size yourself. Below are a number of ways to do this. As noted earlier in this chapter, we are not only interested in whether there is a difference between the intervention and control groups, we also want to know the size of the difference (if any) and an effect size provides this information. Two common effect sizes that are used to describe the impact of trials in education include the standardised mean difference (for continuous data) and the odds ratio (for dichotomous data).

Standardised mean difference: An SMD is used if the outcome variable is continuous and represents a common metric that can be used to compare effects across different trials despite different outcome measures being used between studies. It is also referred to as a d index, with Cohen's d and Hedges' g belonging to this family of effect sizes. It is calculated using Equation 1 (or a variation of it in the case of Hedges' g) where X_1 is the mean score for the intervention group and X_2 is the mean score for the control group:

$$d = \frac{X_1 - X_2}{\text{pooled standard deviation}} \qquad \text{Equation 1.}$$

The SMD can be computed for individual studies if authors report the means and standard deviations for both intervention and control groups, however sometimes not all the necessary information is reported. Conveniently, effect sizes (d) can be calculated from a t-test or F-test using Equation 2:

$$d = \frac{2t}{\sqrt{df_{error}}} \qquad \text{Equation 2.}$$

Where 't' is the value of the t-test for the associated comparison and df_{error} represents the degrees of freedom associated with the error term of the t-test (i.e. n_1+n_2-2). If you have the results of an F-test instead, 't' can be calculated by taking the square root of 'F' ($t = \sqrt{F}$). Of course, you will need to know the direction of the mean difference in order to know whether the effect is favouring the intervention or control group.

By calculating the variance of the SMD (V_d) you can compute the 95% confidence intervals of the SMD using Equations 3 and 4:

$$V_d = \frac{n_1 + n_2}{n_1 n_2} + \frac{d^2}{2(n_1 + n_2)} \qquad \text{Equation 3.}$$

Taking the square root of the variance calculated above ($\sqrt{V_d}$) gives you the standard error and it is possible to calculate 95% confidence limits using Equations 4a and 4b:

Lower bound 95% CI value = $d - 1.96 (\sqrt{V_d})$ \qquad Equation 4a.

Upper bound 95% CI value = $d + 1.96 (\sqrt{V_d})$ \qquad Equation 4b.

Ratio effects: A ratio effect is an appropriate measure of effect when your outcome variable is dichotomous. Risk is the probability that an event will occur and so, taking the example depicted in Table 6.5, the risk of experiencing reading problems in the intervention group is 0.2, i.e. for every 10 children who receive the intervention, 2 will have reading problems. In the control group the risk is 0.4, i.e. for every 10 children who do not receive the intervention, 4 will have reading problems. The risk ratio (RR) is calculated using Equation 5:

$$RR = \frac{\text{Risk of the event occurring in group 1}}{\text{Risk of event occurring in group 2}}$$ Equation 5.

Table 6.5 Hypothetical data relating to the incidence of reading problems after an intervention has been delivered

	Intervention	Control
Reading problems	20	40
No reading problems	80	60

If we calculate the RR for our current example (0.4/0.2 = 2) we can see that children in the control group are twice as likely to have reading problems compared to the intervention group.

Odds are slightly different and a little more difficult to understand. As described in Chapter 5, odds are the ratio of the probability that an event will occur to the probability that the event will not occur. In the current example, the odds of having a reading problem in the control group are 40/60 (or 0.67) and the odds of having reading problems in the intervention group are calculated as 20/80 (or 0.25), i.e. for every 2 children that do have reading problems, 8 will not. The odds ratio (OR) therefore is = 2.68 i.e. 40/60 divided by 20/80. This means that the odds of having reading problems if you do not receive the intervention are over two-and-a-half times higher than the odds of experiencing reading problems if you do receive the intervention.

Interpreting an odds ratio of less than 1 is not very intuitive and to aid interpretability should be avoided if at all possible. You can do this by calculating the multiplicative inverse of the odds ratio, i.e. 1/OR and relating it to the other group. So in this example an OR of 2.68 in favour of the control group is equivalent to an OR of 0.37 in favour of the intervention group. You'll perhaps agree that understanding the impact of the programme in terms of the control group having odds of reading problems over 2.5 times as high as the intervention group is easier than being told that the intervention group is 63% less likely (OR = 0.37) then the control group to experience reading problems.

Combining effect sizes across studies

Once the effect sizes have been extracted (or calculated) from the individual RCTs included in your review, they are then weighted by sample

168   Using randomised controlled trials in education

size, with greater weight being given to larger studies as these are more likely to provide a more precise estimate of the effect size within the population. There is software freely available that is invaluable in terms of organising, writing and managing your review as well as conducting the meta-analysis for you (you need to input the means and SDs for each group extracted from your included studies) such as RevMan, which is produced and maintained by Cochrane (http://tech.cochrane.org/revman). It is also possible to use statistical packages such as Stata and R for meta-analysis; however, the advantage of RevMan is that it has been designed with the sole purpose of conducting a systematic review and has everything that you need in one place. Other software packages are available that will help you screen citations, collate papers and extract data, for example Covidence, EPPI-Reviewer, Distiller or Abstrackr (to name a few).

Figure 6.2 provides the typical output from a meta-analysis produced by RevMan. It reports the identifier for each RCT that was included, the mean and SD for the intervention and control groups (which you as the reviewer manually input after extracting these data from the individual evaluations). It also reports the total number of participants in each group and calculates the weighting variable, effect size and the 95% confidence intervals. A graph, called a forest plot, is produced which depicts the effect size, direction and margin of error (95% CI) for each study. The combined effect size and associated 95% CI is calculated (ES = 0.30 [−0.18, 0.78]) and represented by the large black diamond. If any part of the diamond crosses the vertical zero line then this means that the overall effect is not statistically significant.

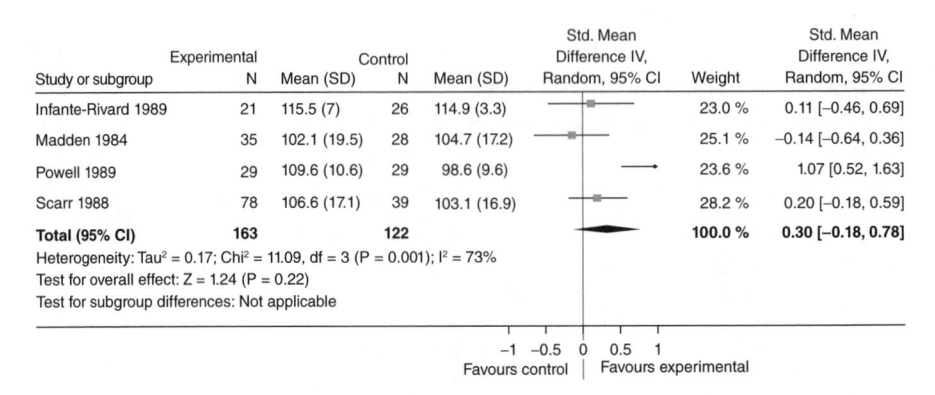

Study or subgroup	Experimental N	Mean (SD)	Control N	Mean (SD)	Std. Mean Difference IV, Random, 95% CI	Weight	Std. Mean Difference IV, Random, 95% CI
Infante-Rivard 1989	21	115.5 (7)	26	114.9 (3.3)		23.0 %	0.11 [−0.46, 0.69]
Madden 1984	35	102.1 (19.5)	28	104.7 (17.2)		25.1 %	−0.14 [−0.64, 0.36]
Powell 1989	29	109.6 (10.6)	29	98.6 (9.6)		23.6 %	1.07 [0.52, 1.63]
Scarr 1988	78	106.6 (17.1)	39	103.1 (16.9)		28.2 %	0.20 [−0.18, 0.59]
Total (95% CI)	**163**		**122**			**100.0 %**	**0.30 [−0.18, 0.78]**

Heterogeneity: Tau² = 0.17; Chi² = 11.09, df = 3 (P = 0.001); I² = 73%
Test for overall effect: Z = 1.24 (P = 0.22)
Test for subgroup differences: Not applicable

−1   −0.5   0   0.5   1
Favours control | Favours experimental

Figure 6.2 Home-based child development interventions for preschool children from socially disadvantaged families (Miller et al., 2011)

Models of error

A fixed effect model of error assumes that all the studies in the meta-analysis share a common effect size and so the observed effect size only varies between studies because of sampling (random) error. This means that if each study had an infinite sample, the sampling error would be zero and the observed effect would be the same as the true effect. In practice the sample size is not infinite and so the sampling error is present. In a fixed effect model all observed variance reflects sampling error.

In a random effects model, we acknowledge that there are likely to be systematic differences between studies that will result in additional variance between effect sizes. Consequently, the observed effect is made up of two distinct elements: true variation in effect sizes in addition to sampling error. Thus, the summary effect produced by your meta-analysis represents an estimate of the mean of all true effects (which make up a distribution of true effects). It is uncommon in education trials to use a fixed effect model of error because in reality study characteristics do tend to differ, especially in relation to the populations sampled and the tools used to measure outcomes.

Variance in effect sizes

Alongside finding out the mean effect of an intervention, understanding how much effect sizes vary around this mean, i.e. the range of effects, is an important goal of meta-analysis. A homogeneity analysis calculates the probability that the variance in effect sizes between studies is due to sampling variance alone and is only relevant in a random effects model. If there is an indication that the variance between studies is not solely down to sampling error then it is helpful to look for study characteristics that are systematically associated with the effect size. There are two statistics, which are useful in terms of deciding whether or not the variation between studies is due to more than simply sampling error.

Tau^2 is an estimate of the variance of the true effect sizes. If it is not statistically significant then this indicates that the variation between study effect sizes is likely to be due only to sampling error. Similarly, I^2 is a measure of inconsistency between studies and describes approximately the proportion of variation in point estimates due to heterogeneity rather than sampling error:

170 Using randomised controlled trials in education

- 0% to 40% indicates that only a small amount of the observed variation is due to true heterogeneity.
- 30% to 60% may indicate moderate heterogeneity.
- 50% to 90% may indicate substantial heterogeneity.
- 75% to 100% may indicate considerable heterogeneity.

It is important to note that I^2 is not an absolute measure of heterogeneity, instead it refers to the proportion of observed (effect size) variance that is due to variance in true effect size rather than sampling error. Neither Tau^2 nor I^2 capture the range of effects observed and this is important, relevant information that should be reported alongside these statistics.

Funnel plots

Funnel plots help to determine whether there is publication bias. For each study in the review it plots the estimated effect size and each study's size (or precision, denoted below by the standard error on the vertical axis). Larger studies will provide a more precise estimate and so have a smaller standard error – for this reason these studies will cluster together towards the top of the plot. As the studies become smaller and less precise (denoted by a higher standard error), there will be greater variation between estimated effects and these studies will be more broadly distributed around the bottom of the graph. If there is no publication bias

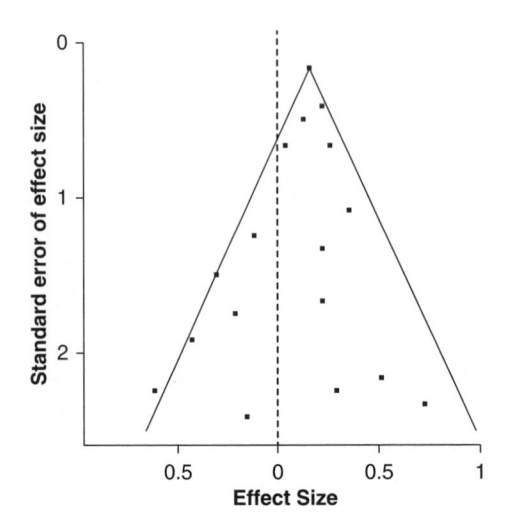

Figure 6.3 Hypothetical example of a funnel plot suggesting no evidence of publication bias

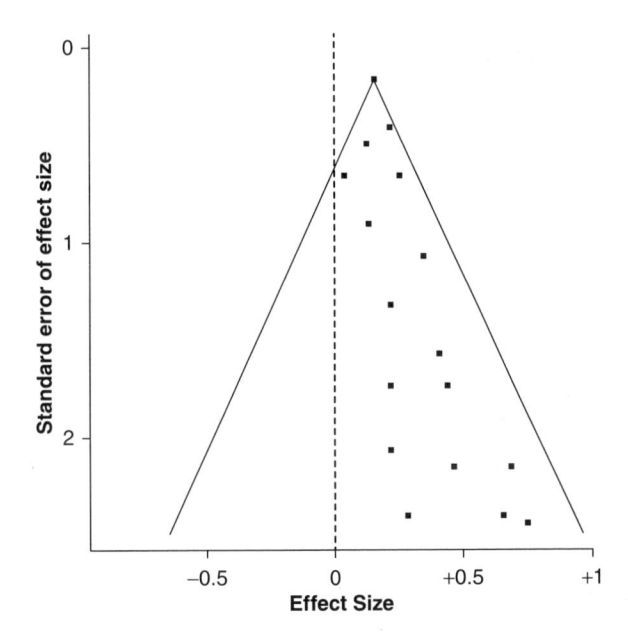

Figure 6.4 Hypothetical example of a funnel plot that suggests publication bias

(see Figure 6.3) then the graph should represent an inverted funnel and be approximately triangular in shape.

It can be seen from Figure 6.4 that the funnel shape is not present and there appear to be studies missing from the left-hand side of the inverted funnel, i.e. those studies that have reported negative findings are missing. This strongly suggests that publication bias is an issue and only the positive trials have been published and included in the review.

Conclusions

The purpose of this chapter has been to highlight the importance of clear, honest reporting of trials and to provide a clear framework for how this can be achieved. This is imperative in its own right. However, it becomes even more so when we attempt to combine studies into a research synthesis and so rely on trialists providing the required information not only in relation to the results but also with respect to the methodological rigour of their study. As guidelines like CONSORT and PRISMA continue to be used by authors and adopted by journals, the quality and standard of reporting of trials in education can only continue to improve.

Further Reading

Reporting RCTs
CONSORT (Consolidated Standards of Report Trials): www.consort-statement.org

Meta-Analysis
Introduction to Meta-Analysis, by M. Borenstein, L.V. Hedges, J.P.T. Higgins and H.R. Rothstein (Wiley, 2011).

Research Synthesis and Meta-Analysis: A Step by Step Approach (Applied Social Research Methods), 5th edn, by H.M. Cooper (Sage, 2010).

The Handbook of Research Synthesis and Meta-Analysis, by H.M. Cooper, L.V. Hedges and J.C. Valentine (Russell Sage Foundation, 2008).

The Cochrane Handbook for Systematic Reviews of Interventions, by J.P.T. Higgins and S. Green (Wiley, 2008).

References

Achenbach, T.M., Becker, A., Dopfner, M., Heiervang, E., Roessner, V., Steinhausen, H. and Rothenberger, A. (2008) 'Multicultural assessment of child and adolescent psychopathology with ASEBA and SDQ instruments: Research findings, applications, and future directions', *Journal of Child Psychology and Psychiatry*, 49: 251–75.

Ajzen, I. (2011) Theory of planned behavior. *Handbook of Theories of Social Psychology Vol One*. London: Sage. p. 438.

Alexander, J.F. and Parsons, B.V. (1973) 'Short term behavior interventions with delinquent families: Impact on family process and recidivism', *Journal of Abnormal Psychology*, 81: 219–25.

Alexander, J.F., Pugh, C., Parsons, B. and Sexton, T.L. (2000) 'Functional family therapy', in D. Elliott (series ed.), *Book Three: Blueprints for violence prevention* (2nd edn). Golden, CO: Venture.

American Educational Research Association (2000) *Ethical Standards of the American Educational Research Association*. Washington, DC: American Educational Research Association.

American Psychological Association (2010) *Publication Manual of the American Psychological Association* (6th edn). Washington, DC: APA.

Ball, S. (1995) 'Intellectuals or technicians? The urgent role of theory in educational studies', *British Journal of Educational Studies*, 43 (3): 255–71.

Biggart, A., Kerr, K., O'Hare, L. and Connolly, P. (2013) 'A randomised control trial evaluation of a literacy after-school programme for struggling beginning readers', *International Journal of Educational Research*, 62: 129–40.

Bonnell C., Fletcher, A., Morton, M., Lorenc, T. and Moore, L. (2012) 'Realist randomised controlled trials: A new approach to evaluating complex public health interventions', *Social Science & Medicine*, 75 (12): 2299–306.

Briggs, D.C. (2008) 'Synthesizing causal inferences', *Educational Researcher*, 37 (1): 15–22.

British Educational Research Association (2000) *Ethical Guidelines*. Available at: www.scutrea.ac.uk/library/beraethguide.pdf [accessed 3 March 2017].

Bronfenbrenner, U. (2009) *The Ecology of Human Development: Experiments by nature and design*. Cambridge, MA: Harvard University Press.

Campbell, D.T. and Stanley, J.C. (1963) *Experimental and Quasi-Experimental Designs for Research*. Boston, MA: Houghton Mifflin Company.

Campbell, M.J. (2004) 'Extending CONSORT to include cluster trials', *British Medical Journal*, 328: 654–5.

Campbell, M.K., Elbourne D.R. and Altman, D.G. (2004) 'CONSORT statement: Extension to cluster randomized trials', *British Medical Journal*, 328: 702–8.

Campbell, M.K. and Grimshaw, J.M. (1998) 'Cluster randomized trials: Time for improvement', *British Medical Journal*, 317: 1171–2.

Cartwright, N. and Hardie, J. (2012) *Evidence-Based Policy: A practical guide to doing it better*. New York: Oxford University Press.

Chaiklin, S. (2003) 'The zone of proximal development in Vygotsky's analysis of learning and instruction', *Vygotsky's Educational Theory in Cultural Context*, 1: 39–64.

Child Welfare Information Gateway (2016) *Evaluation Toolkit and Logic Model Builder*. Available at: www.childwelfare.gov/preventing/evaluating/toolkit.cfm [accessed 3 March 2017].

Cockerill, M. and Thurston, A. (2015) 'Improving fidelity to treatment during randomized controlled trials in schools by engaging teachers in the design process during a development study', in R.M. Gillies (ed.), *Collaborative Learning: Developments in research and practice*. New York: Nova Science Publishers, Inc.

Cohen, L., Manion, L. and Morrison, K. (2011) *Research Methods in Education* (7th edn). London: Routledge.

Cohen, P.A., Kulik, J.A. and Kulik, C.C. (1982) 'Educational outcomes of tutoring: A meta-analysis of findings', *American Educational Research Journal*, 19: 237–48.

Connolly, P. (2011) 'Review of "Engaging science policy: From the side of the messy" by Patti Lather', *British Journal of Sociology of Education*, 32 (3): 471–7.

Connolly, P., Miller, S. and Eakin, A. (2010) *A Cluster Randomised Trial Evaluation of the Media Initiative for Children: Respecting difference programme*. Belfast: Centre for Effective Education, Queen's University Belfast. Available at: www.paulconnolly.net/publications/mifc_fullreport_2010.pdf [accessed 3 March 2017].

Connolly, P., Sibbett, C., Hanratty, J., Kerr, K., O'Hare, L. and Winter, K. (2011) *Pupils' Emotional Health and Wellbeing: A review of audit tools and a survey of practice in Northern Ireland post-primary schools*. Belfast: Centre for Effective Education.

Cronbach, L.J. and Meehl, P.E. (1955) 'Construct validity in psychological tests', *Psychological Bulletin*, 52 (4): 281.

Davies, B. (2003) 'Death to critique and dissent: The policies and practices of new managerialism and of "evidence-based practice"', *Gender and Education*, 15 (1): 91–103.

Dillenbourg, P. (1999) 'What do you mean by collaborative learning?', in P. Dillenbourg (ed.), *Collaborative-learning: Cognitive and computational approaches,* pp. 111–19. Oxford: Elsevier.

Dunn, W.N. (ed.) (1998) *The Experimenting Society: Essays in honor of Donald T. Campbell.* New Brunswick, NJ: Transaction Publishers.

Dunne, L., Thurston, A., Kee, F., Lazenbat, A. and Gildea, A. (2016) 'Research Protocol: A randomized controlled trial of Dead Cool: A partnership between Cancer Focus NI and Queen's University Belfast', *International Journal of Educational Research,* 75: 24–30.

Durlak, J.A., Weissberg, R.P., Dymnicki, A.B., Taylor, R.D. and Schellinger, K.B. (2011) 'The impact of enhancing students' social and emotional learning: A meta-analysis of school-based universal interventions', *Child Development,* 82 (1): 405–32.

EEF (Education Endowment Foundation) (2016) *Annual Report 2015/16.* London: EEF. Available at: http://educationendowmentfoundation.org.uk/public/files/Annual_Reports/EEF_Annual_Report_2015-16_-_print_version.pdf [accessed 3 March 2017].

Eldridge, S., Ashby, D., Bennet, C., Wakelin, M. and Feder, G. (2008) 'Internal and external validity of cluster randomized trials: Systematic review of recent trials', *British Medical Journal,* 336: 876–80.

Elliott, J. (2004) 'Making evidence-based practice educational', in G. Thomas and R. Pring (eds), *Evidence-based Practice in Education.* Maidenhead: Open University Press.

ETS (2016) *Test Collection at ETS.* Available at: www.ets.org/test_link/about [accessed 3 March 2017].

Farrington, D.P. and Welsh, B.C. (2003) 'Family-based prevention of offending: A meta-analysis', *Australian & New Zealand Journal of Criminology,* 36 (2): 127–51.

Finckenauer, J.O. (1982) *Scared Straight and the Panacea Phenomenon.* Englewood Cliffs, NJ: Prentice-Hall.

Fitz-Gibbon, C.T. (1996) *Monitoring Education: Indicators, quality and effectiveness.* London: Cassell.

Fixsen, D.L., Blase, K.A., Naoom, S.F. and Wallace, F. (2009) 'Core implementation components', *Research on Social Work Practice,* 19 (5): 531–40.

Funnell, S.C. and Rogers, P.J. (2011) *Purposeful Program Theory: Effective use of theories of change and logic models, vol. 31.* New Jersey: John Wiley & Sons.

Gearing, R.E., El-Bassel, N., Ghesquiere, A., Baldwin, S., Gillies, J. and Ngeow, E. (2011) 'Major ingredients of fidelity: A review and scientific guide to improving quality of intervention research implementation', *Clinical Psychology Review,* 31 (1): 79–88.

Gifford, B.K. (2010) '"School reform is like cleaning out your garage": A case study of one school district's influence on student achievement', *Dissertation Abstracts International: Section A. Humanities and Social Sciences,* 70 (11): 4133.

GL Assessment (2016) *The New Group Reading Test.* Available at: www.gl-assessment.co.uk/products/new-group-reading-test [accessed 3 March 2017].

Goldacre, B. (2013) *Building Evidence into Education*. Paper available at: http://media.education.gov.uk/assets/files/pdf/b/ben%20goldacre%20paper.pdf [accessed 3 March 2017].

Gorard, S. (2013) 'The propagation of errors in experimental data analysis: a comparison of pre- and post-test designs', *International Journal of Research and Method in Education*, 36 (4): 372–84.

Gordon, D.A., Graves, K. and Arbuthnot, J. (1995) 'The effect of Functional Family Therapy for delinquents on adult criminal behavior', *Criminal Justice and Behavior*, 22 (1): 60–73.

Gortmaker, S. L., Peterson, K., Wiecha, J., Sobol, A.M., Dixit, S., Fox, M.K. and Laird, N. (1999) 'Reducing obesity via a school-based interdisciplinary intervention among youth: Planet Health', *Archives of Pediatrics & Adolescent Medicine*, 153 (4): 409–18.

Gottfried, M.A. and Williams, D. (2013) 'STEM club participation and STEM schooling outcomes', *Education Policy Analysis Archives*, 21: 79.

Gruzelier, J.H., Foks, M., Steffert, T., Chen, M.L. and Ros, T. (2014) 'Beneficial outcome from EEG-neurofeedback on creative music performance, attention and well-being in school children', *Biological Psychology*, 95: 86–95.

Gupta, S.K. (2011) 'Intention-to-treat concept: A review', *Perspectives in Clinical Research*, 2 (3): 109–12.

Hammersley, M. (2004) 'Some questions about evidence-based practice in education', in G. Thomas and R. Pring (eds), *Evidence-based Practice in Education*. Maidenhead: Open University Press.

Hammersley, M. (2008) 'Paradigm war revived? On the diagnosis of resistance to randomized controlled trials and systematic review in education', *International Journal of Research and Method in Education*, 31 (1): 310.

Hargreaves, D.H. (1996) 'Teaching as a Research-based Profession: Possibilities and prospects'. Teacher Training Agency Annual Lecture 1996.

Higgins, J.P.T. and Green, S. (2008) *The Cochrane Handbook for Systematic Reviews of Interventions*. Chichester: Wiley.

Higgins, S., Katsipataki, M., Kokotsaki, D., Coleman, R., Major, L.E. and Coe, R. (2014) *The Sutton Trust-Education Endowment Foundation Teaching and Learning Toolkit*. London: Education Endowment Foundation.

Higgins, S., Kokotsaki, D. and Coe, R. (2012) *The Teaching and Learning Toolkit Technical Appendices*. London: Educational Endowment Foundation.

Hodder Education (2016) *Hodder Education: Learn More*. Available at: www.hoddereducation.co.uk/ [accessed 3 March 2017].

Hodkinson, P. and Smith, J. (2004) 'The relationship between research, policy and practice', in G. Thomas and R. Pring (eds), *Evidence-based Practice in Education*. Maidenhead: Open University Press.

Holland, P.W. (1986) 'Statistics and causal inference', *Journal of the American Statistical Association*, 81 (396): 945–60.

Insight Assessment (2016) *California Critical Thinking Skills Test (CCTST)*. Available at: www.insightassessment.com/Products/Products-Summary/Critical-Thinking-Skills-Tests/California-Critical-Thinking-Skills-Test-CCTST [accessed 3 March 2017].

Institute of Education Services (2006) *What Works Clearing House Study Design Classification*. Available at: http://ies.ed.gov/ncee/wwc/pdf/ studydesignclass.pdf [accessed 16 May 2008].

Johnson, D.W. and Johnson, R.T. (2012) 'Restorative justice in the classroom: Necessary roles of cooperative context, constructive conflict, and civic value', *Negotiation and Conflict Management Research*, 5 (1): 4–28.

Johnson, D.W., Johnson, R.T. and Roseth, C. (2010) 'Cooperative learning in middle schools: interrelationship of relationships and achievement', *Middle Grades Research Journal*, 5 (1): 1–18.

Jones, C.H. (2013) Evaluation of the Incredible Years Parent and Babies Programme in Wales. Doctoral dissertation. Bangor University.

Kaplan, S.A. and Garrett, K.E. (2005) 'The use of logic models by community-based initiatives', *Evaluation and Program Planning*, 28 (2): 167–72.

Kellogg, W.K. (2004) *Logic Model Development Guide*. Michigan: WK Kellogg Foundation.

Kuhn, T. (1962) *The Structure of Scientific Revolutions*. Chicago, IL: University of Chicago Press.

Lachin, J.M., Matts, J.P. and Wei, L.J. (1988) 'Randomization in clinical trials: Conclusions and recommendations', *Control Clinical Trials*, 9 (4): 365–74.

Lancaster, G.A., Dodd S.R. and Williamson, P.R. (2004) 'Design and analysis of pilot studies: recommendations for good practice', *Journal of Evaluation in Clinical Practice*, 10 (2): 307–12.

Lather, P. (2010) *Engaging Science Policy: From the side of the messy*. New York: Peter Lang.

Liberati, A., Altman, D.G., Tetzlaff, J., Mulrow, C., Gøtzsche, P.C., Ioannidis, J.P.A., Clarke, M., Devereaux, P.J., Kleijnen, J. and Moher, D. (2009) 'The PRISMA statement for reporting systematic reviews and meta-analyses of studies that evaluate healthcare interventions: Explanation and elaboration', *British Medical Journal*, 339: b2700.

Maas, C.J. and Hox, J.J. (2005) 'Sufficient sample sizes for multilevel modelling', *Methodology*, 1 (3): 86–92.

Magolda, P. and Ebben, K. (2007) 'From schools to community learning centers: A program evaluation of a school reform process', *Evaluation and Program Planning*, 30: 351–63.

Mayer, J.D. and Salovey, P. (1997) 'What is emotional intelligence?', in P. Salovey and D.J. Sluyter (eds), *Emotional Development and Emotional Intelligence: Educational implications*. New York: Harper Collins.

McGilloway, S., Bywater, T., Ni Mhaille, G., Furlong, M., O'Neill, D., Comiskey, C., Leckey, Y., Kelly, P. and Donnelly, M. (2009) *Proving the Power of Positive Parenting: A randomised controlled trial to investigate the effectiveness of the Incredible Years BASIC Parenting program in an Irish context (short-term outcomes)*. Dublin: Archways. Available at: http://iyirelandstudy.ie [accessed 3 March 2017].

Miller, S. and Connolly, P. (2012) 'A randomized controlled trial evaluation of time to read, a volunteer tutoring program for 8 to 9 year olds', *Educational Evaluation and Policy Analysis*, 35 (1): 23–37.

Miller, S., Maguire, L.K. and Macdonald, G. (2011) 'Home-based child development interventions for preschool children from socially disadvantaged families', *Cochrane Database of Systematic Reviews*, 12: 1–49.

Montgomery, P., Grant, S., Hopewell, S., Macdonald, G., Moher, D., Michie, S. and Mayo-Wilson, E. (2013) 'Protocol for CONSORT-SPI: An extension for social and psychological interventions', *Implementation Science*, 8: 99–106.

Muijs, D. and Harris, A. (2006) 'Teacher led school improvement: Teacher leadership in the UK', *Teaching and Teacher Education*, 22: 961–72.

Oakley, A. (2000) *Experiments in Knowing*. Cambridge: Polity Press.

Oakley, A. (2006) 'Resistance to 'new' technologies of evaluation: Education research in the UK as a case study', *Evidence and Policy*, 2 (1): 63–87.

Oancea, A. and Pring, R. (2009) 'The importance of being thorough: On systematic accumulations of "what works" in education research', in D. Bridges, P. Smeyers and R. Smith (eds), *Evidence-based Education Policy: What evidence? What basis? Whose policy?* Oxford: Wiley-Blackwell.

O'Hare, L., Biggart, A., Kerr, K. and Connolly, P. (2015) 'A randomized controlled trial evaluation of an after-school prosocial behavior program in an area of socioeconomic disadvantage', *The Elementary School Journal*, 116 (1): 1–29.

O'Hare, L. and Connolly, P. (2014) 'A cluster randomised controlled trial of "Bookstart+": a book gifting programme', *Journal of Children's Services*, 9 (1): 18–30.

O'Hare, L. and McGuinness, C. (2015) 'The validity of critical thinking tests for predicting degree performance: A longitudinal study', *International Journal of Educational Research*, 72: 162–72.

O'Hare, L., Santin, O., Winter, K. and McGuinness, C. (2016) 'The reliability and validity of a child and adolescent participation in decision-making questionnaire', *Child: Care, Health and Development*, 42 (5): 692–8.

Oreopoulos, P. and Petronijevic, U. (2013) *Making College Worth it: A review of research on the returns to higher education* (No. w19053). Cambridge, MA: National Bureau of Economic Research.

Paint Stewardship Program (2016) *Oregon Paint Stewardship Pilot Program*. Available at: http://paintstewardshipprogram.com/ [accessed 3 March 2017]

Pawson, R. (2006) *Evidence-based Policy: A realist perspective*. London: Sage.

Pawson, R. and Tilley, N. (1997) *Realistic Evaluation*. London: Sage.

Petrosino, A., Turpin-Petrosino, C., Hollis-Peel, M.E. and Lavenberg, J.G. (2013) *Scared Straight and Other Juvenile Awareness Programs for Preventing Juvenile Delinquency: A systematic review*. Campbell Systematic Reviews 2013:5. DOI: 10/4073/csr.2013.5.

Pring, R. (2004) 'Conclusion: Evidence-based policy and practice', in G. Thomas and R. Pring (eds), *Evidence-based Practice in Education*. Maidenhead: Open University Press.

Pring, R. (2015) *Philosophy of Educational Research* (3rd edn). London: Bloomsbury.

Puffer, S., Torgerson, D.J. and Watson, J. (2003) 'Evidence for risk of bias in cluster randomized trials: Review of recent trials published in three general medical journals', *British Medical Journal*, 327: 785–9.

Raffe, D. and Spours, K. (2007) 'Three models of policy learning and policy-making in 14–19 education', in D. Raffe and K. Spours (eds), *Policy-making and Policy Learning in 14–19 Education*. Institute of Education, University of London.

Raudenbush, S.W., et al. (2011) Optimal Design Software for Multi-level and Longitudinal Research (Version 3.01) [Software]. Available at: www.wtgrant foundation.org [accessed 3 March 2017]

Ravitz, J. (2010) 'Beyond changing culture in small high schools: Reform models and changing instruction with project-based learning', *Peabody Journal of Education*, 85: 290–312.

Reezigt, G.J. and Creemers, B.P.M. (2005) 'A comprehensive framework for effective school improvement', *School Effectiveness and School Improvement*, 16: 407–24.

Rubin, R.S. (2002) 'Will the real SMART goals please stand up', *The Industrial-Organizational Psychologist*, 39 (4): 26–7.

Rumsey, D.J. (2016) *Statistics for Dummies*. New Jersey: Wiley.

Rutter, M. and Maughan, B. (2002) 'School effectiveness findings 1979–2002', *Journal of School Psychology*, 40 (6): 451–75.

Sandieson, R. (2006) 'Pathfinding in the research forest: The Pearl Harvesting method for effective information retrieval', *Education and Training in Developmental Disabilities*, 41 (4): 401–9.

Sandieson, R.W., Kirkpatrick, L.C., Sandieson, R.M. and Zimmerman, W. (2010) 'Harnessing the power of research databases: The Pearl Harvesting methodological framework for information retrieval', *Journal of Special Education*, 44: 161–75.

Sayer, A. (2000) *Realism and Social Science*. London: Sage.

Schonert-Reichl, K.A., Oberle, E., Lawlor, M.S., Abbott, D., Thomson, K., Oberlander, T.F. and Diamond, A. (2015) 'Enhancing cognitive and social–emotional development through a simple-to-administer mindfulness-based school program for elementary school children: A randomized controlled trial', *Developmental Psychology*, 51 (1): 52.

Sexton, T.L. and Alexander, J.F. (2002) Family-Based Empirically Supported Interventions. *The Counseling Psychologist*, 30: 238–61.

Sexton, T.L. and Turner, C.T. (2010) 'The effectiveness of functional family therapy for youth with behavioral problems in a community practice setting', *Journal of Family Psychology*, 24 (3): 339–48.

Shadish, W.R., Cook, T.D. and Campbell, D.T. (2002) *Experimental and Quasi-Experimental Designs for Generalized Causal Inference*. Boston, MA: Houghton Mifflin.

Slavin, R.E. (2008a) 'Perspectives on evidenced-based research in education', *Educational Researcher*, 37 (1): 5–14.

Slavin, R.E. (2008b) 'Response to comments – Evidence-based reforms in education: Which evidence counts?', *Educational Researcher*, 37 (1): 47–50.

Slavin, R.E. and Madden, N. (2008) *Success For All: Research and reform in elementary education*. London: Routledge.

Stone, L.L., Janssens, J.M., Vermulst, A.A., Van Der Maten, M., Engels, R.C. and Otten, R. (2015) 'The strengths and difficulties questionnaire: Psychometric properties of the parent and teacher version in children aged 4–7', *BMC Psychology*, 3 (1): 1.

Storch, S. A. and Whitehurst, G. J. (2002) 'Oral language and code-related precursors to reading: Evidence from a longitudinal structural model', *Developmental Psychology*, 38 (6): 934.

Taylor-Powell, E. and Henert, E. (2008) 'Developing a logic model: Teaching and training guide', *Benefits*, 3: 22.

Thurston, A., Christie, D., Howe, C.J., Tolmie, A. and Topping, K.J. (2008) 'Effects of continuing professional development on group work practices in Scottish primary schools', *Journal of In-Service Education*, 34 (3): 263–82.

Thurston, A., Dunne, L., Miller, S., Gildea, A., Stepien, D. and Tapsell, D. (2015) 'Research protocol: A randomized controlled trial of functional family therapy: An Early Intervention Foundation (EIF) partnership between Croydon Council and Queen's University Belfast', *International Journal of Educational Research*, 70: 47–56. doi: 10.1016/j.ijer.2015.01.001

Torgerson, C.J. and Torgerson, D.J. (2001) 'The need for randomised controlled trials in educational research', *British Journal of Educational Studies*, 49 (3): 316–29.

Torgerson, C.J., Torgerson, D.J., Birks, Y.F. and Porterhouse, J. (2005) 'A comparison of randomised controlled trials in health and education', *British Educational Research Journal*, 31 (6): 761–85.

Torgerson, D.J. and Torgerson, C.J. (2008) *Designing Randomised Trials in Health Education and the Social Sciences*. Basingstoke: Palgrave McMillan.

Trochim, W. (2012) *Design, The Research Method Knowledge Base*. Available at: www.socialresearchmethods.net/kb/design.php [accessed 3 March 2017].

Twist, L., Sizmur, J., Bartlett, S. and Lynn, L. (2012) *PIRLS 2011: Reading achievement in England*. Slough: NFER.

Tymms, P.B., Merrell, C. and Coe, R.J. (2008) 'Educational policies and randomized controlled trials', *The Psychology of Education Review*, 32 (2): 3–7.

Tymms, P.B., Merrell, C., Thurston, A., Andor, J., Topping, K. and Miller, D. (2011) 'Improving attainment across a whole district: school reform through peer tutoring in a randomized controlled trial', *School Effectiveness and School Improvement*, 22 (3): 265–89.

Vallabhajosula, S., Holder, J.B. and Bailey, E.K. (2016) 'Effect of exergaming on physiological response and enjoyment during recess in elementary school-aged children: A pilot study', *Games for Health Journal*, 5 (5): 325–32.

Wardle, J., Guthrie, C.A., Sanderson, S. and Rapoport, L. (2001) 'Development of the children's eating behaviour questionnaire', *Journal of Child Psychology and Psychiatry*, 42 (7): 963–70.

Webster-Stratton, C., Reid, M.J. and Stoolmiller, M. (2008) 'Preventing conduct problems and improving school readiness: Evaluation of the Incredible Years Teacher and Child training programs in high-risk schools', *Journal of Child Psychology and Psychiatry*, 49: 471–88. doi: 10.1111/j.1469-7610.2007.01861.x

Whitty, G. (2006) 'Education(al) research and education policy making: Is conflict inevitable?', *British Educational Research Journal*, 32 (2): 159–76.

Wholey, J.S. (1979) *Evaluation: Promise and performance*. Washington, DC: Urban Institute Press.

Youth Justice Board for England and Wales (2010) *Exploring the Needs of Young Black and Minority Ethnic Offenders and the Provision of Targeted Interventions*. Available at: www.justice.gov.uk/downloads/youth-justice/yjb-toolkits/disproportionality/Exploring-needs-young-bme-offenders.pdf [accessed 3 March 2017].

Zeneli, M., Thurston, A. and Roseth, C. (2016) 'The influence of experimental design on the magnitude of the effect size – peer tutoring for elementary, middle and high school settings: A meta-analysis', *International Journal of Educational Research*. doi: 10.1016/j.ijer.2015.11.010

Index

Page numbers followed by 'f' are figures; those followed by 'o' are outcomes; those followed by 't' are tables.

ability tests 46
abstracts 149–50
Achenbach, T.M. 46
adaptive randomisation 63–6
administration of outcome measurement 47
Ajzen, I. 34
Alexander, J.F. 64
analysis 75–6
   linear regression 76–83
      Doodle Den example 95–105, 96o, 97o, 100o, 100t, 101o, 102o, 103t, 104f, 104t, 105o
   and RCTs 83–91
   methodology (CONSORT guidelines) 154
   sample size and intended analysis 69–73
   sub-group effects 91–4, 92o, 94t
      Doodle Den example 99–105, 100f, 100o, 101o, 102o, 103t, 104f, 104t, 105o
analysis, complex
   analysis plans 145
   assumptions and conditions 143–4
   cluster RCTs 121–41
      assessing the effects of programme fidelity 140–1, 141o
      multilevel modelling 122–31, 124f, 127f, 128f, 129o
      multilevel modelling and binary outcomes 137–40, 137o, 139o, 140t
      multilevel modelling and scale outcomes 131–7, 131o, 132o, 133o, 134o, 135t, 136f, 136o
   intention to treat analysis 142, 155, 156–7
   missing data 143
   non-randomised controlled trials 144–5
   trial data with binary outcomes 108–21
      applying binary logistic regression to trial data 114–21, 115o, 117o, 118t, 119o, 120o, 121t
      binary logistic regression 109–14, 110o, 111o, 114o
assessment. *see* measuring outcomes
assumptions 32, 36, 38f, 39, 41, 143–4
attitudinal measures 45–6
attrition 68, 155, 155f

background noise 51, 52
Ball, S. 18, 19
baseline measurement 71, 83, 155–6, 156t. *see also* pre-test vs post-test scores
behavioural measures 46
bias 149, 162, 170–1, 170f, 171f
Biggart, A. 40, 95
binary logistic regression 109–14, 110o, 111o, 114o
   applying to trial data 114–21, 115o, 117o, 118t, 119o, 120o, 121t

Index

binary outcomes 107–9
　applying binary logistic regression to trial data 114–21, 115o, 117o, 118t, 119o, 120o, 121t
　binary logistic regression 109–14, 110o, 111o, 114o
'black box evaluation' 22, 25, 26, 74
blinding 154
block randomisation 60–3, 62f, 65–6, 67–8, 68f
Bonferroni correction 153
Bonnell, C. 26, 27
Bookstart+ programme 37–40, 44
　analysis 108–21
　　applying binary logistic regression to trial data 114–21, 115o, 117o, 118t, 119o, 120o121t
　　binary logistic regression 109–14, 110o, 111o, 114o
Briggs, D.C. 60
Bronfenbrenner, U. 34

Campbell Collaboration 14, 162
Campbell Collaboration Library 150
Campbell, D.T. 13, 24, 52
Campbell, M.J. 66
Campbell, M.K. 66
Cancer Focus NI: Dead Cool programme 67–8, 68f
Cartwright, N. 58
causal statements 36
causal validity 60
causation 25, 51
Chaiklin, S. 33
cluster RCTs 53–4, 107–8, 121–2
　assessing the effects of programme fidelity 140–1, 141o
　design 66
　multilevel modelling 122–31, 124f, 127f, 128f, 129o
　　binary outcomes 137–40, 137o, 139o, 140t
　　scale outcomes 131–7, 131o, 132o, 133o, 134o, 135t, 136f, 136o
　pre-specifying outcomes and measures 151–2, 152t
　sample size 153
　validity 60
Cochrane Collaboration 162
Cochrane Library 150
Cockerill, M. 58, 59
coefficient of variation 87–8, 93–4
　binary logistic regression 112–13, 115, 115o, 118, 119o
　linear regression 102–3, 102o, 105, 105o
　multilevel modelling 129–31, 131o, 132o, 133, 133o, 136, 136f
cognitive measures 46

Cohen, L. 5, 6, 15, 17, 19, 58
Cohen's d 90–1, 91t, 125, 157, 158t, 160, 165
collaboration 35, 40–1, 57
communication with stakeholders 41
confidence intervals 158–9
Connolly, P. 37, 39, 43, 45, 108, 118, 125, 152t, 155f, 156t, 157t
consent 56–7
CONSORT reporting requirements 148, 149–61
　discussion 161
　introduction and hypothesis 150
　methodology 150–4, 152t
　outcome reporting bias 162
　results 154–61, 155f, 156t, 157t, 158t
　title and abstract 149–50
　trial registration and protocol publication 149
constant 80f, 83o
constructs. see outcomes
contexts 6–7, 22–3, 28
control groups 3–4
　analysis of sub-group effects 91–4, 92o, 94t
　binary logistic regression 115–21, 117o, 118t, 120o, 121t
　description of 151
　ethical issues 23
　example 84f, 86–91, 86f, 87o, 89o, 91t
　importance of 52
　line of best fit 85, 86f, 87–8
　linear regression 95–105, 96o, 97o, 100o, 100t, 101o, 102o, 103t, 104f, 104t, 105o
　multilevel modelling 133–5, 134o, 135t, 138–40, 140t
　'wait-intervention' control 68
controversies 4–6
correlation 51, 78, 123, 153
covariate imbalance 60
covariates 144–5
Creemers, B.P.M. 58
critical realism 12, 24–6, 27
critical social research 16t
Cronbach, L.J. 43
Croydon Council: Functional Family Therapy 64–6, 70–3
cultural differences and export of programmes 28

data
　missing 143
　preparation 165–7
　　ratio effects 166–7
　　standardised mean difference 90, 157–8, 158t, 165–6
data, hierarchical. see multilevel modelling
Davies, B. 18
demographic measures 47

dependent variable 76–7, 77f
  binary logistic regression 108, 109, 111–12, 118, 120
  linear regression 77–83, 78f, 80f, 83f, 83o
  multilevel modelling 127, 128f, 131, 131o
design effect: multilevel modelling 139–40
design of RCTs 53–6, 150
  ethics 56–9
  logic models 31–43, 37f, 38f
  outcome measures 43–8
  principles 50–3
  recruitment and attrition 66–8
  sample size and intended analysis 69–73
  sampling and randomisation 59–66
    adaptive randomisation 63–6
    true/simple and block randomisation 61–3
development studies 57–9
Dillenbourg, P. 34
Doodle Den after-school literacy programme 40, 53
  analysis 95–105, 96o, 97o, 100o, 100t, 101o, 102o, 103t, 104f, 104t, 105o
dummy variable 85–6, 87–8
  analysis of sub-group effects 91–4, 92o, 94t
    Doodle Den example 99–105, 100f, 100o, 101o, 102o, 103t, 104f, 104t, 105o
Dunn, W.N. 24
Dunne, L. 66, 67
Durlak, J.A. 34

Ebben, K. 58
Educational Endowment Foundation 17
educational policy 11, 16–18, 16t, 20
educational research
  history of 14–15
  paradigm wars 6, 15–20, 16t
educational research community: resistance to the use of RCTs 5–6
effect size 152–3
  binary logistic regression 117–18, 118t, 121, 121t
  combining across studies 167–8, 168f
  crime prevention programmes 52, 65
  example 90–1, 91t
  interpreting effect sizes 158–60
  multilevel modelling 135, 135t, 138, 140, 140t
  Optimal Design 69, 70, 71, 72f
  variance in effect sizes 169–70
Effect Size Calculator 90, 94
effect size measures 157–8, 158t
effective sample sizes: multilevel modelling 138–9
Eldridge, S. 66
eligibility criteria 151
Elliott, J. 19, 20, 22
equipoise 57, 66

ethics 6, 18, 23–4, 56–9
ETS test link 47
evidence-based practice: critique of 17–18
exams 46
experimentation and pedagogical practice 12–14
external factors 32, 36, 38f, 39, 41
external validity 27, 151

factor designs 54–6, 55f
fads in education 12–14
Farrington, D.P. 65
fidelity 58, 67, 140–1, 141o
  cluster RCTs 140–1, 141o
Fife Peer Learning Project 54–6, 55f, 66
filter variable 98–9, 104, 117, 120, 133–4, 137
Finckenauer, J.O. 13
Fitz-Gibbon, C.T. 11
fixed effect models 169
Fixsen, D.L. 32
Functional Family Therapy 64–6, 70–3
funnel plots 170–1, 170f, 171f
Funnell, S.C. 35

Garrett, K.E. 31
Gearing, R.E. 33
generalisability 151, 155, 156
Gifford, B.K. 58
Goldacre, B. 12
Gorard, S. 57
Gordon, D.A. 64
Gortmaker, S.L. 43
Gottfried, M.A. 46
gradient: line of best fit 79–80, 80f
Green, S. 157, 164
Grimshaw, J.M. 66
Gruzelier, J.H. 46
Gupta, S.K. 156

Hammersley, M. 6, 18, 19
Hardie, J. 58
Hargreaves, D.H. 12
Harris, A. 58
Hedges' g 157, 158t, 165
Henert, E. 31, 32
hierarchical data. *see* multilevel modelling
Higgins, J.P.T. 157, 164
Higgins, S. 35, 58
Hodkinson, P. 18
Hox, J.J. 244
hypotheses 150

I^2 169–70
ICC 153
impact evaluation 42
implementation factors 32–3

independent variables 76–7, 77f
  additional covariates 144–5
  analysis of sub-group effects 91–4, 92o, 94t
  binary logistic regression 109, 111–13, 114–21, 115o
  dummy variable 85–6, 87–8
  linear regression 77–83, 78f, 80f
  multilevel modelling 127–9, 128f, 132, 133–4, 137, 139, 141
indicators. *see* outcomes
inputs 32, 38–9, 38f
intended analysis and sample size 69–73
intention to treat analysis 142, 155, 156–7
interim analyses 153
interpretivist approach to research 15–16
intervention groups
  analysis of sub-group effects 91–4, 92o, 94t
  binary logistic regression 115–21, 117o, 118t, 120o, 121t
  description of 151
  example 84f, 86–91, 86f, 87o, 89o, 91t
  line of best fit 85, 86f, 87–8
  linear regression 95–105, 96o, 97o, 100o, 100t, 101o, 102o, 103t, 104f, 104t, 105o
  multilevel modelling 133–5, 134o, 135t, 138–40, 140t
interventions
  experimental nature of 12–13
  negative effect of 13–14, 23–4
  theory of intervention 33–4
intra class correlation 153
intra-cluster correlation coefficient 139, 139o
Ireland
  Cancer Focus NI: Dead Cool programme 67–8, 68f
  Maths Peer Tutoring in Irish Medium Schools 61–2, 61t
  Media Initiative for Children: Respecting Difference Programme 54, 125–41
  programmes imported from USA 28
  RCTs as bottom-up initiatives 21
ISRCTN 149

Johnson, D.W. 58
Johnson, R.T. 58
Jones, C.H. 28

Kaplan, S.A. 31
Kellogg, W.K. 31
Kuhn, T. 15

Lachin, J.M. 63
Lancaster, G.A. 57
Lather, P. 16, 16t, 17, 25
Liberati, A. 162

Likert scales 45–6, 45f
line of best fit 78–83, 78f, 80f, 85, 86f, 87–8
linear regression 71, 75–6, 143–4
  analysis 76–83, 77f, 78f, 80f, 83o
  Doodle Den example 96–105, 96o, 97o, 100o, 101o, 102o, 103t, 104f, 104t, 105o
  and RCTs 83–91, 84f, 86f, 87o, 89o, 91t
  SPSS 82, 83o
literature reviews 65. *see also* systematic reviews
location 151
log-odds 111–13, 116, 118–20, 138
logic models 37f
  building 35–7, 37–40, 38f
  components of 32–3
  definition 31–2
  direction of implementation 36, 37f
  direction of thinking 36, 37f
  dissemination of 41
  evaluation function 42
  other functions of 40–3
  and programme theory 33–5
logistic regression 71

Maas, C.J. 244
Madden, N. 67
Magolda, P. 58
Manion, L. 5
Mate-Tricks afterschool pro-social behaviour programme 34
Maths Peer Tutoring in Irish Medium Schools 61–2, 61t
Maughan, B. 43
Mayer, J.D. 33
McGilloway, S. 28
McGuinness, C. 46
measuring outcomes
  ABCD model 45–7
  administration of 47
  pre-specifying 151–2, 152t
  related trial information 47
  SMART outcomes 44
Media Initiative for Children: Respecting Difference Programme 54
  analysis 125–41, 127f, 128f, 129o
    with binary outcomes 137–40, 137o, 139o, 140t
    fidelity 140–1, 141o
    with scale outcomes 131–7, 131o, 132o, 133o, 134o, 135t, 136f, 136o
mediators 32–3. *see also* implementation factors
Meehl, P.E. 43
meta-analysis 14, 23, 64–5, 163–5
methodology (CONSORT guidelines) 150–4, 152t
Miller, S. 152t, 155f, 157t, 168
Minim (software) 154

minimisation 60, 154
MLwiN software
  Media Initiative for Children: Respecting Difference Programme 125–41, 127f, 128f, 129o
    with binary outcomes 137–40, 137o, 139o, 140t
    fidelity 140–1, 141o
    with scale outcomes 131–7, 131o, 132o, 133o, 134o, 135t, 136f, 136o
models of error 169
Montgomery, P. 148
Morrison, K. 5
Muijs, D. 58
multilevel modelling 122–31, 124f, 127f, 128f, 129o, 141–2, 144
  cluster RCTs with binary outcomes 137–40, 137o, 139o, 140t
  cluster RCTs with scale outcomes 131–7, 131o, 132o, 133o, 134o, 135t, 136f, 136o
multiple imputation 143
multivariate regression analysis 66, 71

neo-liberalism and educational policy 11, 17
New Labour 17
No Child Left Behind Act 2001: 16
non-randomised controlled trials 144–5

Oakley, A. 6, 12, 14, 17
Oancea, A. 17
odds 110–13, 111o, 115o, 118, 118t, 121t, 140, 140t, 167
O'Hare, L. 34, 37, 39, 45, 46, 108, 118
on-treatment analysis 156
open systems 28
Optimal Design 69–73, 72f
Oreopoulos, P. 46
outcome chains 35, 40
outcome variable. *see* dependent variable
outcomes 32, 38–9, 38f, 162
  defining and selecting 43–4
  maintaining the status quo 34
  measuring 44–8, 151–2, 152t
  outcome chains 35
  pre-specifying 151–2, 152t
  primary 151–2, 152t
  secondary 151–2, 152t
  SMART 44
  starting design process with 36
outputs 32, 38, 38f, 43

p values 157, 159, 160, 161
Paint Stewardship Program 41
paradigm wars 6, 15–20, 16t
Parsons, B.V. 64

participants. *see also* stakeholders
  intention to treat analysis 142
  missing data 143
  participant flow 154–5, 155f
  ratio of allocation 154
  recruitment and attrition 66–8
  recruitment and eligibility criteria 151, 154
  sub-group effects 91–4, 92o, 94t
  variations among 50–1
Pawson, R. 19, 24, 25, 27
Pearl Harvesting Methodological Framework 163
pedagogical practice and experimentation 12–14
peer tutoring
  Fife Peer Learning Project 54–6, 55f
  Maths Peer Tutoring in Irish Medium Schools 61–2, 61t
  North East England 58–9
per-protocol analysis 156
permission 56–7
Petronijevic, U. 46
Petrosino, A. 13, 14
physiological measures 46
placebo designs 53
positivist approach to research 11, 15–16
power calculations 152, 153
pre-test vs post-test scores 77–83, 77f, 78f, 80f, 83o
  linear regression 96–105, 96o, 97o, 100o, 101o, 102o, 103t, 104f, 104t, 105o
  and RCTs 83–91, 84f, 86f, 87o, 89o, 91t
predictor variables. *see* independent variables
primary outcomes 151–2, 152t
Pring, R. 15, 17, 19
prior knowledge of research methods 8–9
PRISMA statement 162
probabilities 109–10, 110o, 113–14, 114o, 167
process evaluation 42
professional standards 56–7
programme components: logic models 32, 36
programme logic models, building 35–7, 37–40, 37f, 38f
programme theory 33–5
programmes: export of across cultures 28
protocols 145, 149, 163
publication bias 149, 162, 170–1, 170f, 171f
Puffer, S. 60
pupils: involvement in research 6

qualitative methods 7, 8–9, 22, 27
  vs quantitative 15, 25–6
quantitative vs qualitative methods 15, 25–6

R^2 (proportion of variance) 69, 70–3, 81, 83o
Raffe, D. 12
random allocation of groups 4, 25, 52–3, 154

random effects models 169
random number generation 61
randomisation
 cluster RCTs 53–4
 factor designs 54–6
 methodology (CONSORT guidelines) 153–4
 and sampling 59–60
  adaptive randomisation 63–6
  true/simple and block randomisation 61–3
 simple RCTs 53
randomised control trials
 advantages 13, 14
 challenges 5, 6–7
 and context 6–7, 22–3, 28
 and critical realism 12, 24–6, 27
 critique of 5–6, 15–20, 26–8
 defence of 20–4
  and context 6–7, 21–2
  ethics 6, 18, 22–3
  intended purpose of 21–2
  political positioning of 20–1
 ethics 6, 18, 23–4, 56–9
 as the 'gold standard' of research 21
 intended purpose of 21–2
 political positioning of 20–1
 stages 3–4
rank ordering pre-test variables 63, 64
ratio effects 158, 158t, 166–7, 167t
Raudenbush, S.W. 71
Ravitz, J. 58
recruitment 66–8, 151, 154
Reezigt, G.J. 58
registration of trials 149
regularities 28
reporting results. *see* CONSORT reporting requirements
research synthesis. *see* systematic reviews
Respecting Difference Programme. *see* Media Initiative for Children
response variable. *see* dependent variable
results (CONSORT guidelines) 154–61, 155f, 156t, 157t, 158t
 Cohen's reference values in education studies 160
 comparing groups at baseline 155–6, 156t
 discussion 161
 effect size measures 157–8, 158t
 interpreting effect sizes 158–60
 participant flow 154–5, 155f
 sub-group analyses 160–1
 summary results 156–7, 157t
RevMan (software) 168, 168f
'rhetorical devices' used to critique RCT 17–18
risk ratio 166–7
Rodgers, P.J. 35

Rubin, R.S. 44
Rumsey, D.J. 51
'run-in' studies 57–9
Rutter, M. 43

Salovey, P. 33
sample selection bias 60
sample size 59–60, 152–3
 binary logistic regression 120, 120o
 example 89–90, 89o
 and intended analysis 69–73
 logistic regression 98–9
 multilevel modelling 133–4, 134o, 138–40, 140t
 Optimal Design 71–2, 72f
sampling and randomisation 4, 59–60
 adaptive randomisation 63–6
 true/simple and block randomisation 61–3
Sandieson, R. 163
Sandieson, R.W. 163
Sayer, A. 28
Scared Straight programme 13–14, 26
Schonert-Reichl, K.A. 46
schools and experimental interventions 12–13
secondary outcomes 151–2, 152t
selective outcome reporting 149, 162
Sexton, T.L. 64, 65, 73
Shadish, W.R. 25
simple randomisation 60, 61–3
Slavin, R.E. 60, 63, 67
SMART outcomes 44
Smith, J. 18
Spours, K. 12
SPSS 62–3, 62f, 63f, 76
 analysis of sub-group effects 92–4, 92o, 94t
 binary logistic regression 108–21, 109–14, 110o, 111o, 114o
  applying to trial data 114–21, 115o, 117o, 118t, 119o, 120o121t
 example 86–91, 87o, 89o, 91t
 linear regression 82, 83o, 95–105, 96o, 97o, 100o, 100t, 101o, 102o, 103t, 104f, 104t, 105o
 Media Initiative for Children 126
 Split File facility 94
 standardised scores 86, 87o
stakeholders
 benefits of logic models for 31
 collaboration and building logic models 35, 41
 collaboration and 'run-in' studies 57
 communication with 41
 exclusion of 20
 involvement in research 6, 21
standard deviations 89–90, 89o, 98–9
standardised mean difference 90, 157–8, 158t, 165–6

standardised scores 86
Stanley, J.C. 13, 52
statistical knowledge 76
statistics, descriptive 9
status quo, maintaining 34
Stone, L.L. 46
Storch, S.A, 33
study variability 165
sub-group effects: analysis 91–4, 92o, 94t, 160–1
  Doodle Den example 99–105, 100f, 100o, 101o, 102o, 103t, 104f, 104t, 105o
Success for All 67
summary results 156–7, 157t
synthesising evidence from different trials 161–2
  combining effect sizes across studies 167–8
  data preparation 165–7
  funnel plots 170–1, 170f, 171f
  meta-analysis 164–5
  models of error 169
  systematic reviews 162–4
  variance in effect sizes 169–70
  variation between study results 165
systematic research: Functional Family Therapy 64–6
systematic reviews 14, 23, 162–4

Tau^2 169–70
Taylor-Powell, E. 31, 32
teachers: involvement in research 6
terminology across disciplines 35, 41
tests 46
theory of change 31, 33, 34
Thurston, A. 58, 59, 66, 71
Tilley, N. 19, 24, 25, 27
Torgerson, C.J. 12, 52, 53, 57, 66, 147, 148
Torgerson, D.J. 12, 52, 53, 57, 66

trial data with binary outcomes 108–21
  applying binary logistic regression 114–21, 115o, 117o, 118t, 119o, 120o, 121t
  binary logistic regression 109–14, 110o, 111o, 114o
Trochim, W. 52
true/simple randomisation 60, 61–3
Turner, C.T. 65, 73
Twist, L. 45f, 46
Tymms, P.B. 52, 54, 59, 66
Type 1 errors 60, 61, 61t, 65, 153

validity and sampling 59–60
Vallabhajosula, S. 46
variables. *see also* dependent variable; dummy variable; independent variables
  associations between 24–5
  and factor design 54
  and sampling 63–4
variance in effect sizes 169–70
Vygotsky, L. 33

'wait-intervention' control 68
Wardle, J. 46
Webster-Stratton, C. 28
Welsh, B.C. 65
'what works' agenda 16–17, 16t, 18, 20
Whitehurst, G.J. 33
Whitty, G. 20, 22
Wholey, J.S. 40
Williams, D. 46
within-programme analysis 18

z score 76, 86, 96–7, 97o
Zeneli, M. 60
'Zone of proximal development' 33–4
Zpretest 86, 88, 92–3